PRESENTED TO

....

BY

....

DATE

....

GOD'S WORD
FOR GUYS

3-MINUTE DAILY DEVOTIONS

BARBOUR
PUBLISHING

Formerly published as *3-Minute Daily Devotions for Men.*

Editorial assistance by Tracy M. Sumner.

ISBN 978-1-63609-606-3

Scripture quotations marked NIV are taken from the HOLY BIBLE, NEW INTERNATIONAL VERSION®. NIV®. Copyright © 1973, 1978, 1984, 2011 by Biblica, Inc.™ Used by permission. All rights reserved worldwide.

Scripture quotations marked NLT are taken from the *Holy Bible.* New Living Translation copyright © 1996, 2004, 2015 by Tyndale House Foundation. Used by permission of Tyndale House Publishers, Inc. Carol Stream, Illinois 60188. All rights reserved.

Scripture quotations marked MSG are from *THE MESSAGE.* Copyright © by Eugene H. Peterson 1993, 1994, 1995, 1996, 2000, 2001, 2002. Used by permission of NavPress Publishing Group.

Scripture quotations marked NKJV are taken from the New King James Version®. Copyright © 1982 by Thomas Nelson, Inc. Used by permission. All rights reserved.

Scripture quotations marked KJV are taken from the King James Version of the Bible.

Scripture quotations marked AMPC are taken from the Amplified® Bible, Classic Edition, Copyright © 1954, 1958, 1962, 1964, 1965, 1987 by The Lockman Foundation. Used by permission.

Published by Barbour Publishing, Inc., 1810 Barbour Drive, Uhrichsville, Ohio 44683, www.barbourbooks.com

Our mission is to inspire the world with the life-changing message of the Bible.

Member of the
Evangelical Christian
Publishers Association

Printed in China.

INTRODUCTION

Sometimes, as a Christian man, you want a good source of inspiration and encouragement for just a moment or two—a breath of fresh air for your soul. That's why we've compiled *God's Word for Guys: 3-Minute Daily Devotions*, the book you're holding now.

Here is a collection of 365 scripture passages, one for every day of the year, each accompanied by musings from fellow Christian men making the same spiritual journey you are. Within these pages, you'll enjoy just-right-sized readings that can be experienced in as little as three minutes:

Minute 1: Reflect on God's Word
Minute 2: Read real-life application and encouragement
Minute 3: Pray

None of the writers in this book want their words to replace your personal time reading and studying God's Word. Instead, they hope that the daily readings will be a jump start to your own time with the Lord.

Perhaps you can share these moments with friends, family, coworkers, and others you come in contact with every day. They're looking for inspiration and encouragement too.

Your word is a lamp to guide my feet and a light for my path.
PSALM 119:105 NLT

DAY 1
GOD IS THE ONLY PROVIDER

"When you enter the land I am going to give you and you reap its harvest, bring to the priest a sheaf of the first grain you harvest. . . . You must not eat any bread, or roasted or new grain, until the very day you bring this offering to your God."
LEVITICUS 23:9–10, 14 NIV

From the day Moses returned to Egypt to lead his people out, God was preparing them to trust Him for their provision. For four hundred years, as slaves, they had relied on their Egyptian masters for everything. But after a vast array of signs and wonders, God established festivals and offerings to remind the people that He alone would be their provider and sustainer.

Sadly, most of the festivals would have to wait forty years while the Israelites suffered for their unbelief in the desert (Numbers 14).

Then, on the verge of the Promised Land, Moses reminded them: "You may say to yourself, 'My power and the strength of my hands have produced this wealth for me.' But remember the LORD your God, for it is he who gives you the ability to produce wealth, and so confirms his covenant" (Deuteronomy 8:17–18 NIV).

Why so much reminding? Because people are slow to remember God when things go well. But all success is God's doing and a result of His mercy.

Lord, let me never take credit for what You alone have provided.

DAY 2
WALK IN FAITH

The official pleaded, "Lord, please come now before my little boy dies." Then Jesus told him, "Go back home. Your son will live!" And the man believed what Jesus said and started home.

JOHN 4:49–50 NLT

A nobleman traveled some fifteen miles, presumably on foot, from Capernaum to Cana when he heard that Jesus was there. He begged Jesus to come heal his son, who was about to die. Jesus didn't need to travel to Capernaum. He simply told the nobleman that his son would live, and the boy began to heal that same instant.

What lengths are you willing to go to in order to petition God to answer a prayer? Would you walk fifteen miles to a worship service? Would you drive several hundred miles to a retreat center? Would you forgo food for a day as you seek God's face, trusting that He will show up and speak to you? Would you be willing to let others see your desperate faith, as the nobleman did, setting yourself up for possible ridicule?

If you have an urgent need, you won't be afraid to go the extra mile to meet that need. Your willingness to do so shows your faith in God.

Lord, in the past, I've simply asked You to show up during times of need, and You are often more than willing to do so, but help me to go to real lengths to seek You at times.

DAY 3
A SOBER REMINDER

Don't be so naive and self-confident. You're not exempt.
You could fall flat on your face as easily as anyone else. Forget
about self-confidence; it's useless. Cultivate God-confidence.
1 CORINTHIANS 10:12 MSG

In today's passage, Paul sends the church in Corinth a reminder about how easy it is to trust in self and end up falling into sin. This was the blight affecting God's people in the old covenant. They had a taste of God, but "just experiencing God's wonder and grace didn't seem to mean much—most of them were defeated by temptation during the hard times in the desert, and God was not pleased" (1 Corinthians 10:5 MSG). They trusted in themselves and believed they were fine.

Forget about patting yourself on the back or mustering self-confidence. Both are traps. Cultivate God-confidence. How? Seek God during hard times. Trust Him to come through for you. Seek less pleasure and comfort, in favor of obedience and joy in the Lord.

Father, empower me to walk in the Spirit when times get
tough so that my trust in You increases. Help me to see
with spiritual eyes so I can always stay the course.

DAY 4
GLORIFYING GOD'S NAME

*Help us, O God of our salvation, for the glory of
Your name; and deliver us, and provide atonement
for our sins, for Your name's sake!*
PSALM 79:9 NKJV

In this prayer of repentance for Israel's sins, the psalmist appeals to God's holy name, trusting Him for deliverance and atonement—not because Israel deserved it, but because God was merciful, and His name was worth glorifying.

Matthew Henry makes this observation in his commentary—that "deliverances from trouble are granted in love, and are mercies indeed, when they are grounded upon the pardon of sin and flow from that; we should therefore be more earnest with God in prayer for the removal of our sins than for the removal of our afflictions, and the pardon of them is the foundation and sweetness of our deliverances."

How often do you ask God to remove your afflictions rather than your sins? Maybe it's time to flip the script, showing a willingness to glorify God's name while you quietly endure the afflictions that resulted from sin. You'll find peace with God, regardless of whether God delivers you from your afflictions.

*Lord, I confess to being quick to ask for deliverance and slow
to being willing to endure affliction that resulted from my sin.
Going forward, I want to glorify Your name, regardless of
whether or not You choose to deliver me from my afflictions.*

DAY 5
THE PROVISION TRAP

For the love of money is a root of all kinds of evil.
Some people, eager for money, have wandered from
the faith and pierced themselves with many griefs.
1 TIMOTHY 6:10 NIV

So many men feel a burden to provide for their families, and to a certain degree this is good and responsible. There are, however, lines that can be crossed when it comes to providing—when the drive to "provide" turns into a damaging love for money or a driving ambition that could undermine God's work in your life.

Paul writes about the "love of money," but perhaps we try to disguise it as something else. We justify our financial decisions and commitments, calling them wise investments, good stewardship, or planning for the future.

Paul hints at the way to determine whether our ambitions and investments are destructive or positive: What do we long for? Do we long for more money? More influence and power? The admiration of others? These are the very things that can undermine and essentially replace our longing for God. Money in particular supplants God's place in our lives because it can provide for our needs, offer security and comfort, and convince us that we are on the right track.

Paul reminds us that the size of the paycheck isn't necessarily the issue; it's about the object of our desires—what we pursue each day above all else.

Father God, keep me from the love of money.
Let me always remember that You, not money or
things, should be the object of my desires.

DAY 6
LET GOD CHOOSE

Let all those who take refuge and put their trust in
You rejoice; let them ever sing and shout for joy, because
You make a covering over them and defend them.
PSALM 5:11 AMPC

There's waiting on God, and then there's just waiting. You have an idea, and even though you're pretty sure it came from God, you're still waiting to act. There are always more reasons to wait—uncertainty about resources or support or timing—and only one to move. But is God telling you, "Go," enough? You'll never know until you take that first step.

When God calls you to follow Him, you won't know all the steps and stops along the way. All He told Abram was to "go to the land that I will show you" (Genesis 12:1 NLT). All you know for sure is that God will lead you step by step as you obey.

After some ups and downs, Abram eventually learned to trust God. When he and Lot parted company after a land dispute, Abram let his nephew choose the territory he wanted—but really, Abram was letting God choose for him. And whereas Lot chose Sodom, God came to Abram and gave him the rest of the land "as a permanent possession" (Genesis 13:15 NLT). God knows best, so let Him be Himself. You won't regret it.

God, You will take care of me in ways I can't imagine
when I trust You to give me Your best.

DAY 7
STANDING STRONG

When Saul realized that the LORD was with David and that his daughter Michal loved David, Saul became still more afraid of him, and he remained his enemy the rest of his days.

1 SAMUEL 18:28–29 NIV

S aul set his bride price for his daughter, Michal, at one hundred Philistine foreskins, believing David would perish in his attempt to get them. Not only did David survive, but he returned with two hundred foreskins, causing Saul to realize that God was mightily with David. So he greatly feared this astonishing young man from Bethlehem.

David already knew that Saul's intentions couldn't have been honorable, given that Saul had already tried to impale David twice with his javelin (1 Samuel 18:11). But David also knew that God was with him, and he trusted Him. This therefore made him fearless as he went into battle against the Philistines.

Are you currently facing a situation at work or school in which your boss or teacher might not have your best interests in mind? Maybe he or she isn't happy about you being a Christian and plans to make things difficult for you. Based on your response, does he or she see that God is with you? If not, what can you change to help make that a reality?

Lord, my current situation is unnerving. It would be easier to stay quiet about what I believe, but that wouldn't be honoring You. Grant me the courage and strength to represent You well.

DAY 8
PRAY FOR OTHERS WHO TRUST GOD

*Paul and Barnabas appointed elders for them in each
church and, with prayer and fasting, committed them
to the Lord, in whom they had put their trust.*

ACTS 14:23 NIV

B efore their first missionary journey, Barnabas and Paul and other gifted men were worshipping God, praying, and fasting. Now, near the end of that missionary journey, Paul and Barnabas are doing the same with the men they appointed as elders in each city.

What a great way for these converts to step into servant-leader roles within each city church. It's one thing to give your life to Jesus Christ. It's quite another to have dedicated, godly men join you in committing your life to the Lord. This support causes you to sink your roots down deeper than ever.

True, not all Christian men will be appointed as leaders within the local church. Just the same, all should aspire to live up to the qualifications of such leaders. These qualifications are spelled out in 1 Timothy 3:1–7; Titus 1:5–9; and 1 Peter 5:1–4.

The bottom line: Don't worry about whether you'll ever be appointed as a leader. Live as one just the same!

---

*Lord, yes, I aspire to be a servant-leader within my family,
friends, and local church. More than ever, I trust in You!*

DAY 9
FAITH STRETCHING

*When Jesus looked out and saw that a large crowd had
arrived, he said to Philip, "Where can we buy bread
to feed these people?" He said this to stretch Philip's
faith. He already knew what he was going to do.*

JOHN 6:5–6 MSG

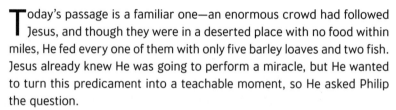

Today's passage is a familiar one—an enormous crowd had followed
Jesus, and though they were in a deserted place with no food within
miles, He fed every one of them with only five barley loaves and two fish.
Jesus already knew He was going to perform a miracle, but He wanted
to turn this predicament into a teachable moment, so He asked Philip
the question.

Philip didn't really pass the test. He chose to depend on his intellect
and consider only the limited options. But his perspective changed greatly
after Jesus performed the miracle.

Does God ever ask you questions during times of prayer? How do
you respond? Do you give a practical answer, like Philip? Or have you
ever considered that God might be asking such questions to open your
eyes so that you'll learn to trust Him in a deeper way? If not, let this
passage be your guide the next time, and watch God work.

---

*Lord, I don't always see with spiritual eyes. I allow everyday
concerns to keep me from trusting Your miracle-working power.
But this passage has taught me that You sometimes allow
needs and problems in order to stretch my faith.*

DAY 10
SERVANT LEADERSHIP

"You call me 'Teacher' and 'Lord,' and you are right, because that's what I am. And since I, your Lord and Teacher, have washed your feet, you ought to wash each other's feet."
JOHN 13:13–14 NLT

Jesus expanded what His followers thought about God and their teachers. If they were going to take over His ministry, they needed to exercise authority and teach others like Him. Never one to settle for teaching by words alone, Jesus took on the role of a servant and washed their feet. He wasn't afraid to disrupt their flawed understandings of authority in order to drive home His point about servant leadership.

Whether you're leading a team at work, a group at church, or just participating in an impromptu gathering, the principle remains the same. You might not literally wash anyone's feet, but Jesus' challenge to imitate His service to others remains.

As your responsibility and authority increase, your call to lead with humility and sacrifice expands as well. The greatest leaders will never hesitate to serve in a lower position or to make sacrifices.

Leaders can get trapped worrying about how to build influence—or how to convince people to follow Jesus' way—but it couldn't be any simpler. You are to serve others and to express your care for them. That's a message no one can miss.

Lord, show me how to serve others today.

DAY 11
SPACE OF GRACE

And now for a little space grace hath been
shewed from the LORD our God.
EZRA 9:8 KJV

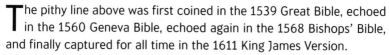

The pithy line above was first coined in the 1539 Great Bible, echoed in the 1560 Geneva Bible, echoed again in the 1568 Bishops' Bible, and finally captured for all time in the 1611 King James Version.

- *"And now"* refers to the year 457 BC.
- *"for a little space"* refers to a brief period of *time*. Ezra probably had that year in mind.
- *"grace hath been shewed"* refers to the blessings of God demonstrated by the king's favor, his royal decree, and his generosity to the Jewish people returning to the Promised Land. It also likely refers to the safe passage of Ezra and many Jewish exiles despite having no military escort (contrast Nehemiah 2:9).
- *"from the LORD our God"* refers to the one true God, Creator of heaven and earth, sustainer of the entire universe, and sovereign over all men—from the greatest emperors to the poorest slaves. He, and He alone, could show the abundant demonstrations of grace treasured by Ezra.

When was the last time you experienced a little "space of grace" from God? Maybe it's been a long time. Or maybe it's your current reality. Either way, ask God to give you some today.

Lord, thank You for demonstrating so much grace in my life.
You know how things have been going for me lately.
I pray for another space of grace, please.

DAY 12
RESCUE ME, LORD

"In your distress you called and I rescued you, I answered you
out of a thundercloud; I tested you at the waters of Meribah."
PSALM 81:7 NIV

As Israel set out from the Desert of Sin, traveling from place to place as the Lord commanded, they arrived at Rephidim (near Meribah), where they didn't have any water to drink (Exodus 17:1). Today's verse says this was a test. God wanted to see whether His people would be patient and trust Him to provide, or whether they'd grumble and complain over their lack. Unfortunately, they grumbled and complained.

How might God be testing you and your family right now? Are you struggling to make the mortgage payment this month due to unforeseen expenses? Is your car in the shop for costly repairs? Are your cabinets bare?

In your distress, call out to God and He will rescue you. His help might be different than what you're expecting, but it will arrive. Meanwhile, patiently trust in Him. He knows your every need long before you knew it, and He already has a plan to meet it.

Lord, I can't see any way around my circumstances, but I'm
trusting You to meet my need. I know You to be a faithful,
loving God who is more than willing to send help. You know
my circumstances. Take me through them, Lord. Rescue me.

DAY 13

WHO REALLY NEEDS THE LESSON?

*The woman was a Greek, a Syro-Phoenician by birth, and
she kept asking Him to cast the demon out of her daughter.
But Jesus said to her, "Let the children be filled first, for it is not
good to take the children's bread and throw it to the little dogs."
And she answered and said to Him, "Yes, Lord, yet even the
little dogs under the table eat from the children's crumbs."*

MARK 7:26–28 NKJV

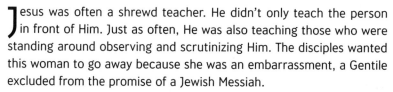

Jesus was often a shrewd teacher. He didn't only teach the person in front of Him. Just as often, He was also teaching those who were standing around observing and scrutinizing Him. The disciples wanted this woman to go away because she was an embarrassment, a Gentile excluded from the promise of a Jewish Messiah.

For the disciples' ears, Jesus intentionally compared her to a dog—and a few Jewish heads must have nodded. *Yeah, that's right. She's not one of us.* But the mother was undeterred, and because of her faith this "dog" received the miracle she asked for! What a lesson to the disciples: a dog with faith is better than a man with a Jewish last name.

Faith is the only thing that impresses God. No family history or heritage matters; not the denomination or church you grew up in. Faith alone puts you in touch with the Savior.

Father, count me a dog if necessary, but a dog of faith.

DAY 14
CHASING RICHES

*Don't wear yourself out trying to get rich; restrain
yourself! Riches disappear in the blink of an eye; wealth
sprouts wings and flies off into the wild blue yonder.*
PROVERBS 23:4–5 MSG

Whoever first uttered the cliché "You can't take it with you" was making the point that life is about more than making money and that it's wise to slow down, relax, and enjoy at least some of your time here on earth.

The Bible speaks positively about hard work for the purpose of earning money, but today's verse offers some balance. Solomon, who had learned a thing or two about hard work and riches during his years as Israel's third monarch, offered some wise advice: a man of God shouldn't become so focused on work that he wears out his body, soul, and spirit.

Furthermore, he points out that some may find that what they worked so hard to earn can vanish, sometimes in the blink of an eye. (The 2008 housing crash, anyone?)

Nothing in God's Word should be read as discouraging you from working hard to make a good life for you and your family. But take the time to slow down and enjoy life, spend time with your friends and family, and get to know your God better.

---

*Lord, help me to trust You in my work life and financial life,
and help me to glorify You in them in every way.*

DAY 15
TRUE RICHES

I love your commands more than gold, more than pure gold.
PSALM 119:127 NIV

The Old Testament's first three Wisdom books affirm the exceedingly great value of divinely revealed truths.

Job offers a full chapter. In the closing verse, Job says, "And to man He said, 'Behold, the fear of the Lord, that is wisdom, and to depart from evil is understanding' " (Job 28:28 NKJV).

Psalms has three verses. The first says, "They are more precious than gold, than much pure gold; they are sweeter than honey, than honey from the honeycomb" (19:10 NIV). The second says, "The law from your mouth is more precious to me than thousands of pieces of silver and gold" (119:72 NIV). And the third is quoted at the top of this page.

Proverbs offers five verses. See if you can catch the pattern that emerges. The first says: "Wisdom is more profitable than silver, and her wages are better than gold" (3:14 NLT). The second says: "Choose [Wisdom's] instruction rather than silver, and knowledge rather than pure gold" (8:10 NLT). The third: "[Wisdom's] gifts are better than gold, even the purest gold, my wages better than sterling silver!" (8:19 NLT). The fourth: "How much better to get wisdom than gold, and good judgment than silver!" (16:16 NLT). And fifth: "Wise words are more valuable than much gold and many rubies" (20:15 NLT).

Lord, I fear You and want the true riches You give.

DAY 16
WORDS OF LIFE

*"It is the Spirit who gives life; the flesh profits nothing.
The words that I speak to you are spirit, and they are life.
But there are some of you who do not believe."*
JOHN 6:63–64 NKJV

One day, Jesus was teaching His disciples (not just the Twelve or the Seventy, but a larger group) that they must eat His flesh and drink His blood to have spiritual life. Many of these followers rejected this shocking teaching.

In reality, Jesus' teachings were spiritual and not to be interpreted literally, but these halfhearted people were unwilling to dig deeper to unpack what He was saying. They weren't committed followers.

How do you react when you encounter a hard teaching in the Bible—one that doesn't line up with your personal doctrine or your current behavior? Are you quick to dig deeper, comparing it with other scriptures on the subject, or do you reject it like these shallow followers did? Jesus is still speaking to His disciples through His Word. How willing are you to examine it thoroughly so you'll know you have a comprehensive understanding?

*Lord, much of my personal doctrine was settled some time ago,
but I never want to start thinking that I have it all figured out.
I'm willing to change when Your Word confronts one of
my beliefs or behaviors. Make me teachable, Lord.*

DAY 17

PROCLAIMING THE LORD'S DEATH

For whenever you eat this bread and drink this cup,
you proclaim the Lord's death until he comes.
1 CORINTHIANS 11:26 NIV

Communion is the most somber of celebrations because the Church looks back on what Christ did for us, recognizing that our sins led to His death, while also recognizing that His death led to our redemption. So Christians of all denominations partake in faith, and the mere act proclaims the Lord's death to a lost and dying world.

Why proclaim His death? Because He's the Lamb of God who takes away the sin of the world by laying down His life as the ultimate sacrifice. Nothing else shows the world that the Church is different—set apart for God's use—more than when they proclaim the Lord's death.

Regardless of how often your church celebrates communion, stir yourself up to earnestly desire to be there to partake in it. It's a glorious opportunity to wipe your slate clean and start fresh, while also encouraging unbelievers who might be seated around you to do the same the next time they have an opportunity. If they see that the Church is serious about sin, perhaps they'll be inspired to be so as well.

Lord Jesus, I look forward to the next time my church offers
communion. I'll be faithful to examine myself, to confess
my sin, and to proclaim Your death until You return.

DAY 18
THE LORD'S ANOINTED

"No!" David said. "Don't kill him. For who can remain
innocent after attacking the LORD's anointed one?"
1 SAMUEL 26:9 NLT

Abishai, one of David's men, was convinced that God had given Saul over to David when they slipped into Saul's camp and found him sleeping. But David wouldn't have anything to do with killing Saul. He still saw him as God's anointed, in spite of everything Saul had done.

Have you considered today's verse in light of the way you speak about political leaders, or any other leaders? It's not always easy to understand why God allows some to rise to power and not others—especially when such leadership holds views that are contrary to scripture. But somehow, in God's perfect plan, they're the Lord's anointed, at least for a time.

That's not to say you shouldn't support someone who is campaigning against them, or that you shouldn't hold them accountable. But to assassinate their character isn't the answer. Instead, pray for the leader's conversion, and pray for the power to keep your tongue. And then trust that God has the future figured out.

Lord, I confess that I don't always mind my tongue when it comes
to leaders, but I haven't considered the fact that they, like Saul—
in spite of all their flaws—are Your anointed. Forgive me, Lord.
Help me to set a better example to others going forward.

DAY 19
HOW TO BLESS OTHERS

*"May the LORD bless you and protect you. May the
LORD smile on you and be gracious to you. May the
LORD show you his favor and give you his peace."*
NUMBERS 6:24–26 NLT

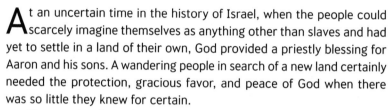

At an uncertain time in the history of Israel, when the people could scarcely imagine themselves as anything other than slaves and had yet to settle in a land of their own, God provided a priestly blessing for Aaron and his sons. A wandering people in search of a new land certainly needed the protection, gracious favor, and peace of God when there was so little they knew for certain.

The people of Israel rarely had smooth sailing with God. They were disobedient, rebellious, and grumbled even when God blessed them. They were rarely on their best behavior, but God mercifully encouraged them to pray for protection, peace, and the favor of God. In fact, despite their struggles, God encouraged them to imagine Him smiling upon them as He extended His unearned grace to them.

As you think about how to pray for others, consider praying that those in danger will receive God's blessing and protection. Ask God to guide them through uncertain times and to mercifully provide blessings for them. Bless them by interceding for God's favor and peace to be manifested in their lives.

---

*Loving Father in heaven, remind me often to pray
for people You've placed in my life. Please be
present for them in tangible, gracious ways.*

HANDLING ANGER PROPERLY

Fools vent their anger, but the wise quietly hold it back.
PROVERBS 29:11 NLT

This may come as a surprise to some Christian men, but the Bible teaches that the emotion of anger isn't necessarily a sin. God Himself expressed His anger in scripture (see Psalm 7:11; Mark 3:5). And the apostle Paul made a distinction between anger and *sinful* anger when he wrote, " 'In your anger do not sin': Do not let the sun go down while you are still angry" (Ephesians 4:26 NIV).

Godly anger—also known as righteous indignation—can motivate men to act in ways that glorify God and further His kingdom. It moves you to defend those who are being wronged or mistreated, or to stand up for a biblical principle you see being violated.

But sinful anger, the kind of anger that moves you to contend for your own selfish desires, can damage relationships, cause unneeded pain to those you love, and hurt your witness for Christ.

Life will afford you many opportunities to feel anger. But when you feel that emotion rising up within you, stop and ask yourself if the way you're considering expressing that anger will hurt others or displease your Father in heaven. If the answer to that question is yes, then patiently hold your words in check, and choose to find a godly, healthy way to express how you feel.

Righteous God, help me to be angry only at the right things and to display that anger only in ways that please and glorify You.

DAY 21
YOU ARE SURROUNDED BY SACRED REMINDERS

The heavens are yours, and the earth is yours; everything in the world is yours—you created it all. You created north and south. Mount Tabor and Mount Hermon praise your name.

PSALM 89:11–12 NLT

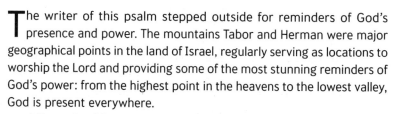

The writer of this psalm stepped outside for reminders of God's presence and power. The mountains Tabor and Herman were major geographical points in the land of Israel, regularly serving as locations to worship the Lord and providing some of the most stunning reminders of God's power: from the highest point in the heavens to the lowest valley, God is present everywhere.

Where should you start with your awareness of God today? This psalm makes it quite simple: step outside. The mountains, streams, fields, flowers, sunrises, and sunsets serve as reminders of God's care for you and for all of creation. Perhaps you're struggling to experience God in creation because you aren't expecting to find Him there.

Would it change how you take walks or approach prayer if you remembered that every single rock, flower, blade of grass, and splash of water has been created and maintained by God's loving creativity?

There are songs and shouts of praise in creation that are resounding just for God. You have an invitation to step outside and join in.

Lord, may I see Your presence and love around me today.

DAY 22

BLESSED WHILE YOU SLEEP

It is vain for you to rise up early, to sit up late, to eat the
bread of sorrows; for so [the Lord] gives His beloved sleep.
PSALM 127:2 NKJV

Solomon talks twenty-one times about sleep. It's probably not surprising. After all, God invented sleep, you spend nearly a third of your life sleeping, and the quality of your sleep affects your waking hours and vice versa. Here are some facts and insights about sleep:

- God blesses you as you sleep (verse quoted above).
- Your quality of sleep varies. Sometimes you sleep well after a hard day's work, sometimes overwork makes for restless sleep, and sometimes you can miss a night of sleep (Ecclesiastes 5:12).
- What's more, sometimes you can't sleep thinking of a loved one, and sometimes you sleep lightly and are ready to rise at a moment's notice (Song of Songs 5:2).
- Then again, sleeping with any woman other than your wife will bring severe punishment. Good and wise men tend to sleep well, but wicked men can't sleep until they commit another heinous act. Someone who makes a foolish financial promise shouldn't sleep, lazy men sleep their way to poverty and ruin, but wisdom will bless you while you sleep (Proverbs 3:24; 4:16; 6:4; 6:9, 29).

Lord, I want to enjoy Your blessings while I sleep. Help me balance life's demands and walk in wisdom all my days.

DAY 23
THE POWER OF QUIET

"Be still, and know that I am God; I will be exalted
among the nations, I will be exalted in the earth."

PSALM 46:10 NIV

Men are natural doers, workers, initiators. Achievement means a lot to men. Work is part of a man's identity. And when work is done, there's more! Sports, hobbies, family events, church, community involvement—so many opportunities to be doing something.

Consequently, most men are too busy to be still or quiet for very long. It takes effort, but when God commands it, there's a reason. And what better reason than knowing your Father in heaven better? Men are so busy working out solutions to problems, creating the next thing, or meeting obligations that they forget God is the Lord of all creation.

Though most people don't constantly have God on their minds and hearts, He will be exalted one day above all other concerns. He will exert Himself for His own glory globally. But you can enjoy the power of His presence now when you embrace the power of *quiet*. All you need to do is refrain from busyness to know Him.

God promises it will be worth the effort. He says, "I will give you hidden treasures, riches stored in secret places, so that you may know that I am the LORD, the God of Israel, who summons you by name" (Isaiah 45:3 NIV).

Father, You are the reward of my quiet
moments, my treasure above all else.

DAY 24
KNOW YOUR WORTH

*"But He knows the way that I take; when He has
tested me, I shall come forth as gold."*
JOB 23:10 NKJV

In the temple treasury, Jesus pointed out a poor widow who had quietly contributed two very small bronze coins. Her gift demonstrated her implicit trust in God's ability to supply all her needs. The widow's mites were worth far more than everything the rich had donated (Mark 12:41–44). Even when you can't afford it, trust God and give.

In one of His parables, Jesus talked about a wealthy and successful farmer who had laid up enough to retire. He was quite proud of his accomplishments. Little did he know, however, that he would die that very night (Luke 12:16–21). Never trust earthly wealth.

In two shorter parables about the kingdom of heaven, Jesus said it is worth selling everything you have to obtain it. The kingdom of God is worth more than all your accumulated wealth here on earth (Matthew 13:44–46). Buy it.

In Matthew 6:26; 10:29–31; and Luke 12:6–7, Jesus pointed out the birds, talked about how God cared for them, and assured His listeners that God valued them much more. Receive His love.

In Matthew 16:26 and Mark 8:36–37, Jesus says the world's vast wealth is nothing compared to the value of your soul. Give it to God.

---

*Lord, I give You my trust, for You are worthy of it.
Help me to never fail to trust You.*

DAY 25
LONGING TO WORSHIP

How amiable are thy tabernacles, O LORD of hosts! My
soul longeth, yea, even fainteth for the courts of the LORD:
my heart and my flesh crieth out for the living God.

PSALM 84:1–2 KJV

This unknown psalmist longed to worship the Lord with other believers in the tabernacles. Bible commentator Adam Clarke points out that the word *tabernacles* refers to "all the places in or near the temple where acts of Divine worship were performed. The holy of holies, the holy place, the altar of incense, the altar of burnt-offering. . .all called here God's tabernacles or dwelling-places; for wherever God was worshipped, there he was supposed to dwell."

Today, Christians worship in church buildings, school buildings, workplaces, cafés, parks, and homes. In fact, wherever two or three are gathered in Jesus' name, He's with them. Do you trust that when you worship, He will indeed show up? He will!

If your soul doesn't long to worship the Lord the way the psalmist describes, and if it doesn't cry out to the living God, something is wrong. Ask the Lord to renew your spirit.

Father, sometimes my worship is dry. Sometimes my want-to
is lacking. Sometimes I go through the motions. I know it's
often due to my wayward heart. Renew my spirit, O Lord.
Draw me closer. Lead me beside still waters. Lead me in
the paths of righteousness, for Your name's sake.

DAY 26
GRACE UNDER FIRE

"Do not worry about how or what you should speak. For it will be given to you in that hour what you should speak; for it is not you who speak, but the Spirit of your Father who speaks in you."
MATTHEW 10:19–20 NKJV

Well, you went and did it. You took a leap of faith and talked about your faith in a public forum. You listened first, trying to understand the other people's situations and thoughts, and you did your best, presenting the gospel clearly and with compassion.

No matter how it went, know that God's grace is with you when you're under fire. Look past the emotions of the moment, good or bad, and know that He cares—about you, about the people you spoke with, and about working to the best possible solution for all involved.

Whether you have a feeling of peace or one of unease, rest in this: you have been faithful to what God called you to do, and that's a success. "But I have trusted, leaned on, and been confident in Your mercy and loving-kindness; my heart shall rejoice and be in high spirits in Your salvation. I will sing to the Lord, because He has dealt bountifully with me" (Psalm 13:5–6 AMPC).

Father, I shared Your love and truth with people. Now the results are in Your hands. Open their hearts, and give me wisdom for any responses they may have.

DAY 27
BEFORE ABRAHAM

*Then the Jews said to Him, "You are not yet fifty years
old, and have You seen Abraham?" Jesus said to them,
"Most assuredly, I say to you, before Abraham was, I AM."*
JOHN 8:57–58 NKJV

In today's verses, Jesus makes the ultimate claim. He uses the phrase "I
AM"—a phrase the Jews would have been familiar with as meaning "even
from everlasting to everlasting," John Wesley writes in his commentary.
"This is a direct answer to the objection of the Jews, and shows how
much greater he was than Abraham."

You've probably encountered political correctness in your office or
at school. If so, you've heard coworkers or classmates make the claim
that all paths lead to heaven, no matter the belief system. But as soon as
you point out that Jesus claims to be God in the flesh, many will accuse
you of being intolerant. Proclaim it anyway. Be as wise as serpents and
as harmless as doves as you do so.

Jesus has indeed always existed, distinct from, yet one with, the
Father and the Holy Spirit. And He's the only way to heaven (John 14:6).
Hold on to those truths.

---

*Lord, many people are resistant to the gospel, so what I
encounter on a regular basis is nothing new. I believe that
Jesus is the great I AM, and I'm willing to continue to
push against a culture that believes otherwise.*

DAY 28
DO GOOD. . .EVEN WHEN IT HURTS

Who is going to harm you if you are eager to do good?
But even if you should suffer for what is right, you are
blessed. "Do not fear their threats; do not be frightened."
1 PETER 3:13–14 NIV

Have you ever done everything you can to demonstrate godly love to someone, only to have that person repay your good with evil—evil words, evil attitudes, and evil actions? When faced with such situations—and they are a part of life here on earth—many Christians are tempted to turn to God and protest, "It's just not fair!"

No, it's not fair when a Christian suffers for doing what is good and right in God's eyes. But today's verse gives a twofold promise for the believer in such a situation. First, it promises that even if doing good is accompanied by persecution, the man of God needn't fear any lasting harm as a result. Second, it promises that God sees his suffering and will find a way to bring him blessing in the midst of it.

Those are some amazing, comforting promises, aren't they? Your part in claiming them is to trust God enough to continue doing what you know is right in His eyes.

Father in heaven, I commit myself to doing good for You
and for others and to leaving the results in Your hands.

DAY 29

DIRECT CONNECTION TO THE FATHER

"I tell you the truth, you will ask the Father directly, and he will grant your request because you use my name. You haven't done this before. Ask, using my name, and you will receive, and you will have abundant joy."

JOHN 16:23–24 NLT

When Jesus told His disciples about their access to God the Father, He informed them that this was unfamiliar ground. They had never done anything quite like approaching God as their loving Father.

Jesus provides an ongoing promise that applies to every Christian, but are you taking Him up on it daily? Jesus even offers a clue to determine whether you're fully availing yourself of your connection with the Father: Are you experiencing the abundant *joy* He promised?

While there surely are many challenging circumstances in life that could cause you sorrow, there is joy to be found in your connection with God. If you're presenting your requests to God on the basis of your relationship with Jesus, then you'll experience the joy of the Lord in your life.

What you ask will certainly need to be in accordance with the will of Christ. This isn't a blank check. Rather, God is inviting you into the abundant joy of living daily as His beloved child. You have an open invitation to bring your requests to Him.

Father, I trust that You have given me full access to You as a son.

DAY 30
GOD IS NEAR

Where can I go from your Spirit? Where can I flee from
your presence? If I go up to the heavens, you are there;
if I make my bed in the depths, you are there.
PSALM 139:7–8 NIV

David's questions in today's verses might make it seem as if he actually wanted to find a way to separate himself from God, but that wasn't true. Earlier in the psalm, he listed many of the ways that God was close to him. Instead, he was making the case that God is everywhere and always sustains His people.

That's not to say that His people don't hide from Him or pull away from Him during times of sin or hardship. But the great news is He's never far away. You can trust that about Him. Does this fact provide great comfort to you, or does it strike fear in your heart? The truth is it should probably do a little of both. You can't hide from God, but in spite of your sin, He sees you through the lens of Christ.

What can you do to be more aware of His presence in your everyday activities? How might becoming more aware change your routines and further your sanctification process?

Father, I can't escape Your presence. I praise You
for being such a personal God that You never leave
me alone. You love me too much to abandon me.

DAY 31
GOD'S INFINITE FAME

Your name, O LORD, endures forever; your fame,
O LORD, is known to every generation.
PSALM 135:13 NLT

*F*ame isn't a word you'd expect to read in the Bible.

In scripture, God was the first one to talk about fame. He told Pharaoh, "I have spared you for a purpose—to show you my power and to spread my fame throughout the earth" (Exodus 9:16 NLT; also see Romans 9:17). Later, Moses urged God to remember His fame and not destroy His disobedient people (Numbers 14:15).

King David's fame spread throughout Palestine and beyond (1 Chronicles 14:17). His fame was a gift from God for His glory. King Solomon's fame spread throughout the known world (1 Kings 1:47; 3:13; 4:31; 10:1; 2 Chronicles 1:11–12; 9:1). Again, his fame was a gift from God because of his humility during the first decades of his reign.

Similarly, centuries later King Hezekiah's fame spread throughout the Levant and beyond (2 Chronicles 26:8; 26:15), and Mordecai's fame spread throughout the entire Persian Empire (Esther 9:4).

Mostly, however, God's Word talks about the Lord's worldwide and eternal fame (Psalms 102:12, 21; 135:13; Isaiah 64:2; 66:19). Ultimately, every knee will bow and every tongue confess that Jesus Christ is Lord of all (Isaiah 45:22–25; Romans 10:9–10; 14:11; Philippians 2:10–11).

Lord, You know my heart. I have gladly confessed
that Jesus Christ is my Lord. Help me to brag
about Your fame again this coming week.

DAY 32

THE JOY OF YOUR SALVATION

*You have forgiven and taken away the iniquity
of Your people, You have covered all their sin.
Selah [pause, and calmly realize what that means]!*
PSALM 85:2 AMPC

Today's verse is a clear presentation of the gospel in the Old Testament. The writer understood that humankind could never atone for its own sin—that God would need to take it away from His people and cover it, to be remembered no more.

In historical context, the writer was referring to when God's people were brought back from Babylonian captivity.

Can you think of a time when you had to deal with the consequences of your sin—a time in which you felt far from God but then experienced a complete restoration the way this writer did? How did you express the joy you felt? Did you tell others? Write about it? Sing about it? Worship? Dance for joy? Any of these responses would be appropriate.

If you can't think of a time in which you had to deal with the consequences of your sin and then were able to celebrate God's faithfulness, you're probably not looking hard enough. As David prayed in Psalm 51:12 (NIV), "Restore to me the joy of your salvation."

---

*Lord, my sin is a burden to me. It's heavy, and it
weighs me down. But You are a forgiving God,
and I trust in You to completely pardon me.*

DAY 33
BEYOND COMPREHENSION

"God thunders marvelously with His voice; He does great things which we cannot comprehend. For He says to the snow, 'Fall on the earth'; likewise to the gentle rain and the heavy rain of His strength."

JOB 37:5–6 NKJV

Job's friend Elihu does a good job of describing God's majesty in Job 36–37, pointing out His absolute control over nature to show that nothing goes unnoticed with Him. For God tells the rain and snow to fall on the earth, and they do.

Why does any of this matter? Because the ecosystem is wholly dependent on the weather, just as you are dependent on the ecosystem for food and air. And God is faithful to send snow and rain to provide for you.

It's easy to wake up, check the weather, and then view the weather patterns that occur as random. In reality, nothing is random. God rules and reigns as He sees fit. Don't complain about the weather. Instead, consider observing it so you can be just as wowed by God's handiwork as Elihu was. And then praise God for the snow and rain, letting Him know that you trust in Him for providing them.

Father, I'm in awe when I consider that You can just speak and the weather obeys. And I'm humbled when I consider that You speak such commands to provide for me and my family.

DAY 34

THE IMPORTANCE OF "ONE ANOTHER"

"A new command I give you: Love one another. As I have loved you, so you must love one another. By this everyone will know that you are my disciples, if you love one another."

JOHN 13:34–35 NIV

During His earthly ministry, Jesus brought to His followers some radical new (new to them) teachings about the Law, about the nature of their relationship with God, and about love. He taught that by-the-letter "obedience" to the Law of Moses wasn't nearly as important as obedience to the spirit of the Law. He gave them a glimpse of the loving nature of their heavenly Father and taught them the vital importance of loving one another.

The New Testament is filled with references to "one another," starting with Jesus' commandment that His followers love one another in the same way He loved them—selflessly, sacrificially, and compassionately. Here are just a few examples from the pen of the apostle Paul:

- *"Be devoted to one another in love. Honor one another above yourselves" (Romans 12:10 NIV).*
- *"Live in harmony with one another" (Romans 12:16 NIV).*
- *"Serve one another humbly in love" (Galatians 5:13 NIV).*
- *"Be kind and compassionate to one another" (Ephesians 4:32 NIV).*

Clearly, God never intended for followers of Jesus Christ to live self-focused lives. On the contrary, He has commanded you to be lovingly devoted to your brothers and sisters in the faith.

Loving God, remind me often that You want me to be others-focused and not the kind of man who tries to live out his faith all alone.

DAY 35
FLEE FROM HER

*I discovered that a seductive woman is a trap more
bitter than death. Her passion is a snare, and her soft
hands are chains. Those who are pleasing to God will
escape her, but sinners will be caught in her snare.*

ECCLESIASTES 7:26 NLT

If any man was qualified to warn other men about seduction, it would be Solomon. He had seven hundred wives and three hundred concubines, and they turned his heart away from the Lord to worship Ashtoreth and Molech (1 Kings 11:3–5). "In this way, Solomon did what was evil in the LORD's sight; he refused to follow the LORD completely, as his father, David, had done" (1 Kings 11:6 NLT).

If you could take a peek at what God has recorded about your dealings with worldly women, what might it say? Would it say you have been pleasing to Him by escaping such snares? Or would it say their soft hands were like chains, binding you and keeping you from walking in the Spirit as you ought?

Those who are pleasing to God will escape the seductress before she turns their hearts away from God. It's not too late. Trust in God's power and run.

---

*Father, Solomon's description of the seductress struck
home with me. Give me power from on high to stay out of
the clutches of such women so I can be pleasing to You.*

DAY 36

GOD IS PRESENT IN TIMES OF SORROW

"I have told you all this so that you may have peace in me.
Here on earth you will have many trials and sorrows.
But take heart, because I have overcome the world."
JOHN 16:33 NLT

Appearances can be deceiving, and that was especially so during the final hours before the arrest, trial, and execution of Jesus. How could the disciples believe in a moment like this that He had overcome the world?

Jesus trusted the Father to remain with Him as He faced His greatest hour of trial. In the same way, Jesus promised to remain with His disciples during their own trials, giving them peace and hope that could overcome all appearances of being defeated.

Whether you're going through a difficult season or you anticipate one in the near future, consider that, regardless of circumstances, Jesus *has* overcome the world. That hardly guarantees smooth sailing, as His impending death made clear in this passage. Rather, there's nothing that can separate you from God. God remains with you even in your lowest moments and deepest sorrows.

Much as the good shepherd didn't abandon his sheep in the darkest valley, God will not abandon you. On the other side of your sorrow is the joy that God is victorious.

Lord, help me to take a step of faith into
Your victory and peace today.

DAY 37
NO COMPROMISE

"If we are thrown into the blazing furnace, the God we serve is able to deliver us from it. . . . But even if he does not, we want you to know, Your Majesty, that we will not serve your gods or worship the image of gold you have set up."

DANIEL 3:17–18 NIV

Three Hebrew men of God—Shadrach, Meshach, and Abednego—were faced with a situation many might see as a true dilemma, meaning a choice between two equally bad options. Those two options were to either (1) worship King Nebuchadnezzar's gold idol or (2) be tossed into a blazing hot furnace.

However, these men of God didn't see their choice as a dilemma at all. In fact, for them, there really wasn't a choice to make. They weren't going to serve the king's gods or bow to his idol. Period. And if that meant dying in a fiery furnace, so be it.

Can you remember a situation in which you were asked to do something you knew wouldn't please God? Maybe a situation at your own business or at your place of employment?

Living in this fallen world means you may be faced with choices between honoring God and compromising your faith. Can you trust God enough to make the right choice?

---

*Lord, I will serve and obey You and You alone,
even when it means facing all sorts of difficulties.*

DAY 38
THE FLOW OF NATIONS

And it shall come to pass in the last days, that the mountain of the LORD's house shall be established in the top of the mountains, and shall be exalted above the hills; and all nations shall flow unto it.

ISAIAH 2:2 KJV

The news is full of reports of persecution, oppression, abuse, and war. Humankind often doesn't treat each other very well. It's nearly too much to bear in big doses. And it's difficult not to wonder if the world is void of hope. It won't always be this way, though.

Isaiah sees a vision in which the Lord's house, which many believe to be the Church (the people of God), shall be established on this earth, exalted above the hills (for the gospel shall reign supreme above all else), and all nations shall flow unto it like a mighty river.

Imagine some of the most hostile nations on earth bowing the knee to King Jesus. Imagine the sweet sound of the gospel rolling off the lips of once-distant lands. Imagine the darkness being pushed back by the flood of light. Don't lose hope, no matter what you see going on around the world right now. It won't always be like this.

Lord Jesus, I confess to allowing the events of this world to dictate my mood sometimes, but this verse brings me great hope as I consider Your faithfulness.

DAY 39

SPIRITUAL EARS TO HEAR

"My sheep hear My voice, and I know them, and they follow Me.
And I give them eternal life, and they shall never perish;
neither shall anyone snatch them out of My hand."

JOHN 10:27–28 NKJV

When the Jews asked Jesus if He was the Christ, He spoke plainly to them, also telling them that they were not of His sheepfold. If they were part of His flock, they would have followed Him, rather than questioning Him.

His sheep know His voice—it has a ring of truth to it for the converted heart. It has *the* ring of truth to it. If any man has spiritual ears to hear, let him hear.

The voices around you might be loud, making demands on your time and calling you to work, volunteer, serve—or even escape to a nearby lake for a weekend fishing excursion. You hear all of them and often respond accordingly.

But do you still hear Jesus' voice when He calls out or whispers to you? Or has it been a while? If you aren't tuned in to His Word, it's time to set aside some time to focus on Him above all else.

Lord Jesus, my spiritual ears aren't always in tune with You. I often place a higher value on the voices of others than on Yours. Forgive me, Lord. Draw me close. Speak to me. I want to hear from You.

DAY 40
DID HE REALLY JUST SAY THAT?

"Teacher, I brought You my son, who has a mute spirit. . . . So I spoke to Your disciples, that they should cast it out, but they could not." He answered him and said, "O faithless generation, how long shall I be with you? How long shall I bear with you? Bring him to Me."

MARK 9:17–19 NKJV

It's hard to imagine Jesus getting exasperated with people who needed His help, but in this passage Jesus is clearly annoyed. With everyone. The father of the mute boy, His disciples, and the whole of Jewish society.

And it's not the only time Jesus became impatient with people's lack of faith. Consider this statement: "If that is how God clothes the grass of the field. . .how much more will he clothe you—you of little faith!" (Luke 12:28 NIV). Or ponder this incident: "Jesus appeared to the Eleven as they were eating; he rebuked them for their lack of faith and their stubborn refusal to believe those who had seen him after he had risen" (Mark 16:14 NIV).

Jesus can only be known by faith—even back then, when standing in His physical presence. How are you responding to Him today? In faith, or causing Him to be "amazed at [your] lack of faith" (Mark 6:6 NIV)?

I pray, O God, as the father of this boy did.
Help me overcome my unbelief.

DAY 41

REMEMBER THE DAYS OF LONG AGO

I remember the days of long ago; I meditate on all your works and consider what your hands have done. I spread out my hands to you; I thirst for you like a parched land.

PSALM 143:5–6 NIV

It's believed that David composed this psalm while on the run after Absalom's rebellion. Surely he was recalling the days of old when God continually delivered him from Saul's hands. And in remembering God's faithfulness, he entered worship mode, lifting his hands in his thirst for the Lord. In so doing, he provides an example.

Are you going through a trial right now that feels familiar—one you've endured in the past but hoped never to face again? Remember the days of long ago. Remember God's faithfulness.

Consult your journal or talk to the person who prayed with you and walked with you through the trial the first time. Doing so will remind you about the little ways God provided. It will fill you with great hope that God will indeed show up again. Then allow those memories to lead you into a spirit and time of worship.

Lord, You have always been faithful to show up when I needed You. And You've always been faithful to send believers my way to remind me of Your faithfulness. Thank You, Lord. I worship and praise You.

DAY 42
A GRACIOUS GOD

But you, Lord, are a compassionate and gracious God,
slow to anger, abounding in love and faithfulness.
PSALM 86:15 NIV

Bible commentator Matthew Henry believed that David didn't write this psalm "under any particular occasion," but instead, it was a go-to prayer for him whenever he was in a time of need. David was a man after God's own heart, but he was also a grave sinner—one who probably needed to remind himself frequently that God is compassionate and slow to anger.

If you grew up with a father figure who ruled with an iron fist, or if you attended a church in which rules were more important than your relationship with Christ, you may still struggle to have a correct understanding of God's nature. You might see Him as an overbearing deity who is just waiting for you to mess up so He can bring the hammer down on you. But this isn't who God is. Instead, He's everything David describes in today's verse and more.

This would be a great verse to write in the front pages of your Bible so you can turn to it frequently. And you might want to incorporate it into your daily prayers as you seek to reorient your view of God's loving nature.

Father, help me to see You and Your character rightly.
Help me to see You in the same light that David—
himself a grave sinner—saw You.

DAY 43
DEAD MAN WALKING

*Then Jesus shouted, "Lazarus, come out!" And the
dead man came out, his hands and feet bound in
graveclothes, his face wrapped in a headcloth.*
JOHN 11:43–44 NLT

This familiar story is often told from Jesus' perspective, or from Lazarus'
two sisters' perspective. But have you ever considered it from Lazarus'
perspective? He was good friends with the Savior, the Messiah, and yet,
when Lazarus took ill, Jesus didn't come to his aid right away. In fact,
He didn't show up until after the illness had claimed his life.

Perhaps you or someone you love is dealing with a serious or even
terminal illness. You know that the Lord could heal you or your loved
one, but for some reason, He has chosen not to. Don't lose heart. God
will be glorified, just as Jesus said to Martha in John 11:40 (NLT): "Didn't
I tell you that you would see God's glory if you believe?"

Do you have that sort of faith—one that rests in the fact that the
Lord is glorified in both the life and death of His saints? To live is Christ
and to die is gain (Philippians 1:21). You can count on the fact that on
the last day, Jesus will call your body forth from the grave when He
returns for His saints.

---

*Lord Jesus, I look forward to Your return, when You will
make all things right and usher me into Your presence.*

DAY 44
PAID IN FULL

They trust in their wealth and boast of great riches. Yet they
cannot redeem themselves from death by paying a ransom
to God. Redemption does not come so easily, for no one can
ever pay enough to live forever and never see the grave.
PSALM 49:6–9 NLT

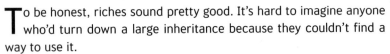

To be honest, riches sound pretty good. It's hard to imagine anyone who'd turn down a large inheritance because they couldn't find a way to use it.

But at the same time, as with so many blessings in this life, there has to be a balance. Money is a useful tool, but it has significant limits. It can't guarantee good health, a happy marriage, or well-behaved kids. And above all, it can't save a soul from the corruption of sin and the inevitability of death. Money just doesn't have that kind of value.

There is, however, a suitable currency that can save people from sin and death: "For even the Son of Man came not to be served but to serve others and to give his life as a ransom for many" (Matthew 20:28 NLT). Jesus' life was the only payment valuable enough to bring anyone freedom, and He offers it freely through faith. No amount of riches, no payment scraped together by human effort, could ever come close to doing what Christ did in His great mercy.

Father, help me to keep money and its limits clearly in mind.
Remind me that You alone are my refuge and hope.

DAY 45
AN UNEXPECTED PATH TO WISDOM

Teach us to realize the brevity of life,
so that we may grow in wisdom.
PSALM 90:12 NLT

The psalmist focuses on the hardship and brevity of life with a breathtaking and unvarnished perspective. Life is fleeting and painfully short, and even more striking, God sees every person's failures and sins. There is nowhere to hide, and there's no way to get an extension on life beyond what everyone else has.

How should believers respond to this seeming tragedy? With faith and trust in God, surely. But how?

Perhaps the most important step you can take is to fully enter into the sorrow and tragedy of this psalm. You don't have to stay in a state of fear and dread about the reality of death. Rather, facing the brevity of life can lead to better choices and wisdom. Who would knowingly waste a short life on the foolish pursuit of pleasure? Who would risk God's anger when everything could be swept away in a moment?

The limits and boundaries of life can sharpen your thinking and lead to better long-term investments of your time. God hasn't abandoned you to the sorrow and suffering of this world. In fact, the wise, who live in fear of God, will receive God's comfort. The sooner you recognize God's comforting presence, the better you'll spend your time each day.

Lord, show me how to use my time well today.

DAY 46
A STEADFAST FAITH

LORD, I have called daily upon You;
I have stretched out my hands to You.
PSALM 88:9 NKJV

Psalm 88 is a lament. The psalmist starts by pouring out his heart to the Lord, the God of his salvation, and he goes on to express the depths of his despair. He even seems to believe that God is the cause of it, saying He has laid him in the lowest pit, afflicted him, and put away his acquaintances, leaving him isolated. But that doesn't stop him from calling out to God.

Does your faith look similar when you're in the depths of despair? Are you able to be honest with the Lord, telling Him that your burden is heavy but that you will continue to seek Him every day? Or is your faith unable to hold up under such pressure? You'll know the answer to these questions if you tend to pull away from Him during difficult times.

If you want a faith that endures, continue seeking God even when you don't understand what He's up to. Trust Him with your circumstances. Trust Him with your future. Believe that He has your best interests at heart—that is, purifying you and helping you grow.

Father, I often don't understand my circumstances.
But I'm resolved to seek Your face every day, regardless,
knowing that tribulation produces perseverance;
and perseverance, character; and character, hope.

DAY 47
CRYING AND LAUGHING

To every thing there is a season, and a time to every purpose under the heaven. . .a time to weep, and a time to laugh.
ECCLESIASTES 3:1, 4 KJV

Y ou may be persuaded that grown men shouldn't cry, but as you look through the pages of the Bible, you see again and again that men of God weren't afraid to make themselves vulnerable by showing their emotions. From Jacob and Esau weeping as they embraced to King David publicly lamenting his son Absalom, Bible men often wept.

And they just as frequently laughed and enjoyed humorous situations. They even had a proverb: "A feast is *made* for laughter" (Ecclesiastes 10:19 KJV, emphasis added), so you can be sure that they looked forward to times when they would cut loose and laugh heartily.

Whether you laugh and cry in public or hold in your emotions stoically, the literal meaning of these passages from Ecclesiastes 3 is that during the course of your life, you can expect seasons of both sorrow and joy, times that would be enough to make a grown man cry as well as others that cause him to burst into uncontrollable laughter.

Thank God for the happy times. Enjoy them to the full. Know that you will also experience times of sorrow—but remember that you won't have to walk them alone.

Lord, I sometimes wish that I could have only happy times and would never experience stress, hardship, or sorrow. But I know that's not realistic. Thank You that You are always with me, in the happy times and in the difficult times as well.

DAY 48
A PICTURE OF DEPENDABILITY

As Scripture says, "Anyone who believes
in him will never be put to shame."
ROMANS 10:11 NIV

I n modern psychology, those who have a difficult time trusting in or depending upon another person are said to have "trust issues." Sometimes those trust issues come as a result of a father who repeatedly proved himself to be undependable.

While some earthly fathers weren't as dependable as they should have been, you never have to worry about this with your Father in heaven. He always keeps His promises and is always there for you if you simply call out to Him.

Jesus, who knew your heavenly Father better than anyone, said this of Him: "Which of you, if your son asks for bread, will give him a stone? Or if he asks for a fish, will give him a snake? If you, then, though you are evil, know how to give good gifts to your children, how much more will your Father in heaven give good gifts to those who ask him!" (Matthew 7:9–11 NIV).

When you come to God in faith for something—your salvation or some other pressing need—you can trust in Him to generously give you what you ask for. When you place that kind of trust in your heavenly Father, He will never let you down or leave you wondering where He is. Even when it seems He's *not* there, He's still there.

Loving Father in heaven, never let me forget that
I can always depend on You for all things.

DAY 49
THE LEAST

For I [Paul] am the least of the apostles, who am not
worthy to be called an apostle, because I persecuted
the church of God. But by the grace of God I am what
I am, and His grace toward me was not in vain.
1 CORINTHIANS 15:9–10 NKJV

Paul's background wasn't a secret. Prior to his conversion, he persecuted the Church. He watched approvingly as Stephen was stoned (Acts 22:20). It's no wonder Paul considered himself the least of the apostles. But the grace of God changed him.

It's difficult to have an inflated ego when you have such a checkered past. Maybe that's your story too. Surely you did things in the past that you regret, but if you've called on the name of the Lord for salvation, you've tasted the same grace of God that Paul is talking about in today's verse.

Do you consider yourself the least of the men at your church? Or in your Bible study? Or have you been around the church long enough that your ego has become inflated? Paul had quite the religious background (see Philippians 3:3–6), but he had no confidence in his post-conversion flesh. Nor should any Christian.

Lord, apart from Your grace, I am nothing—a worm among worms.
With Your grace, I am redeemed but still among the least in Your
kingdom. For I know my own heart too well to believe otherwise.

DAY 50
YOU CAN TRUST GOD'S WORD

No prophecy of Scripture is of any private interpretation,
for prophecy never came by the will of man, but holy men
of God spoke as they were moved by the Holy Spirit.
2 PETER 1:20–21 NKJV

Trying to live a victorious life of faith without reading your Bible is like trying to put together a complex piece of electronic gear without reading the instruction manual. Neither is going to go well.

The apostle Paul wrote, "All Scripture is God-breathed and is useful for teaching, rebuking, correcting and training in righteousness, so that the servant of God may be thoroughly equipped for every good work" (2 Timothy 3:16–17 NIV).

The phrase "God-breathed" as Paul used it is important because it echoes what the apostle Peter wrote in today's verse. It literally means that every word of the Bible is straight from the mouth of God, who used men as His own human fountain pens to record what He has to say to every believer who has ever lived or ever will live.

The Bible is an amazing book, and God went to amazing lengths to give it to His people. You can trust it explicitly and completely, knowing that it is the communication straight from the heart and mind of the God who knew you'd need an instruction manual.

Father, thank You for giving me Your written Word, which
contains everything I need to live a life that pleases You.

DAY 51

BECOME TRUSTWORTHY

Concentrate on doing your best for God, work you won't
be ashamed of, laying out the truth plain and simple.
2 TIMOTHY 2:15 MSG

Trust God and you can become more trustworthy. While no one is entirely trustworthy, when God is the one you follow, you'll be inclined to become more than a promise maker.

God's desire for you is to reflect His character in your actions, responses, and words. You have the opportunity to inspire others to catch a glimpse of what trust is then point them to the ultimate source of trust.

Do work you won't be ashamed of. Help others to trust God's simple truth. That's today's message, and it gives you a goal God can help you achieve.

God is trustworthy because He always does what He says He will do. You become trustworthy when you obey what He asks. You can learn what He requires by reading God's Word and doing what it says. The Bible isn't an advice column, a book of suggestions, or one of many inspirational texts to consider. The Bible is God's guide to the best life. God and His words can be trusted.

Dear God, I would love to be considered worthy of Your trust, and
to do that, I must obey what You've asked me to do. Your Word
tells me that when You can trust me with small things, You'll entrust
bigger things to my care. Help me become more trustworthy.

DAY 52

THE WISE, THE FOOLISH, THE TRUSTED

Wisdom is enshrined in an understanding heart;
wisdom is not found among fools.

PROVERBS 14:33 NLT

Proverbs is a great collection of wise sayings. Many powerful truths are found in its short thoughts. In this book of wisdom, we learn that fools can't be trusted. We also learn that God's wisdom and understanding *are* worthy of trust.

Even though God declares He is the source of trust, fools won't believe it and will refuse to trust Him. They tend to do the opposite of everything wise. They trust in other foolish humans' ideas. They try to convince the wise that they're the foolish ones. Those who are foolish highly regard deception but fail to recognize true wisdom as a priceless treasure.

If wisdom is water, then foolishness is oil that separates when in contact with water. Foolishness is repelled by wisdom, and while the wise are willing to teach, the foolish don't want to learn.

The foolish make up their own rules, so there's no reason to trust them. The source of true wisdom is God, so it's foolishness to fail to trust Him. God's wisdom can be trusted, and those who accept His wisdom are worthy of trust.

Lord, thank You for making it clear that the foolish can't be trusted because their beliefs constantly change. Help me pursue Your wisdom. Help me trust You, the God who never changes.

DAY 53

IS YOUR SHELTER STRONG ENOUGH?

Those who live in the shelter of the Most High will find rest in the shadow of the Almighty. This I declare about the LORD: He alone is my refuge, my place of safety; he is my God, and I trust him.

PSALM 91:1–2 NLT

The writer of this psalm compares trusting God to living in a shelter that provides safety and refuge from the worst parts of life. Danger and challenges still come, but within this shelter there is relief and hope for the future. When everything else falls away and proves itself unreliable, God alone remains as the one true source of safety.

Perhaps you can begin to meditate on this psalm today by asking whether you're in a state of rest and peace regardless of your life circumstances. Are you aware of God's presence and comfort? Do you have the peace of God even if your life is in turmoil?

If you don't have this sense of trust and peace in God, this could be a sign that you need to step into God's shelter instead of your own. Any man-made structure or source of security will topple when the circumstances of life grow difficult.

Lord, I surrender my own security and future into Your loving care. I trust You to guard me in the trials of life.

DAY 54
GIVING GENEROUSLY AND WISELY

Give freely and spontaneously. Don't have a stingy heart.
The way you handle matters like this triggers GOD, your God's,
blessing in everything you do, all your work and ventures.
DEUTERONOMY 15:10 MSG

Often it seems contrary to sound reason to give "freely and spontaneously." Aren't you supposed to follow a well-thought-out budget and not deviate from it with impulse purchases? Yes, you are. But God makes a difference between selfish personal expenditures and unselfish giving to the needy. And He promises to bless you for your generosity.

A word of caution, however: some people can be just as irresponsible in giving as they can be in impulse buying. They have so *much* empathy that, without thinking things through, they would give away their car or drain their bank account. Remember, "wisdom brings success" (Ecclesiastes 10:10 NKJV). And bear in mind: you are to care for your family first and foremost (Matthew 15:5–6; 1 Timothy 5:8).

But there are times to follow your heart instead of your head—and that's when God's Spirit is speaking to you. The New King James Version states clearly, "You shall surely give to [your poor brother], and your heart should not be grieved when you give" (Deuteronomy 15:10 NKJV). If you *know* that God wants you to give, then absolutely, give—even if your natural mind tries to hold you back.

However, if you have reasonable doubts about whether it's wise to give at this time, then don't. "Whatever is not from faith is sin" (Romans 14:23 NKJV).

Generous Father, help me to trust You enough to be
a cheerful giver. Help me also to be wise in my giving.

DAY 55
COME, LORD JESUS!

It will happen in a moment, in the blink of an eye,
when the last trumpet is blown. For when the trumpet
sounds, those who have died will be raised to live forever.
And we who are living will also be transformed.
1 CORINTHIANS 15:52 NLT

In today's verse, the Church is promised resurrection. A trumpet will sound and the dead in Christ shall rise to be transformed into resurrected bodies, and those who are living will be transformed. This is the great promise of Christianity. Jesus will return for His Church in the most glorious event since the day He willingly died for you on the cross.

"And cannot the same power now change us into saints in a moment?" asks John Wesley in his commentary. "Surely it can. And since a day is coming when the church will rise or be transformed in a single moment, how does such a promise help you determine who you will spend time with now and how you will spend your time, money, and energy?"

Knowing that the final trumpet can sound at any minute, it's time to get busy doing kingdom work and leave the foolish pursuits of this world behind.

Lord Jesus, I look forward with great anticipation to the final
trumpet. As I live with the resurrection in mind, may it shape every
decision I make and every action I take. Amen! Come, Lord Jesus.

DAY 56

MINISTERING ON A TIGHT BUDGET

Peter said, "I don't have any silver or gold for you.
But I'll give you what I have. In the name of Jesus
Christ the Nazarene, get up and walk!"

ACTS 3:6 NLT

Peter lacked the financial resources to help the beggar, but he was rich in other things that he gladly shared. Helping this man stand and walk brought Peter and John a good deal of attention, some that helped them preach the gospel and some that brought persecution and suffering. However, their focus in the moment was this man who was unable to walk.

Peter stepped out in faith, perhaps uncertain of where his actions would lead, but in the end, many benefited from his compassionate ministry.

It's tempting to assume either that money is what will fix most problems or that not being able to donate money can rule you out as a contributor. Peter's faith is a reminder that followers of Jesus have blessings to share that are far greater than money.

Whether praying for actual physical restoration or spiritual liberation, you have access to God's power and mercy for the benefit of others. Pay attention to the moments today when you can bless others and even step out in faith to ask God for something miraculous.

Lord, use me to bless those who are in need.

DAY 57
A LIVING FAITH

What good is it, my brothers and sisters, if someone claims to have faith but has no deeds? Can such faith save them? . . . Faith by itself, if it is not accompanied by action, is dead.

JAMES 2:14, 17 NIV

Do you find today's verse a little troubling or, at the very least, confusing? If so, you're not alone. Taken in isolation, these words seem to say that without good works, you can't be saved.

However, this passage is a clear example of how context means everything. When you take these words as part of the bigger picture of New Testament teaching about your salvation, you understand that your good works are not a *means to the end* of your salvation but rather are a *result* of that salvation.

The New Testament is clear that you're not saved through your own works, no matter how good they are. But when you have God's Spirit dwelling inside you as a result of coming to Jesus Christ for salvation, your Spirit-inspired attitude will always result in good works.

Are you looking for ways to put your faith into action? Then ask God what good works He'd like you to take part in today. But never forget that your good works here on earth can't save you for eternity, and they can't earn you additional favor with God. What they *can* do, however, is make your faith more real to you and others.

Father in heaven, You've been good and generous to me in so many ways. Show me how I can show others goodness and generosity so that I can bring glory to You.

DAY 58

WHEN BEING HARD IS GOOD AND WHEN IT'S NOT

*But when they saw him walking on the lake, they thought
he was a ghost. They cried out, because they all saw him
and were terrified. Immediately he spoke to them and said,
"Take courage! It is I. Don't be afraid." Then he climbed
into the boat with them, and the wind died down. They were
completely amazed, for. . .their hearts were hardened.*

MARK 6:49–52 NIV

Professional fishermen are a tough bunch. It's hard work, not suited to the lazy or the soft. If you were a fisherman in first-century Palestine, you were usually a hardworking guy, made strong by a difficult life. In fact, just about everyone in the ancient world would be considered hardened by today's standards. It was often an unforgiving environment where only the hardy survived. That's when it's good to be hardened.

But it's not good to be hard when it comes to spiritual lessons. To be dull to the things God has made known about His power and provision is to miss the next lesson. The disciples were amazed that Jesus was walking on the water despite the fact that He had just fed thousands from a handful of food.

Are there lessons God has shown you that you haven't taken to heart yet?

*Jesus, help me to remember Your great deeds and to trust
You for even more. Let me not be hard of heart.*

DAY 59
A BETTER GIFT

*"But only you and your sons may serve as priests in connection
with everything at the altar and inside the curtain. I am
giving you the service of the priesthood as a gift. Anyone else
who comes near the sanctuary is to be put to death."*

NUMBERS 18:7 NIV

When God organized the system of worship for the ancient Israelites, He appointed the Levites to serve as assistants to Aaron and his sons, who alone were priests before God. The priesthood was an honor, and the Lord confirmed with a promise that anyone else who tried to take on that responsibility would die.

Today, however, believers have been offered this very honor because they have been born into "a royal priesthood" (1 Peter 2:9 NIV) under a "better covenant" (Hebrews 7:22 NIV). Christians aren't part of Aaron's priesthood, but rather of Melchizedek's (Hebrews 7:17). Melchizedek, who came long *before* Levi, was a king and a priest of God; his name means "King of Righteousness." This is the priesthood of Jesus and is every believer's calling.

Are you taking hold of the gift that you have in Christ? Are you living in freedom and power as a priest whose gift comes from "the power of an indestructible life" (Hebrews 7:16 NIV)? If not, embrace the better gift—it's your birthright.

*King of Righteousness, thank You for including me
in a priesthood that endures forever in Christ.*

DAY 60
WHEN AN ENEMY FALLS

*Do not gloat when your enemy falls; when they stumble,
do not let your heart rejoice, or the LORD will see and
disapprove and turn his wrath away from them.*
PROVERBS 24:17–18 NIV

---

*S*chadenfreude is a German word for feeling pleasure or joy at the troubles or failures of another person. While there may not be an exact English equivalent for this word, it's safe to say that the emotion itself is a common one to humanity.

Have you ever felt at least a small twinge of satisfaction or pleasure when someone you know—say a competitor in business or someone who hasn't dealt with you in the way you felt you deserved—fell on difficult times? If so, then you should know that God doesn't approve of that way of thinking.

Jesus instructed His followers to pray for their enemies and adversaries, not to wish ill on them—and *certainly* not to rejoice at their downfall (Matthew 5:44). When you walk in obedience to this command, in effect you're saying, "God is bigger than any conflict I have with another person, and I'm going to trust God enough to respond to that person's suffering in a way that pleases Him."

---

*Lord, guard my heart from feeling pleasure or joy when my
adversary suffers or fails. Instead, remind me to pray for
that person knowing that You will deal with him as You see fit.*

DAY 61
THE ONE WHO REVEALS

Then Simeon blessed them, and said to Mary His mother,
"Behold, this Child is destined for the fall and rising of many
in Israel, and for a sign which will be spoken against. . .
that the thoughts of many hearts may be revealed."
LUKE 2:34–35 NKJV

God had promised Simeon that he wouldn't die until he had seen the Messiah. That promise was fulfilled the day Jesus was brought to the temple to be consecrated. But with this promise came a problem: this Messiah would be a welcome sight to some but a controversy to others.

Jesus, the Word (*logos*) of God, would be "sharper than any two-edged sword, piercing even to the division of soul and spirit, and of joints and marrow," and He would be "a discerner of the thoughts and intents of the heart" (Hebrews 4:12 NKJV). He would become the greatest threat to the self-righteous, and the greatest friend to the sinner seeking forgiveness.

Then, as now, it all came down to the heart. Open your own heart to the Messiah today so that you can experience the full healing of His love. If you feel reluctant, ask God to reveal why, and confess any sin. Don't be afraid of the great Revealer—He came to raise up the humble and give new life.

Father, reveal my inner thoughts so that I may receive
Your grace to change and become like Your Son.

DAY 62
LIVING WHAT YOU UNDERSTAND

To him who knows to do good and does not do it, to him it is sin.
JAMES 4:17 NKJV

There are sins of omission as well as sins of commission. How often do men fail to do something good out of lethargy, procrastination, or simply a lack of concern? Solomon instructed, "Do not withhold good from those to whom it is due, when it is in the power of your hand to do so" (Proverbs 3:27 NKJV). As we see in the next verse, he was talking about giving generously to people when you just don't feel like it.

There are many complex situations where you won't *know* the correct thing to do. In hindsight, yes, you may see clearly what you should've done, but if you simply don't know at the time what you should do, you won't be held accountable. But most of the Bible's important teachings are very plain and simple. There's little that's puzzling about them. The problem, however, is that they can be difficult to obey.

Mark Twain said, "It ain't those parts of the Bible that I can't understand that bother me, it is the parts that I do understand." Whatever context Twain meant this in, it's very relevant here. For example, most Christians are deeply bothered by Jesus' command "Love your enemies" (Matthew 5:44). They reason that He couldn't really have meant that literally. So they withhold love and forgiveness from people they don't like.

Once you understand clearly what you ought to do, however, it's a sin if you don't follow through and do it.

Father, move my heart toward acts of love,
especially toward those who I may not think deserve them.

DAY 63
QUESTION AUTHORITY

And as He was walking in the temple, the chief priests,
the scribes, and the elders came to Him. And they said
to Him, "By what authority are You doing these things?
And who gave You this authority to do these things?"

MARK 11:27–28 NKJV

There's been a bumper sticker around for years that says: "Question Authority." It's most often interpreted in a radical, antiestablishment sense. While verifying human authority for its validity may be a good practice, questioning the authority of Christ is a different matter.

The day before the Jewish leaders approached Jesus to question His authority, He had disrupted their religious system by driving dishonest merchants from the temple. The leaders demanded answers since they were the ones profiting from the corrupt system. They believed they had authority and that Jesus was the disruptor when, in fact, it was the other way around. If the temple was God's house, then His Son had every right to kick people out.

Authority doesn't just grant privilege—it requires accountability. The Jewish leaders embraced privilege but rejected accountability. Jesus addressed their hypocrisy, but, of course, they chose to reject the Messiah's rebuke.

While you can see the Pharisees' obvious mistake, is there anything you're trusting in that Jesus might like to overrule? Is there anything you're insisting is your "right" that He may disagree with?

Jesus, may Your authority always have the final say in my life.

DAY 64

COURAGE TO SHARE THE GOSPEL

Peter and John replied, "Do you think God wants us to obey you rather than him? We cannot stop telling about everything we have seen and heard."

ACTS 4:19–20 NLT

What stops Christians from sharing the gospel? The religious teachers in Jerusalem hoped that intimidating Peter and John would prevent them from performing miracles and telling people about Jesus. However, Peter and John had a clear mission for their lives and knew what God had asked them to do.

Their boldness didn't happen overnight. They had been with Jesus, witnessed His resurrection, and were convinced. This focused their lives on what mattered most.

If you struggle with boldness or courage in speaking about your faith, Peter and John offer a helpful clue about where to begin: What have you seen and heard? The boldness to share the gospel comes from spending time with Jesus, experiencing transformation, and then speaking out of the work of God in your life.

If you make time to be with Jesus daily, the courage to speak will come naturally. What you have seen and experienced will be too good *not* to share, regardless of what some people may think.

Lord, I trust that You can give me the words to speak to others.

WORKPLACE HUMOR

Nor should there be obscenity, foolish talk or coarse joking,
which are out of place, but rather thanksgiving.
EPHESIANS 5:4 NIV

I f you work in a professional environment or a business that constantly interacts with the public, the language you hear on a daily basis is apt to be clean and courteous. But there are many trades (particularly all-male workplaces) where cursing and off-color humor are common—particularly if certain coworkers are outspoken unbelievers who habitually use graphic curse words and find crude sexual jokes funny.

While you don't want to come across as a straitlaced old fogy, it's important that you don't encourage their behavior. If you go along with their jokes, laughing politely to avoid offending them, they'll be emboldened to keep going. It's best to let them know up front that this is not your type of humor. There are ways to do this without giving offense. You can simply consistently refrain from smiling at their jokes.

Of course, you have little control over their reaction. Some men will take the cue and turn down the volume around you. Others may mock you for being "puritanical." Don't be surprised. Peter says, "You have spent enough time in the past doing what pagans choose to do. . . . They are surprised that you do not join them in their reckless, wild living, and they heap abuse on you" (1 Peter 4:3–4 NIV).

Whatever others around you do, continue to follow Christ with a clear conscience.

Father in heaven, help me to glorify and obey You, even when
those around me speak and act in ways that don't please You.

DAY 66

AS YOU MAKE YOUR PLANS. . .

Commit to the LORD whatever you do,
and he will establish your plans.
PROVERBS 16:3 NIV

If you've ever been involved in planning for a new project or a new direction at work, you know that there's one all-important step you need to take before those plans can become a reality: your managers or bosses need to sign off on it. Without their approval, you're likely to run into serious problems.

The same thing can be said for the Christian who wants to launch out into some kind of new ministry or professional or personal endeavor. In today's verse, Solomon offers a great bit of wisdom when it comes to planning. The best kind of planning, he tells you, starts with committing your vision for something to your ultimate boss, your heavenly Father, and continues as you allow Him to give ongoing direction.

Many seemingly great plans—even plans for what looked like a God-appointed ministry—have failed because those with the vision didn't first submit their work to God.

Planning is an important part—a bedrock, in fact—of all great and important things you do. It's simply not a good idea to launch out on some new endeavor without it. So by all means plan, but as you make your plans, don't forget to submit what you're thinking about doing to God for His approval and His direction.

Lord God, I know You want me to submit myself
to You as I make my plans. Help me to always
bring my plans to You for Your approval.

DAY 67
GOD'S ENDGAME

My son, do not despise the chastening of the LORD,
nor detest His correction; for whom the LORD loves He
corrects, just as a father the son in whom he delights.
PROVERBS 3:11–12 NKJV

If God constantly sends hardship, financial problems, or health issues into your life, you can begin to get mentally exhausted. You may even think that He allows you to experience grief because He hates you. But the opposite is true. The Lord chastens you because He *loves* you. He especially delights in you and rejoices to see you do your best.

The Lord says, "The people I love, I call to account—prod and correct and guide so that they'll live at their best" (Revelation 3:19 MSG). It's no fun being repeatedly called to account for your actions and decisions. It's frustrating when the boss calls you to his office once again to account for a mistake you made and asks, "Why did you do that?"

At times, you wish God would just let your sloppy behavior slide. And if He didn't care for you as much as He does, He just might do that. But He has a purpose in continually correcting you. He's refining you, and He invites you to actively join in the process. Paul wrote, "Those who cleanse themselves. . .will be instruments for special purposes, made holy, useful to the Master and prepared to do any good work" (2 Timothy 2:21 NIV).

God seeks to make you into a better person, capable of great things. Are you okay with that?

Loving Father, thank You for loving me enough to discipline me,
correct me, and strengthen me for what You have for me.

DAY 68
FIGHT LIKE MEN

Keep your eyes open, hold tight to your convictions, give it
all you've got, be resolute, and love without stopping.
1 CORINTHIANS 16:13–14 MSG

Are you facing an aggressive, belligerent enemy in some area of your personal life? Is one of your children going through a crisis that demands much of your time and energy? Are financial problems putting you at risk of losing your home? These and many other serious challenges test your resolve and show what you're made of.

When Nehemiah and his men were surrounded by enemies who threatened to overwhelm them, he encouraged them, saying, "Don't be afraid of the enemy! Remember the Lord, who is great and glorious, and fight for your brothers, your sons, your daughters, your wives, and your homes!" (Nehemiah 4:14 NLT). Or as David instructed his son Solomon when he was about to face great challenges, "Take courage and be a man" (1 Kings 2:2 NLT).

You're already used to dealing with a certain level of problems and difficulties in your daily life. But sometimes problems go on and on and become very serious threats. At that point, they can seem so overwhelming, so impossible to deal with, that you feel like simply throwing up your hands in despair and saying, "I give up!" But that is precisely the point when you need to be resolute. Have courage and don't give up the fight.

Father in heaven, some things are well worth fighting
for and giving all I've got. Give me the strength to win
battles and withstand the onslaughts of the enemy.

TRUSTING GOD TO ACT

*Wait for the LORD; be strong and
take heart and wait for the LORD.*
PSALM 27:14 NIV

There will be points in your life when you're utterly incapable of affecting the outcome of a situation you find yourself in. At times like that, you have no choice but to wait for the Lord and trust Him to act. Often, it then takes great faith to believe that God is with you, because He might seem very distant, or like He's turned away from you. This is why Isaiah said, "I will wait on the LORD, who hides His face from the house of Jacob; and I will hope in Him" (Isaiah 8:17 NKJV).

If you've sinned and disobeyed the Lord, chances are good that He actually *has* turned His face from you and isn't listening to your prayers (see Isaiah 59:1–2). But if you have sincerely repented, then there are no longer any issues between you, and you simply have to believe that God loves you and will act on your behalf.

This takes faith. You might go through a time of testing just like Job, who was convinced for several months that God was against him. During such lonely sojourns, you must trust God's Word, not your feelings, and believe that "the mercy of the LORD is from everlasting to everlasting upon them that fear him" (Psalm 103:17 KJV).

---

*God of power and strength, when I'm going through
a difficult time, remind me that You are for me and
that You will eventually come through for me.*

GOD'S HOLINESS AND JUSTICE

Mighty King, lover of justice, you have established fairness. You have acted with justice and righteousness throughout Israel. Exalt the LORD our God! Bow low before his feet, for he is holy!

PSALM 99:4–5 NLT

When God imagines a future with righteousness and holiness, justice is always part of the mix. God is praised for His love of justice and the way that He has established fairness as a standard in the world.

God's concern doesn't just stop with personal conduct. The righteousness of systems and laws also matters a great deal to Him. God's concern for people is wide-reaching and holistic.

As you worship the Lord today, keep in mind that He cares for both your personal holiness and the justice that you personally experience. That care is also extended to your neighbors and people around the world.

Worship of God has long been linked with His consistent care for justice and fairness. Today may be a good day to listen to the stories of others in your community or networks. Are there people you know who have experienced injustice or have been treated unfairly? How can you be present in their pain? How can you honor their story? A holy and just God prompts His people to listen well to those who have suffered.

Lord, help me to mourn with those who mourn today and to listen well.

DAY 71
FILTHY LIPS

*"It's all over! I am doomed, for I am a sinful man. I have
filthy lips, and I live among a people with filthy lips.
Yet I have seen the King, the LORD of Heaven's Armies."*

ISAIAH 6:5 NLT

I magine having the vision Isaiah described in Isaiah 6:1–4. He saw the
Lord sitting on a lofty throne. Six-winged seraphim were attending to
Him, saying, "Holy, holy, holy is the LORD of Heaven's Armies!" Their
voices shook the temple to its foundations and the entire building was
filled with smoke.

It had to be a terrifying sight. Isaiah was privy to the holy of holies
and realized he was doomed, for he was a sinful man with filthy lips.

The closer you get to the Lord, the more He will expose your
uncleanliness. He is too holy to do otherwise. But don't fret. God made
Isaiah holy when one of the seraphim touched his unclean lips with a
burning coal to purify them. And, praise God, He also made you holy
when Christ died for you.

The second that the seraphim pronounced Isaiah's forgiveness,
Isaiah volunteered to tell others about it. How about you? Are you busy
sharing the cleansing message of the gospel?

---

*Lord, I too am a sinful man with filthy lips, and I live among
a people with filthy lips. Yet You sent Your Son to offer me
forgiveness. How can I do anything but tell others about Him?*

DAY 72
UNITY IN THE SPIRIT

They were all filled with the Holy Ghost. . . . And the multitude
of them that believed were of one heart and of one soul.
ACTS 4:31–32 KJV

Y ou received the Holy Spirit into your heart, the core of your being, when you put your faith in Jesus (see Galatians 4:6). Many people are very interested in what the Spirit can do for them—as well they should be, since it is He who saves them and gives them wonderful gifts! But they often overlook one of the chief purposes of the Spirit—to bring Christians into unity.

"By one Spirit we were all baptized into one body" (1 Corinthians 12:13 NKJV), so although we are each individual members, we "are all one in Christ Jesus" (Galatians 3:28 NKJV). We all share in "the communion of the Holy Spirit" (2 Corinthians 13:14 NKJV).

The very same Holy Spirit who dwells in your heart also dwells in the hearts of all other believers, and He loves every one of them as much as He loves you. This is why Christians are to love one another sincerely, and why "the members should have the same care one for another" (1 Corinthians 12:25 KJV).

You may be a rugged individualist and be inclined to look out chiefly for yourself, but if you do so, you're missing out on the big picture. When God sent His Spirit into your heart, He made you to live in fellowship with other Christians.

Father God, remind me and empower me to look out for
other believers just like I would a natural brother or sister.

DAY 73
EXCELLING AT WORK

Do you see a man who excels in his work? He will stand
before kings; he will not stand before unknown men.
PROVERBS 22:29 NKJV

It is easy to get caught up in working for the applause of men—or simply to put food on the table—because both produce tangible results. But a man who excels in his work can do so for other reasons. As Christians, we are called to work to the glory of God (Colossians 3:17).

A man who excels in his work is diligent. He studies the systems that are in place and tweaks them to make them even better. He knows the needs of his customers and he exceeds them. He keeps his word. He is prompt, accurate, and quick to adjust his course when he sees the need to do so.

Joseph was sold into slavery by his brothers, but he worked hard and found favor with Potiphar, the governor of Egypt, who eventually elevated Joseph to second-in-command. He literally stood before royalty, as the verse above says. But even those of us who will never meet nobility for our strong work efforts will stand before the King of kings to give account someday.

If you aren't already doing so, what would it look like for you to excel at work for God's glory?

Lord God, show me ways to glorify You in my work—
even if it means doing difficult things like loving an
unlovable boss or going above and beyond my work
description to benefit my department or company.

DAY 74
EYES ARE UPON YOU

"Let your light so shine before men, that they may see your good works and glorify your Father in heaven."

MATTHEW 5:16 NKJV

It's important that you live your Christian faith sincerely, not just put on a show when you think people are watching. However, like it or not, people *are* watching you all the time and constantly judging whether you're living what you preach. This includes fellow believers and your own children. That's why Paul said, "Be an example to all believers in what you say, in the way you live, in your love, your faith, and your purity" (1 Timothy 4:12 NLT).

Unbelievers are watching too—both the curious who are attracted to the gospel and the antagonistic who're looking for an excuse to criticize the faith. Peter refers to them, saying, "It is God's will that your honorable lives should silence those ignorant people who make foolish accusations against you" (1 Peter 2:15 NLT).

People are constantly watching you. That's God's *plan*—one of His chief ways of letting the world see what the gospel can do for a person. Jesus said that believers are the light of the world, a city set on a hilltop where everyone can see them and think about them.

And people are *especially* watching you when you go through hardships, whether they're misfortunes, illnesses, or persecution. Paul said, "God has displayed us. . .for we have been made a spectacle to the world" (1 Corinthians 4:9 NKJV).

Lord God, how I act when I'm suffering communicates Your message of hope more effectively than a sermon. Help me always to let the light of Your gospel shine through me.

DAY 75
WHEN MAN'S LAWS VIOLATE GOD'S LAWS

But when Daniel learned that the law had been signed, he went home and knelt down as usual in his upstairs room, with its windows open toward Jerusalem. He prayed three times a day, just as he had always done, giving thanks to his God.

DANIEL 6:10 NLT

How would you respond if a law were passed forcing you to violate your conscience in regard to something about which God has clearly spoken? That's exactly the situation Daniel found himself in. King Darius had just issued a decree forbidding anyone from worshipping or praying to anyone but him. This under the threat of becoming lunch to a den full of hungry lions.

Daniel had plenty to be concerned about, so, being powerless to change the law, he did the only thing he could: he prayed. After learning of the law, he went to his upstairs room three times every day and prayed to the God who could save him and keep him faithfully serving Him.

There is plenty happening in today's culture that can move a man of God to anger, even fear. That's not necessarily a bad thing, provided those emotions move him to prayer.

Lord, I see many things in today's culture—things I know don't please or honor You—that bring me to a point of anger or fear. Remind me always to bring those things to You in prayer.

KEEPING ABOVE REPROACH

I will search for faithful people to be my companions. Only those who are above reproach will be allowed to serve me.

PSALM 101:6 NLT

Remaining holy and above reproach takes more than personal commitments. The decisions of your colleagues, acquaintances, and friends can all have a significant impact on your values and the choices that you make.

In his quest to remain blameless before God, the psalmist writes about taking time to find faithful people, not settling for those who may have divided loyalties. The stakes were surely higher for someone in a position of authority, but many of the principles apply to believers today.

Your community matters a great deal for your spiritual health. If you're surrounded by people striving to know God and to grow in awareness of His presence, then you'll most likely be encouraged to pursue God with greater passion and set aside more of your time for spiritual pursuits.

Compromising company can lead to compromises in your personal life. Are you surrounded by people who are living by faith, trusting God, and practicing repentance when they fail? You won't always make the right decisions, and that's when being surrounded by a faithful community can make all the difference.

Lord, lead me to people who are faithful and committed to You.

DAY 77
THE TWO COMMANDMENTS

"The most important [commandment]," answered Jesus,
"is this: 'Hear, O Israel: The Lord our God, the Lord is one.
Love the Lord your God with all your heart and with all your
soul and with all your mind and with all your strength.'
The second is this: 'Love your neighbor as yourself.'
There is no commandment greater than these."

MARK 12:29–31 NIV

Jesus was unequivocal about what were the most important commandments in the Law. In fact, He stated in Matthew 22:40 (NIV), "All the Law and the Prophets hang on these two."

Interestingly, neither is found in the Ten Commandments (which usually get more attention and discussion). Does that mean the Ten Commandments aren't important? No, it means they are *written* upon these two concepts the way they were once written on two tablets of stone. They can't be applied or even understood correctly apart from these two commandments.

Now, if you thought the Ten were tough to obey, these two are utterly impossible. That's because no commandment of God can be truly obeyed without the heart involved. Simple outward adherence isn't enough. That's merely legalism. You're in desperate need of the one who fulfilled God's Law (Matthew 5:17)—particularly the Two Commandments. Let Him live in you and obey them through you. That's the only way.

Father, I want to obey from the heart. Thank You
for living in me and strengthening me to obey.

DAY 78
THE FRAGRANCE OF CHRIST

In the Messiah, in Christ, God leads us from place to place in one
perpetual victory parade. Through us, he brings knowledge of Christ.
Everywhere we go, people breathe in the exquisite fragrance.

2 CORINTHIANS 2:14–15 MSG

As Paul traveled from place to place, the gospel was having its way
with people—so much so that he referred to his travels as a perpetual
victory parade. Of course, he faced hardships in his missionary journeys.
(He wrote about these in depth in 2 Corinthians 11:16–33). But the gospel
still prevailed, bringing in the fragrance of Christ, much like a woman's
perfume follows her wherever she goes.

Would you describe your own travels as a perpetual spiritual victory
parade? Does the fragrance of Christ follow you into worship? Into local
cafés? Into work? Surely it does if you belong to and trust in Christ.

The Christian's true joy comes as he finds fulfillment in Jesus and
then seeks to share Him with others. How can you be more intentional
in doing so? By sending cards of prayerful encouragement to those who
need it? By making time to talk to the lonely person across the street
about Jesus? Something else?

Lord, too often I suspect that people can't get a whiff of Christ
as I interact with them because I'm caught up in my personal
issues. Help me to expand my reach for Your name's sake.

DAY 79
START SMALL

You, LORD, will keep the needy safe and will protect us
forever from the wicked, who freely strut about when
what is vile is honored by the human race.

PSALM 12:7–8 NIV

It's hard to share your faith. You know the gospel, you believe it, and maybe you even feel like you could share it effectively. But doing so would complicate your relationships, maybe even cost you at work. Anytime you move beyond life's surface to the deeper questions, it gets messy.

The world is full of messy beliefs, habits, politics, religion—and you can probably find it all right there in your neighborhood. However, you're uniquely and completely equipped to make a difference. Rather than fearing the response of the lost, or being overwhelmed by the scope of the need, remember that it's God's Spirit at work in you, helping you and even giving you the words to say when you share about Jesus and face trouble as a result (Luke 12:12).

Make yourself available, then start small. Jesus said, "Go to the lost, confused people right here in the neighborhood. Tell them that the kingdom is here. . . . Don't think you have to put on a fund-raising campaign before you start. You don't need a lot of equipment. *You* are the equipment" (Matthew 10:6–7, 9–10 MSG).

God, give me an opportunity to start small—even
at home or in my neighborhood. You have given me
everything; help me to live as generously.

DAY 80
HAVE YOU MET MY SON?

When all the people were being baptized, Jesus was
baptized too. And as he was praying, heaven was opened
and the Holy Spirit descended on him in bodily form like
a dove. And a voice came from heaven: "You are my
Son, whom I love; with you I am well pleased."

LUKE 3:21–22 NIV

John the Baptist had created quite a stir with his ministry. Like the prophet Elijah, John had rebuked sin at the highest levels of government. He was fearless and impressive, and the people believed a prophet had come after four hundred years of silence from God.

But the Bible records no miracles or signs from John. Likely, God wanted no confusion on the part of His people as John pointed to the miracle-working Messiah. The anticipation was mounting for the Promised One.

And there was no mistaking the announcement that came at Jesus' baptism: a physical expression of the Holy Spirit and the voice of the Father Himself. You'd think that would have settled the matter. It didn't. For three years, Jesus had to prove Himself over and over. Even the resurrection didn't convince everyone.

What "introductions" to Jesus has God given you? What truths from Christ have changed your life? Build on those, and thank God for reinforcing them with each new day.

Father, thank You for introducing Your Son to me!

DAY 81
WHEN EVERYTHING FALLS APART

But you, O LORD, will sit on your throne forever. Your
fame will endure to every generation. You will arise
and have mercy on Jerusalem—and now is the time to
pity her, now is the time you promised to help.
PSALM 102:12–13 NLT

A s the people of Jerusalem suffered and watched their confidence in the future fade away, they could only turn in one direction for their hope. The Lord was the one constant who couldn't be removed by war, famine, or plots of their enemies. The hope of Jerusalem rested wholly on God's mercy and future action. As the people grasped just how powerless they were, they realized that the real hope for their lives came from God.

Tragedies will come. Your life will be disrupted in one way or another, if it hasn't been already. As you experience this loss and uncertainty, you'll also have an opportunity to trust more completely in God's enduring presence.

That isn't to say losses will be immediately replaced and difficulties will abruptly cease. The people of Israel waited an entire generation for Jerusalem to be restored. However, a season of loss and struggle is often the chance to gain clarity on what is unmovable and to more fully trust in God.

Lord, help me to depend more completely on You.

DAY 82
COLLECTING GOOD

*"No good tree bears bad fruit, nor does a bad tree bear
good fruit. Each tree is recognized by its own fruit. People do
not pick figs from thornbushes, or grapes from briers. A good
man brings good things out of the good stored up in his heart,
and an evil man brings evil things out of the evil stored up in
his heart. For the mouth speaks what the heart is full of."*

LUKE 6:43–45 NIV

Have you ever known someone who was a serious collector? Maybe coins or stamps or World War II memorabilia? Maybe you collect something in earnest.

There are three things serious collectors have in common: they know their subject, they are passionate about it, and they are always on the lookout for new items. What if every believer were a serious collector of "good"?

Goodness is a relative term when applied to people. But compared to God, "there is no one who does good" (Psalm 14:1 NIV). Jesus said, "No one is good—except God alone" (Mark 10:18 NIV). However, the New Testament is filled with admonitions to do good and be good. What's the balance?

Jesus says a good man has *stored up* good in his heart. Like a collector. No collector owns it all. But he pursues it, loves it, and wants to bring it out for all to see.

---

*Father, You alone are good, and I want to collect
as much of Your goodness as I can.*

DAY 83
THE ONLY HOPE

Have mercy on me, O God, according to your unfailing love;
according to your great compassion blot out my transgressions.

PSALM 51:1 NIV

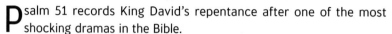

Psalm 51 records King David's repentance after one of the most shocking dramas in the Bible.

David, who had slain Goliath, who had endured years of King Saul's persecution before being crowned king himself, had committed adultery with a woman after seeing her bathing. After she became pregnant, David had her husband placed in the front of a heated battle so he'd be killed and cover up David's sin. It was well after the baby's birth—months perhaps—that the prophet Nathan confronted and convicted David.

Considering this, how can David be described *by God* as a man "who kept my commands and followed me with all his heart, doing only what was right in my eyes" (1 Kings 14:8 NIV)? And why wasn't the Law enforced? Adultery and murder were punished by death (Leviticus 20:10; Numbers 35:31).

The only explanation comes in today's verse: *unfailing love* and *great compassion*. David threw himself totally on the one who could "blot out" his transgression. He had sinned greatly, but in his heart's cry there is no hint of self-help, no explanations or excuses. For David to be forgiven, it was God or nothing. It was God plus nothing. This is your only hope as well, whether you've sinned greatly or quietly.

Father, forgive me because of Your great love and compassion.

DAY 84
GOD GRANTS WEALTH

You may say to yourself, "My power and the strength of my hands have produced this wealth for me." But remember the LORD your God, for it is he who gives you the ability to produce wealth.
DEUTERONOMY 8:17–18 NIV

Deuteronomy 8:1–18 cautions that if your possessions increase, don't get the idea that you produced this wealth. Instead, you are to remember the days when you had next to nothing and trusted God to provide for you—and He did.

If you congratulate yourself, God may see to it that you lose your gains to teach you to trust Him again. Then this saying will come to pass: "You have sown much, and bring in little. . .and he who earns wages, earns wages to put into a bag with holes" (Haggai 1:6 NKJV).

Even if you long to dream up the perfect get-rich-quick plan, God may shoot a hole in your balloon and cause it to dissipate overnight (Psalm 64:6–7). Even if it worked for other people, God can see to it that it *doesn't* work for you—like joining a multilevel marketing scheme too late. Remember, God is the one who gives wealth. . .or not.

Lord, help me never to put my trust in my own ability to gain wealth. Help me to always remember that, ultimately, You are my provider, the one who gives me the ability to earn wealth.

DAY 85
TRUSTING GOD IN A STORM

"Where is your faith?" he asked his disciples.
LUKE 8:25 NIV

———————

You may have the faith to handle small day-to-day crises—such as finding a last-minute replacement for a worker who didn't show up—but can you trust in God's power and care when an emergency strikes? Or do you buckle and come unglued?

One day, Jesus and His disciples were sailing across the Sea of Galilee, with Jesus asleep in the boat, when a sudden squall swept down upon them. Instantly, the sea began raging, so that they were in danger of being swamped. The disciples woke Jesus, terrified that they would drown. Jesus rose, rebuked the wind and the waves, and the storm abruptly ceased.

But note that He then asked where *their* faith was. Clearly, Jesus expected any one of *them* to have been able to pray and trust God for the miracle. You might not have the faith to stop a storm, but you are certain to face many crises during the course of your life that will seem as serious as a storm. So if your faith is small now, pray like Jesus' disciples prayed, for God to increase your faith (Luke 17:5).

Trouble is bound to come, so prepare for it.

Dear Father, increase my faith so that I will be able to trust You for a miracle in the day of testing, and having done all, to stand, I pray.

DAY 86

LOVE LEADS TO OBEDIENCE

GOD sticks by all who love him,
but it's all over for those who don't.
PSALM 145:20 MSG

Commentators point out that Psalm 145 is one of the "alphabetical psalms" in which each verse (except one, in this case) starts with a Hebrew letter and is ordered alphabetically. This is believed to have been done to aid children so they could memorize and sing it, planting the truth of God deep in their hearts.

As they reached today's verse, the Hebrews would have known the importance of loving God. And they would have known that loving God is more than mere lip service. Love leads to obedience. Second John 6 (MSG) says, "Love means following his commandments, and his unifying commandment is that you conduct your lives in love. This is the first thing you heard, and nothing has changed."

And in Luke 6:46 (NIV), Jesus asks a large group of His disciples, "Why do you call me, 'Lord, Lord,' and do not do what I say?" You cannot separate love for God and obedience to Him. Take inventory of your life, comparing your actions to the commands of God. You will never obey Him perfectly, but your desire to obey should be evident.

Lord, I know I fall short of Your commands every day.
The closer I examine my heart, the more disobedience
I see. But my ultimate desire is to obey You.

DAY 87
CONSTANT REMEMBRANCE

*Examine me, GOD, from head to foot, order your battery of
tests. Make sure I'm fit inside and out so I never lose sight of
your love, but keep in step with you, never missing a beat.*

PSALM 26:2–3 MSG

Take stock of what God has been doing in and around you. It's all too
easy to lose sight of what it took to make you His, which is why God
commanded His people to hold regular remembrances of His works,
like the Passover (Exodus 12:14). Human nature is to forget the things
worth remembering.

Look past the familiarity of the story. As surely as the lamb's blood
provided cover for the Jews from the plague of death, so Christ's blood
saved you from eternal damnation. And when God delivered His people,
He was also looking down the road to the day when you would receive
Him as Lord and Savior.

That's worth celebrating! Return to that place of wonder, reminding
yourself of your need for God, the trust of a child relying on his dad for
his needs (Matthew 18:3). Avoid saying, "I've seen too much, know too
much, to ever be that innocent again." The moment you surrendered to
God was the truest moment of your life. Trust its lessons.

---

*Father, never let the awe and wonder of what You
did to save me become stale to me. Thank You
for giving me life and eternity with You.*

DAY 88
LAUNCHING OUT INTO MINISTRY

If a Levite moves from one of your towns. . .and comes in all
earnestness to the place the LORD will choose, he may minister. . .
like all his fellow Levites who serve there in the presence of the LORD.
DEUTERONOMY 18:6–7 NIV

The Levites weren't given a tribal homeland but dwelt in cities throughout Israel (Joshua 21:1–42). Also, a select number worked full-time in the temple. How did they earn a living? God promised, "I give to the Levites all the tithes in Israel. . .in return for the work they do" (Numbers 18:21 NIV). He also specified that "they shall live on the food offerings presented to the LORD" (Deuteronomy 18:1 NIV).

However, the Israelites frequently neglected to tithe. As a result, the Levites were forced to stop God's work and return to supporting themselves (Nehemiah 13:10).

Perhaps like the bright-eyed, idealistic Levite in the first verse, you've felt God leading you to serve Him full-time. Know that you must trust Him. He has promised to supply all your needs (Philippians 4:19), but not all the people He has commanded to give are faithful to give (v. 15). You may often experience hardship as a result. So enter ministry prepared to trust God during tight financial times.

Dear Lord, whenever I step out to serve You, help me to
trust that You'll supply my needs. Help me not to become
disillusioned or bitter if I go through lean times.

DAY 89

HONEST SELF-APPRAISAL

If we say that we have no sin, we deceive ourselves, and the truth is not in us. If we confess our sins, He is faithful and just to forgive us our sins and to cleanse us from all unrighteousness.

1 JOHN 1:8–9 NKJV

Over the years, there have been numerous movements within Christianity teaching that believers can attain sinless perfection here on earth. However, the apostle John, speaking under the inspiration of God's Spirit, warned Christians against believing they had attained sinlessness.

Today's verse begins, "If we say that we have no sin, we deceive ourselves, and the truth is not in us." You could easily personalize this passage this way: "If I'm honest with myself, I have to admit that I sin. Whether it's in my thoughts, in my attitudes, or in my actions. . .I sin."

But this verse concludes with an amazing promise: If you confess your sin, God *will* forgive you. This calls for some serious and honest self-appraisal, and that is why King David prayed, "Search me, God, and know my heart. . . . See if there is any offensive way in me" (Psalm 139:23–24 NIV).

All sin is a huge deal to God. But you can be grateful that His willingness to forgive is even bigger.

Lord, thank You for loving me in spite of my sins and imperfections. Thank You also for forgiving me when I simply confess those sins to You.

DAY 90
A TIME TO TRUST

"Take nothing for your journey," he instructed them.
"Don't take a walking stick, a traveler's bag, food,
money, or even a change of clothes."
LUKE 9:3 NLT

When Jesus sent His twelve apostles throughout Galilee to preach the gospel, He had them depend on the hospitality of the Galileans to provide their needs. So the Twelve stepped out minus the usual travel gear and garb. Later He asked, "When I sent you out. . .did you need anything?" They replied that they had lacked nothing. "But now," He said, "take your money and a traveler's bag" (Luke 22:35–36 NLT).

There will be times in your life when the Lord will tell you to count on others' help and generosity—and you need to trust that they're going to come through for you. There will be other times when the Lord requires you to trust Him alone and not put any confidence in careful planning or safety nets. However, usually He requires you to make practical preparations, to work hard, and to earn money to pay your own way.

Whatever God has you doing, trust His wisdom, and remember that ultimately, He is your provider. Stay in tune with God, and trust Him to tell you when to do what.

Lord God, I pray that You would show me when I am to
make as many preparations as I can, and when I am
to simply trust in You to provide for and protect me.

DAY 91

DO YOU SEE GOD AS A LOVING PARENT?

He has removed our sins as far from us as the east
is from the west. The LORD is like a father to his children,
tender and compassionate to those who fear him.

PSALM 103:12–13 NLT

When the psalmist looked for a metaphor to describe God, he settled on the image of a father caring for his children and treating them with compassion, regardless of their failures. There's no mistaking that God desires obedience and trust from His children, but He's not about to cast away His beloved children if they sin. In fact, God makes a point of separating His children from their sin. Their sins play no part in what He thinks of them.

Can you imagine that God looks at you without any thought of your past failures and mistakes? Whatever story from your past that makes you cringe or causes you to feel unworthy before God, He has chosen to completely forget.

This is not an excuse to sin. Like any parent, God desires to be close to you and wants what's best for you. That includes your obedience. However, God has taken your worst parts and thrust them from you as far as possible.

Thank You, Lord, for making me Your beloved child and
removing my sins from what You think of me.

DAY 92
INCONVENIENT EMERGENCIES

If you see your fellow Israelite's donkey or ox fallen on the road, do not ignore it. Help the owner get it to its feet.
DEUTERONOMY 22:4 NIV

Helping others takes time. But the problem is, when you see someone who needs help, you're often on your way to work and can't afford to be late. Or you're on your way to an appointment. You have to trust God that He will take care of the consequences if helping someone takes time you can't really spare.

God went on to say, "If you see the donkey of one who hates you lying under its burden, and you would refrain from helping it, you shall surely help him with it" (Exodus 23:5 NKJV). Help your *enemy* when he has car problems or has spilled a load? Isn't God judging him? Didn't God make him trip up? Shouldn't you smile as you pass by and let him stew in his own juice?

No, God says, help him. You *really* have to trust Him on this, when your sense of vindictiveness is crying out for you to turn a blind eye "and you would refrain from helping." You have to overcome your selfish nature, stop, roll up your sleeves, and help someone in a situation like that.

Lord, You gave such practical commands, wanting us to love one another. Help me not to look away from my neighbor's trouble when he needs my help.

DAY 93

HARD-HEARTED?

When Pharaoh saw that the rain, the hail, and the thunder had ceased, he sinned yet more; and he hardened his heart.

EXODUS 9:34 NKJV

Pharaoh is the villain, right? You would never harden your heart the way he did. And yet, anyone can become calloused, sometimes even those who know God. God blesses you, you get used to it, and as soon as He puts out one fire in your life, you forget about Him and move on—until there's another fire. But God is not your heavenly fireman. He's your heavenly Father, and He wants you to have an everyday relationship with Him.

Religion can become a cover for hard-heartedness too—the kind that limits God to your perception of Him. Peter experienced a wake-up call in this area a few times, including when God interrupted his pious-sounding offer to build tents for Jesus, Moses, and Elijah during the transfiguration. God told him, "This is My beloved Son, in whom I am well pleased. Hear Him!" (Matthew 17:5 NKJV).

Anytime you try to add something to Jesus—Jesus plus works, Jesus plus service, Jesus plus your sterling reputation—you're missing the point. All those other things are important, but your priority in life is to know God better and to follow Jesus wherever He leads, whatever you must sacrifice to do so.

God, keep my heart tender toward You, open to Your plans and priorities. Forgive me for when I've let mine take precedence.

DAY 94
INTERNAL RENEWAL

Therefore we do not lose heart. Though outwardly we are wasting away, yet inwardly we are being renewed day by day. For our light and momentary troubles are achieving for us an eternal glory that far outweighs them all.
2 CORINTHIANS 4:16–17 NIV

Paul knew his time on earth was short. If he didn't die from an ailment, beatings, drowning, or starvation, he knew he would die for his faith. Even so, he didn't lose heart, going so far as to refer to extreme hardship as "light and momentary" in light of the fact that the internal man was being renewed day by day.

If you're over the age of thirty-five, you probably know exactly what Paul was talking about when he said you're wasting away outwardly—sore knees, a bad back, shoulder pain, on and on it goes. But praise God, the more a Christian wastes away outwardly, the more he's being renewed inwardly as the Holy Spirit transforms him.

Is this true in your life, experientially? If so, rejoice in God's faithfulness. If not, today is the day of your salvation. Turn from your sin, and begin to experience internal renewal.

Lord, I often find it difficult to separate the way I feel physically from the way I feel spiritually. But here, Paul explains that as my body fails, I can praise You for internal renewal. May it be so, Lord.

SHARING WITH THE POOR

*When you shake the olives off your trees, don't go back
over the branches and strip them bare—what's left is
for the foreigner, the orphan, and the widow.*
DEUTERONOMY 24:20 MSG

God made it clear to the Israelites that not *all* the grain of their fields, nor *all* the grapes of their vineyard, nor *all* the olives of their olive trees belonged to them. The fallen stalks of grain, the hard-to-reach grapes, and the stubborn olives were to be left for the poor. God cared for the destitute and commanded the Israelites to provide for them (see Deuteronomy 24:19–22).

Some may complain that the government spends hard-earned tax dollars on welfare programs for those who just don't want to work. But there are many legitimately needy people who benefit from this help. You or someone in your family may have availed yourself of this assistance at times.

God often blesses you so that you can share with others (Ephesians 4:28). He will even nudge your heart to help others when you don't feel like you can really afford to. That's what God is like. He considers the needs of the poor and wants you to consider them as well (Psalm 41:1; Proverbs 29:4). Give wisely, but trust that God knows what He's doing.

*God, help me to obey You when You tell me to give of my belongings
or my cash to help the needy. And give me wisdom, I pray.*

DAY 96
BEARING YOUR BURDENS

*Blessed be the Lord, Who bears our burdens and carries
us day by day, even the God Who is our salvation!*
PSALM 68:19 AMPC

Often you may feel that you have a heavy load to bear and that the Lord has left you to carry it alone. At least, it sometimes feels like He's not there. One day, Moses felt the full weight of all the Israelites upon him and complained to God, "Why did you tell me to carry them in my arms like a mother carries a nursing baby?" (Numbers 11:12 NLT).

But is it true that God stands aloof from your troubles? No. The Bible says: "Give all your worries and cares to God, for he cares about you" (1 Peter 5:7 NLT). God cares *immensely*. In fact, He wants to carry not only your burden but you as well.

Isaiah wrote, "He shall gather the lambs with his arm, and carry them in his bosom" (Isaiah 40:11 KJV). And when you can no longer carry anyone or anything, but must yourself be carried, God promises: "Even to your old age. . .will I carry you: I have made, and I will bear; even I will carry" (Isaiah 46:4 KJV).

God has, in fact, been carrying you all along. So don't stop trusting Him.

*God, I trust that You are bearing my full weight in
Your powerful hands and will also carry my burdens.
I can't carry them by myself. They're too much.*

DAY 97
A REASON FOR COURAGE

"Be strong and courageous. Do not be afraid or terrified because of them, for the LORD your God goes with you; he will never leave you nor forsake you."

DEUTERONOMY 31:6 NIV

Moses told the Israelites that the Lord was going to be the first to enter Canaan. "The LORD your God Himself crosses over before you; He will destroy these nations from before you" (Deuteronomy 31:3 NKJV). Knowing that the Almighty was going to be fighting at the vanguard of their army was good reason not to fear.

There was more. God would not only go *ahead* of their army but would also be *with* each soldier individually as he plunged into battle. God promised never to leave them or forsake them. He would never stop fighting for them and never stop protecting them. How can you lose if you trust *those* kinds of promises?

The writer of Hebrews quotes these very words to Christians in Hebrews 13:5 (NKJV), "I will never leave you nor forsake you"—inspiring them to boldly respond: "The LORD is my helper; I will not fear" (v. 6). Whatever danger or threat you face, don't give in to fear. Be strong. God is with you, and He fights for you.

God, thank You that this Old Testament promise to the Israelites is still true today. I can appropriate it in my walk with You now. The Israelites trusted this promise and conquered Canaan. Help me trust it too.

DAY 98
DON'T STOP TRUSTING

Ask and keep on asking and it shall be given you;
seek and keep on seeking and you shall find; knock and
keep on knocking and the door shall be opened to you.
LUKE 11:9 AMPC

Jesus told a story about a man who had a friend arrive at midnight, but he had nothing to feed him. But he knew that his neighbor had lots of bread. So he hurried to his neighbor's house and rapped on the door. At first, his friend refused to get out of bed and give him some loaves, but as Jesus said, "Although he will not get up and supply him anything because he is his friend, yet because of his shameless *persistence and insistence* he will get up and give him as much as he needs" (Luke 11:8 AMPC, emphasis added).

That's why Jesus said, "Knock *and keep on knocking* and the door shall be opened to you." In the original Greek, this sentence has the present imperative and present participles, which are often used to give the idea of repeated action. So keep on knocking when heaven seems to be turning a deaf ear.

Don't give up. Don't stop trusting that eventually God will answer. Because if what you are asking for is within His will, He *will* answer.

Father, forgive me for the times I've impatiently given up,
thinking You didn't hear or didn't care. Help me to trust
that if I persevere, You will eventually answer.

DAY 99
GOD'S GRASSHOPPERS

But the men who had gone up with [Caleb] said, "We can't attack those people; they are stronger than we are." And they spread among the Israelites a bad report about the land they had explored. . . . "We saw the Nephilim [giants] there. . . . We seemed like grasshoppers in our own eyes."
NUMBERS 13:31–33 NIV

The journey from Egypt to the Promised Land was roughly two hundred miles (Exodus 13:17–18). On the way there, God forged a collection of slave families into a nation that would trust Him. For a little over a year, He guided them through faith-building experiences. He provided manna, gave laws, tested them in battle, and displayed His power over and over.

But the Israelites were slow to learn to trust Him. They complained and rebelled at every hardship, even talking of stoning Moses and returning to Egypt (Numbers 14:4).

Finally, on the edge of the Promised Land, only two of the twelve spies believed they could enter. The rest complained that they were only "grasshoppers" compared to the "giants" of Canaan. But God always knew His people would face giants. When you look at yourself, you *should* be seeing nothing more than a grasshopper—a grasshopper with the promises of a faithful God. He will take you into the land, and you will rejoice in *His* victory.

Father, thank You for allowing a "grasshopper"
to live in Your power and promises.

DAY 100
THE BRAVE HEART OF FREEDOM

*Moses said to the people, "Always remember this day. This is
the day when you came out of Egypt from a house of slavery.
GOD brought you out of here with a powerful hand."*

EXODUS 13:3 MSG

It should have been a day of rejoicing. God had released Israel from captivity. No longer would they need to make bricks all day long. No longer would they need to cower before brutal slave drivers. God had delivered them, but the people had trust issues.

So many choices had been made for the Israelites that they struggled to embrace freedom. The people actually suggested that things had been better when freedom was a dream and hope was drowned out by harsh Egyptian commands.

When *normal* is abuse, addiction, and anger, freedom can seem like a very radical idea. Many former captives return to familiar chains because they don't value the day freedom visited and invited them to leave bondage behind.

You can trust in the God who breaks chains, repairs hearts, and restores futures. He can. He has. He will. His power is great enough to deliver a new normal. He can destroy the heavy chains that have kept you from the good He has planned for you.

*Lord, help me remember the day freedom came to visit. May I
refuse to be chained to a past that You have freed me from.
Thanks for removing my life from the slavery of sin.*

DAY 101
WAITING FOR BLESSINGS

*And all these blessings shall come upon you and overtake
you if you heed the voice of the Lord your God. Blessed shall
you be in the city and blessed shall you be in the field.*

DEUTERONOMY 28:2–3 AMPC

In Deuteronomy 25–26, God gave the Israelites laws, then said in chapter 28 that if they obeyed, He'd bless them in the city, bless them in the field, bless their food, bless their possessions, bless their children—He'd bless them in every possible way. "The Lord shall make you have a surplus of prosperity" and "shall open to you His good treasury" (Deuteronomy 28:11–12 AMPC).

You don't always see these blessings immediately. You often have to wait for some time and trust that God is going to make good on His promises, bring your crop to full harvest, give an ample return on your investment, or cause your child to mature. All these things take time. In the meantime, you may wonder what became of His great promises.

Trust God. Have patience. "Has he ever spoken and failed to act? Has he ever promised and not carried it through?" (Numbers 23:19 NLT). James adds: "Consider the farmers who patiently wait for the rains in the fall and in the spring. They eagerly look for the valuable harvest to ripen" (James 5:7 NLT).

---

*Dear Father, thank You that You promised to bless me for obeying
You and that You will abundantly fulfill Your promises!*

DAY 102
BECAUSE OF WHO HE IS

"O my God, incline Your ear and hear; open Your eyes and see our desolations, and the city which is called by Your name; for we do not present our supplications before You because of our righteous deeds, but because of Your great mercies."

DANIEL 9:18 NKJV

There's something about being a father that brings out the giving spirit in a man. Whether or not his children "deserve" it, his desire to give to them remains. That's because he loves his kids, and the nature of love is to give, even when the recipient isn't necessarily worthy of the gifts and hasn't done anything to earn them.

The prophet Daniel understood this part of God's fatherly character, and that's why he acknowledged that his people could come to the Lord requesting His favor because He is a loving, merciful God and not because of any kind of righteousness or merit on their parts. God loves, and therefore He gives. That's just His nature.

This is, in some ways, the very definition of humility before God. It's knowing that, in and of yourself, you have nothing to offer God but your empty, outstretched hand, waiting to receive what you know you don't deserve but what God, your loving heavenly Father, deeply desires to give you.

Father, thank You that the favor You so generously pour out on me has nothing to do with my performance or worthiness and everything to do with who You are.

DAY 103
BE PECULIAR

*Leaders who know their business and care keep a sharp
eye out for the shoddy and cheap, for who among us
can be trusted to be always diligent and honest?*
PROVERBS 20:8–9 MSG

If you want to know if something is fake, pay a visit to someone who spends most of his time around what's genuine. He can tell the difference. An experienced jeweler knows the variations between quality and flawed gemstones. A chef knows the difference between food made with fresh ingredients and food made with ingredients that have spent quality time with a freezer. A seasoned bank teller has an easy time spotting a counterfeit bill.

This world is filled with the negligent and the dishonest. It's awash with knockoffs in a world of the shoddy and the cheap. So when you come across the authentic and honest, they seem peculiar.

You need someone in your sphere of friendships who can help you value honesty and trustworthiness. It may be uncomfortable to have someone hold you to account, but this is a training tool God can use to separate you from the dishonesty that is all too easy to pick up.

---

*Lord, I want to be known for a life of something more than what's
shoddy and cheap. I know I won't always be diligent and completely
forthright, but I want to be. Keep working on me, and bring
friends into my life who can help me walk this journey with You.*

DAY 104
FOLLOWING ORDERS

God means what he says. What he says goes. His powerful
Word is sharp as a surgeon's scalpel, cutting through
everything, whether doubt or defense, laying us open
to listen and obey. Nothing and no one can resist God's
Word. We can't get away from it—no matter what.
HEBREWS 4:12–13 MSG

Soldiers know what it's like to follow commands. They either trust their commanding officer by following orders, or they learn trust through discipline and undesirable assignments.

Their story is reflected in the lives of Christian veterans. No soldier would consider an order from their commander to be a suggestion, and Christians learn that God never asks us to simply *consider* following His commands. They're meant to be obeyed.

Again: commands are not suggestions to be considered. Get comfortable realizing that God means what He says, and what He says goes.

From battle zones around the world there's gratitude to share and lessons to learn. Serve well, follow orders, trust your commander, and remember that at the end of honorable service there's an acknowledgment of a job well done.

Dear God, I want to be a veteran in Your service. Let me
know that You're my commanding officer and that Your
orders are to be followed. May I share what I learn with those
new to Your service and help them understand the value of
trusting Your plans without knowing the end results.

CONFLICTS AND ROADBLOCKS

A perverse person stirs up conflict,
and a gossip separates close friends.
PROVERBS 16:28 NIV

The word *perverse* is defined as a desire to behave in a way that's unacceptable, even when aware of a negative outcome. No wonder today's verse says that kind of person creates conflict. The word *gossip* is defined as unchecked descriptions of the actions or decisions of other people—typically including unconfirmed details conveyed as fact. That's why gossips put roadblocks between friends.

You probably noticed the connection between creating conflict and keeping friends apart. Acting before thinking, or sharing without considering how it could hurt, creates an absolute trust-buster. Friendship is damaged by a lack of restraint and the sharing of unconfirmed, hurtful stories.

God helps you understand what trust in a friendship looks like. Just as unrestrained behavior and gossip separate people, discretion and caring truthfulness keep friends close. Just as trust in God leads to greater closeness to Him, so too does trust between friends.

Lord, help me see perverse behavior and gossip for what they are. Help me notice them in others. Help me recognize them in myself. And help me resist these things by speaking carefully and sharing the truth in love. May I care enough about others that they can trust me. Thank You for caring enough about me that I have learned to trust You.

DAY 106
CALAMITY AVOIDANCE

Those who guard their mouths and their
tongues keep themselves from calamity.
PROVERBS 21:23 NIV

Today's verse shows that God wants you to take responsibility for what you say. He wants your words to be trustworthy, but that can only happen when you cooperate with God.

Your mouth can get you into trouble. God wants you to stop the speech that hurts before it's ever spoken. He wants you to live in such a way you don't have to regret a poor choice of words.

You will fail. You will say things that damage. But each situation brings a new opportunity to show wisdom by guarding your mouth and listening before you share opinions.

The word *calamity* is described as "an event causing great and often sudden damage or distress"—in other words, a disaster. This is what it's like when you speak thoughtlessly in the hearing of others. Today's verse says this kind of damage can be avoided when you're willing to seriously consider ways to keep your words from causing trouble.

Lord, I want to follow You so completely that the words
I speak mirror what I'm learning and not the frustration
I may be feeling. Help me guard my words and avoid the
disaster of broken relationships and wrong thinking.

DAY 107
A MORE CONSISTENT WALK

"Therefore, come out from among unbelievers, and separate yourselves from them, says the LORD. Don't touch their filthy things, and I will welcome you. And I will be your Father, and you will be my sons and daughters."

2 CORINTHIANS 6:17–18 NLT

While instructing the church at Corinth to avoid partnerships with unbelievers, Paul quotes several Old Testament passages (which you see in today's verses) that reiterate what he was saying. Meanwhile, he points out that such obedience comes with a promise: God welcomes those who separate themselves from unbelievers.

Throughout the centuries, Christians have struggled between the tension of what Paul said here and what Jesus said in John 17:14 about Christians remaining in the world while not belonging to it. It's a complicated proposition, but both admonitions are true.

What does the struggle look like in your household? Are you instructing your children to be lights for Jesus among the lost children at school while also warning them against the pitfalls of this world? Are you talking to the lost while also rejecting their lifestyle? The world won't be very appreciative of the fact that you're living differently, but God will welcome you.

Lord, navigating the tension between wanting to be a witness for You while also wanting to avoid everything this world holds sacred is difficult sometimes. Lead me to walk more consistently.

DAY 108
MISPLACED TRUST, MISTAKEN CONCLUSIONS

"At that time we had plenty of food and were well off and suffered no harm. But ever since we stopped burning incense to the Queen of Heaven. . .we have had nothing and have been perishing by sword and famine."
JEREMIAH 44:17–18 NIV

Jeremiah had spent decades imploring his people to return to the Lord. He had repeatedly explained that all the famines, wars, and troubles they'd experienced were God chastising His wayward people in order to turn them back to Him. Now, in the last, dying days of their nation, the Jews decided to return and worship the deity they'd neglected—the "Queen of Heaven," the Babylonian goddess Ishtar!

If you've ever tried chasing a chicken into a barn, you'll understand Jeremiah's intense sense of frustration. The chicken runs *this* way and *that* way, and *that* way and *this* way—every way *but* through the barn door.

Are you frustrating God by placing your trust in a false hope, a mistaken worldview, a wrong doctrine, and refusing to return to Him? Don't insist on putting your trust in things other than the Lord, or in the end, you'll arrive at the wrong conclusion. Your train will finally pull into the station, but it will be the wrong station. Listen to God today, and return to Him.

Lord, may I be sensitive to Your Spirit and get the point You're trying to communicate to me. May I draw close to You in every area of my life.

DAY 109
LIKE THE CHILDREN JESUS WELCOMED

*Jesus said, "Let the children come to me.
Don't stop them! For the Kingdom of Heaven
belongs to those who are like these children."*

MATTHEW 19:14 NLT

In first-century Israel it was not unusual for parents to disown children. Parents could treat their children like property. Husbands could sell their wives. So when Jesus said, "Let the children come to me," this was beyond revolutionary.

Jesus didn't view children as a substandard group. He even went so far as to say that children can be examples of what trust looks like. To Jesus, children weren't a nuisance. They were pictures of the way everyone should come to Him.

You might come to Jesus as a skeptic thinking He needs to prove Himself. But Jesus is building a kingdom on a foundation of love, enhanced by grace, and growing when people like you trust God like the children Jesus welcomed.

Jesus removed barriers for the forgotten, lost, and marginalized to come to Him. He warned those who thought differently to stay out of the way. If you think there are barriers keeping you from Jesus, please remember those obstacles are not put in place by the one who came to rescue you.

*Dear God, help me look past the barriers I have erected
and see Your invitation to forgiveness. May I come to You
trusting Your answers are greater than my questions.*

DAY 110
ABUNDANT LIFE

*GOD, my shepherd! I don't need a thing. . . . Your beauty
and love chase after me every day of my life. I'm back
home in the house of GOD for the rest of my life.*

PSALM 23:1, 6 MSG

Psalm 23 is a comforting passage, often read at sickbeds or funerals. But even with its famous reference to God's presence in the valley of death's shadow, the psalm is really about life. Most of its words describe God's presence, protection, and provision as you go *through* life's mountaintops and valleys.

God wants you to walk with Him so you get the most out of life (John 10:10). You can see His desire for relationship with His people when He told Moses how to introduce Him to Israel: "I am the LORD. . . . I will redeem you with a powerful arm and great acts of judgment. I will claim you as my own people, and I will be your God" (Exodus 6:6–7 NLT).

God had been known as God Almighty to the patriarchs, but here He opened a whole new level of intimacy. It's even deeper today—through Jesus, you are an adopted son of God. Consider what that means for you, the resources at your disposal to do your Father's work, experience His blessings, and just enjoy knowing Him.

*Father, I can't wait to come home to You, but until then,
let me walk more closely with You each day.*

DAY 111
TRUSTING GOD'S LEADING

*Whether it is good or evil, we will obey the voice
of the Lord our God, to Whom we are sending
you [to inquire], that it may be well with us.*
JEREMIAH 42:6 AMPC

A small group of Jews were camped nervously beside the road to Egypt. Lawless Jews had killed the Babylonian governor and many others, and now the shaken survivors feared retribution from the Babylonians. They told Jeremiah to ask God what they should do, whether to trust Him and stay in Judah, or to flee to Egypt. They promised they'd obey no matter what He answered.

But they didn't *really* trust Him, because when God told them to stay, promising to protect them in Judah, they insisted they were heading to Egypt.

What about you? Do you truly trust God's leading when you're in a crisis? Or do you just go through the motions of seeking His guidance, putting on a show of spirituality for those watching but secretly counting on God putting His stamp of approval on the "reasonable" decision you favor?

If you truly want things to go well with you, you must trust God, obeying Him even when His leading seems to make little sense—even when it appears to be illogical or inexplicably difficult.

*God, help me to trust You sincerely and be willing to follow You
whether what You lead me to do seems easy or difficult.*

DAY 112
BEING THANKFUL

Thank [God] in everything [no matter what the circumstances may be, be thankful and give thanks], for this is the will of God for you [who are] in Christ Jesus.
1 THESSALONIANS 5:18 AMPC

Yes, Paul actually is saying to thank God no matter *what* circumstance you find yourself in. You are to have a thankful attitude and to give audible thanks even when you're having a terrible day. It's God's will for you.

Can you trust Him on *this* one? Does God really expect this of you? Yes. Jesus tells you to count yourself blessed when persecuted. He said, "Rejoice in that day and leap for joy! For indeed your reward is great in heaven" (Luke 6:23 NKJV). After being beaten for Jesus' sake, the apostles "departed. . .rejoicing that they were counted worthy to suffer shame for His name" (Acts 5:41 NKJV). And Paul and Silas sang praises to God after being beaten (Acts 16:22–25).

This may be shaping up to be one of your least favorite commandments, but give it a chance. God advises it for your own good. If you're consistently thankful, even in serious troubles, (a) you'll have a much happier life overall; (b) you'll make it through rough times easier; and (c) you really will be greatly rewarded in heaven.

Father, I thank You for my troubles, my persecutions, the injustices, and even the pain. Help me to continually have a thankful attitude.

DAY 113
THE DNA OF SIN

Only fools say in their hearts, "There is no God." They are corrupt, and their actions are evil; not one of them does good! God looks down from heaven on the entire human race; he looks to see if anyone is truly wise, if anyone seeks God. But no, all have turned away; all have become corrupt. No one does good, not a single one!

PSALM 53:1–3 NLT

Evil is one of the hardest concepts to discuss with atheists. Even if they're willing to acknowledge that evil exists in some form, they don't believe it comes from within and is expressed outwardly, but rather, that it's something outside of ourselves that only a few choose. Even so, "evil" behavior is often excused, blamed on a lack of education, environmental conditions, mental disorders, poor parenting. . .any source but man's own inherent corruption.

Believers understand that the flesh is corrupt, "that in me (that is, in my flesh) nothing good dwells" (Romans 7:18 NKJV). But sometimes Christians don't acknowledge their dilemma for what it is. They embrace a Savior but often make excuses for their corrupt actions. They make almost as many excuses for sin as the "fools" who say there's no God to sin against.

But to acknowledge Christ is to happily acknowledge weaknesses and take hold of His power and His gift of freedom as sons of God.

Father, help me to openly acknowledge my sin and moral failures and my need for Your redemption.

DAY 114
CHECKLIST RELIGION

"Teacher, what good thing must I do to get eternal life?"
MATTHEW 19:16 NIV

A rich man met Jesus. He consulted his mental checklist and compared his past actions with what Jesus said he needed to do.

Don't murder? *Check.* Don't commit adultery? *Check.* Don't steal? *Check.* Don't lie? *Check.* Honor your parents? *Check.* Love your neighbor? *Check.* The rich man had to have felt pretty good about his spiritual résumé. He quickly said, "All these I have kept. What do I still lack?" (Matthew 19:20 NIV).

Jesus said, "Go, sell your possessions and give to the poor, and you will have treasure in heaven. Then come, follow me" (Matthew 19:21 NIV). In this final to-do list, Jesus offered trust and friendship. The trust was wrapped up in believing God was worthy of greater faith than money. The friendship invited the man to stay close and follow.

This is a beautiful picture of why Jesus ushered in a new covenant that moved from a checklist religion to a trusting friendship with God. Don't sacrifice a relationship with God for a wall filled with spiritual merit badges. Maybe you want to impress God, but it ultimately leads you to trust your own efforts while resisting God's help.

---

*Lord, I want to celebrate the things You've done
for me, not the few things I've done right. I believe
obedience transforms my heart, but Your love extends
an invitation to trust and follow. I want to do both.*

DAY 115
SEND ROOTS DEEP

So then, just as you received Christ Jesus as Lord,
continue to live your lives in him, rooted and built up in
him, strengthened in the faith as you were taught.
COLOSSIANS 2:6–7 NIV

When you accepted Jesus as Lord, His Spirit entered your heart and brought you eternal life. This verse then encourages you to *continue* to live as God's child, loving Him and obeying Him. Build your life on Him, sink your roots deep down into His truth, the scriptures, and be nourished by Him.

The idea is for the roots of your faith to become completely intertwined with Jesus, even as a tree's roots reach deep into the rich soil and spread completely throughout it. Today's verse says to be "strengthened in the faith," and both sinking your roots deep and receiving constant nourishment strengthen you.

First, if your roots go deep and wide in Christ and His teachings, you'll be solidly rooted and unshakable. "Therefore, my beloved brethren, be steadfast, immovable, always abounding in the work of the Lord" (1 Corinthians 15:58 NKJV). Second, you'll receive constant nourishment. Paul prayed, "That He would grant you. . .to be strengthened with might through His Spirit in the inner man" (Ephesians 3:16 NKJV).

Dear Lord, establish me firmly in Your truth. Help me to
search throughout Your Word, seeking spiritual nourishment.
And help me to be solid and unmovable in You, I pray.

DAY 116
NOTHING COMPARES TO JESUS

I count everything as loss compared to the possession of the priceless privilege (the overwhelming preciousness, the surpassing worth, and supreme advantage) of knowing Christ Jesus my Lord.

PHILIPPIANS 3:8 AMPC

What does it mean to "know" Jesus? You might think that it simply means knowing that a carpenter from Galilee named Jesus died on a cross, and that God accepted His sacrifice as payment for humanity's sins. But is that all Jesus was? A good man? An enlightened teacher? An anointed miracle worker?

No. Jesus was far, far more. Before time began, He shared incomparable glory with God His Father in heaven (John 17:5). He is the eternal Word who is *with* God and who *is* God—and who created everything in the entire universe (John 1:1–3). He is the express image of God in all His glory (Hebrews 1:3). When John saw Jesus in heaven in His full magnificence and power, he was overcome with awe and fell down at His feet as one dead (Revelation 1:13–17).

To know Jesus is to know Him as God. If you could see Him for even a moment as John saw Him, you would agree that everything in this world is worth very little compared to the precious privilege of knowing Jesus.

Dear Jesus, help me to know You, to truly know You for who You are—the immortal Son of God, God in the flesh.

DAY 117

A TRUSTWORTHY HEAVENLY FATHER

See what great love the Father has lavished on us, that we should be called children of God! And that is what we are!

1 JOHN 3:1 NIV

Many Christians struggle with the idea of God being their loving heavenly Father. They're okay with "Lord and Savior," but a God who so loves them that He calls them His very own children? For some, that can be a tough one to grasp.

A man's memories of his earthly father often color his impressions of God. And when that earthly father falls short in fulfilling his role as a dad, it makes it difficult for a man to fully embrace the idea of a God who loves him as a father loves his child. Yet the Bible makes this clear in both the Old Testament and the New Testament.

Even the very best earthly fathers are imperfect, fallen human beings prone to making mistakes. But it's not that way with God. He's perfect in every way, including in His fatherly love for His people. His love is like nothing even the very best earthly father can pour out on his children.

God has repeatedly identified Himself as your loving heavenly Father. You can trust Him to love you as His valued son.

Loving heavenly Father, thank You for pouring out Your love on me, a love so deep and broad that You consider me Your child.

PERSPECTIVE CHECK

*Then the LORD asked Moses, "Who makes a person's mouth?
Who decides whether people speak or do not speak, hear or do
not hear, see or do not see? Is it not I, the LORD? Now go! I will
be with you as you speak, and I will instruct you in what to say."*

EXODUS 4:11–12 NLT

On one hand, it's okay to admit anxiety and doubt to God; in fact, He tells you to (1 Peter 5:7). On the other hand, doubt can betray a lack of trust in God's ability to keep His promises. Moses, for example, made it clear that he wasn't up to the task God was calling him to do. In return, God made it clear that that was the point.

God knows your shortcomings and will help you overcome them when you obey Him. He equips those He's called. Do you trust Him enough to obey when it gets hard? Your view of God is crucial to your faith. When you have doubts, remind yourself of what you know to be true about Him.

God's will is found in His Word (see Jeremiah 29:11; 1 Timothy 2:3–4; 1 Thessalonians 4:3; 5:18; Micah 6:8; Luke 9:23). The more you know Him, the clearer you'll see Him—including the inescapable truth that nothing is impossible for your God.

*Lord God, You made me for Your good purposes and
to know You. Guide me in my pursuit of You.*

IRRATIONAL ASTROLOGY

"Do not act like the other nations, who try to read their future in the stars. Do not be afraid of their predictions, even though other nations are terrified by them."
JEREMIAH 10:2 NLT

Hundreds of millions of people believe in astrology, including more than a few Christians. But did you know that astrology is based on the pagan belief that the sun and planets are gods, and *that's* how they influence events on earth?

Astrology has no scientific basis. There is no logical explanation for how it might work. For example, what gravitational forces do planets exert on the people they supposedly influence? How can it be argued that the very distant, tiny *dwarf* planet Pluto (which supposedly rules only Scorpios) is equal in influence to the monstrous star called the sun (which supposedly rules only Leos)? It's ludicrous!

If you put any credence in astrology or astromancy (daily predictions), you're trusting important life decisions to pagan superstition. Some people like to have the planets (or stars) handy to blame when things go wrong, but as Shakespeare said in the play *Julius Caesar*, "The fault, dear Brutus, is not in our stars, but in ourselves."

Put your trust in God, not in irrational astrology. God has planned a wonderful future for you, so trust Him to guide you.

God, please forgive me if I put any credence in such superstitious folly. Help me to put my trust firmly in You and Your Word, I pray.

DAY 120
GOD IS MERCIFUL

*Return, faithless Israel, says the Lord, and I will not cause
My countenance to fall and look in anger upon you, for I am
merciful, says the Lord; I will not keep My anger forever.*
JEREMIAH 3:12 AMPC

The Israelites had entered into a covenant with God, had dedicated themselves and their children and all they owned to Him. But they then failed to keep their vows. They'd been faithless. This angered God, and He began to chastise them, removing His blessings and warning that if they didn't repent, total judgment would come.

But if they *did* repent. . .that was an entirely different matter! God promised that He would then put aside His anger, relent from sending judgment, and graciously, mercifully receive them.

If you've sinned against the Lord, you may hesitate to return to Him, fearful that He will only grudgingly and conditionally forgive you, unload a series of lectures on you, and still be seething with anger afterward—ready to toss you out for the slightest infraction. But even in Old Testament days, under the Law of Moses, God made it clear that He wasn't like that.

God says, "I am merciful." Do you trust that He's telling the truth? Of course He is! So return to Him today.

---

*God, help me to put the full weight of faith in Your
promise that You're merciful. Help me trust Your Word
completely and find forgiveness and peace.*

DAY 121
PRAISE HIM ALWAYS

Praise God in his sanctuary; praise him in his mighty heavens. Praise him for his acts of power; praise him for his surpassing greatness.

PSALM 150:1–2 NIV

Some believe that the Israelites sang this entire psalm of praise to God as they entered the sanctuary with their baskets of firstfruits on their shoulders. They praised Him for His mighty heavens, His acts of power, and His surpassing greatness, then went on to name several instruments to use to praise Him. This creates quite a word picture.

Charles Spurgeon, in his commentary, wrote about this psalm: "We have now reached the last summit of the mountain chain of Psalms. It rises high into the clear azure, and its brow is bathed in the sunlight of the eternal world of worship."

Do today's verses express your heart and demeanor as you enter a worship service? Or are you more caught up in the cares and concerns of this world? Or maybe even thinking about what you'll do later that day? A lack of focus happens to every Christian at some point, but you can take steps to avoid it.

Why not memorize this short psalm, or the first two verses, and sing it to yourself or recite it silently as you enter the worship service?

Father, I praise You for who You are and what You've done. You and You alone are worthy of my praise.

DAY 122

ESTABLISHED BY GOD TO WALK WITH GOD

For You have delivered my soul from death.
Have You not kept my feet from falling, that I
may walk before God in the light of the living?
PSALM 56:13 NKJV

If you've ever been on a mountain hike in the dark, you know it's much harder than doing it in the daylight. It takes a lot more effort and the dangers of an accident are multiplied. The Bible often connects "walking" and "light" as spiritual metaphors, saying:

- "Your word is a lamp for my feet, a light on my path" (Psalm 119:105 NIV).
- "Blessed are those who have learned to acclaim you, who walk in the light of your presence, LORD" (Psalm 89:15 NIV).
- "It is when a person walks at night that they stumble, for they have no light" (John 11:10 NIV).
- "But if we walk in the light, as he is in the light, we have fellowship with one another, and the blood of Jesus, his Son, purifies us from all sin" (1 John 1:7 NIV).

God saves His people from darkness for a reason—that they should walk with Him in the light He provides. He's looking for real hiking companions. God desires you to walk with Him in true and abundant life. You can be certain that He Himself will keep you from stumbling along the way.

Good Father, thank You for establishing
me and helping me to keep in step with You.

DAY 123
FIRST-NAME BASIS

*Moses protested to God, "Who am I to appear
before Pharaoh? Who am I to lead the people of Israel
out of Egypt?" God answered, "I will be with you."*
EXODUS 3:11–12 NLT

M oses didn't jump at the chance to deliver Israel. He had spent his first forty years in Egypt and blown his exit badly. He spent the next forty years in the wilderness, staying out of trouble but hiding from his past. So, in a sense, he was right; he had no business going back to Egypt or leading God's people. But in God's eyes, that made him the perfect candidate. At that point, Moses didn't need to see himself as he was, but to see God as He is.

God can handle your doubts, if you don't let them obscure your view of Him. Don't let fear make you forget who is calling you to serve Him. You have chosen to ally yourself with the great "I AM" (Exodus 3:14). In Hebrew, it's *Ehyeh*, which is God's identity, His name. Almighty God wanted Moses to know Him on a deeply personal level, anticipating the access you now have to Him through Jesus.

The next time you face an overwhelming situation, remember that God is with you. You know Him on a first-name basis: Jesus.

---

*Jesus, here I am. I make myself available for whatever You want
me to do today, knowing that You are with me and for me.*

DAY 124
A CHANGE OF HEART

If you will turn (repent) and give heed to my reproof,
behold, I [Wisdom] will pour out my spirit upon you,
I will make my words known to you.
PROVERBS 1:23 AMPC

Wisdom cries out from the streets, in markets, at noisy intersections, and at the entrance of the gates (where people gathered, met, and discussed important matters), according to Proverbs 1:20–21. In other words, the wisdom of God is not bound by walls. It seeks you out, commanding you to repent. As you submit and repent, wisdom will be readily available to you moving forward.

Have you found this to be true? Have you been confronted with your sin by reading the Word, listening to a sermon, or talking to a friend, and then quickly repented? And after doing so, did you notice that you were given wisdom from on high for rooting out that sin?

God uses rather ordinary means to get the attention of the believer. His call to repent is always clear. Now is the perfect time to expect God to make a change in your heart.

Father, make me aware of Your voice. I want to hear Your
call to repentance in areas in my life that I haven't eve
considered to be sinful. I want to walk in Your wisdom.

DAY 125
REFUTE ARGUMENTS

[Inasmuch as we] refute arguments and theories and reasonings
and every proud and lofty thing that sets itself up against
the [true] knowledge of God; and we lead every thought
and purpose away captive into the obedience of Christ.

2 CORINTHIANS 10:5 AMPC

Since the fall, mankind has been relying on itself as the arbiter of truth. And the godless rest in their own reasoning, as if they were an end unto themselves.

Paul often battled false philosophy. He "reasoned and argued" from the scriptures with the Jews in Thessalonica for three Sabbaths about the need for Jesus to die and rise from the dead (Acts 17:2 AMPC). Later, he encountered Epicurean and Stoic philosophers and engaged them in discussion (Acts 17:18).

The darkness is not pushed back with physical weapons. Instead, one of the ways it loses ground is as the people of God refute faulty arguments, theories, and reasonings as Paul says in today's verse.

Are you engaging in civil discussion with people who oppose the Christian worldview? If not, how will they ever learn that their reasoning is faulty? You don't have to be a scholar. Simply preach Christ crucified and hold fast to the resurrection. God will be with you.

Father, I don't always feel adequate to contend for the faith
the way I should. Forgive me for the times I've fallen short.
Embolden me to present the faith to critics, for Your glory.

STOP CROWING

*When things were going great I crowed, "I've got it made.
I'm GOD's favorite. He made me king of the mountain."
Then you looked the other way and I fell to pieces.*

PSALM 30:6–7 MSG

King David knew how easily he could shift his gaze from trusting God toward the trouble God would need to rescue him from once again. Psalm 30 is a glimpse into the heart of a king who often fell into the error of thinking that his personal brownie points made God love him more than most. David kept forgetting he had a wayward heart. This thoughtless combination sometimes led to dark days, sin, and sad psalms.

You can set yourself up for a similar dilemma. You can feel when things are going well that it means God is blessing you and loves you. When things aren't going great, you can think God is upset and withholding blessings.

Your personal level of pride and doubt often determines what God's response will be. When you crow like King David and say, "I've got it made—I'm God's favorite," you can expect Him to send a crash course on humility. That's because when you trust in yourself, you'll find yourself doubting Him.

*Dear God, may I come to each moment in life knowing Your plan
for me can be trusted and there is nothing I can add to it that
will improve it. Help me leave pride behind when I follow You.*

DAY 127
THE ULTIMATE BANQUET

*On this mountain the LORD Almighty will prepare a
feast of rich food for all peoples, a banquet of aged
wine—the best of meats and the finest of wines.*

ISAIAH 25:6 NIV

A time is coming when God's people will attend a feast made possible
by Jesus the Messiah. Jesus referred to this feast in Matthew 8:11
(NIV), saying: "I say to you that many will come from the east and the
west, and will take their places at the feast with Abraham, Isaac and
Jacob in the kingdom of heaven." It'll be an all-inclusive feast, for both
the Jew and the Greek who has called on the name of Jesus.

It should be no surprise that as you currently break bread with
friends and family, it leads to some of the most intimate conversations
you experience. When you sit down with the intention of pulling away
from the cares of this world, you are freer to focus on the people
around your table. Imagine having such an experience with *the Lord of
Armies*—the Lord Almighty, the Lord of Hosts—showing His power over
all. It will be the ultimate banquet.

*Lord of Armies, I'm so looking forward to this banquet.
Indeed, You are the Lord of Hosts and I'm honored that
You cared so much about my attendance that You sent
Your only Son to die to pay for my entrance.*

THE LORD'S PLEASURE

*He does not delight in the strength of the horse; He takes
no pleasure in the legs of a man. The LORD takes pleasure
in those who fear Him, in those who hope in His mercy.*

PSALM 147:10–11 NKJV

Secretariat, the majestic horse that won the Triple Crown in 1973—including his historic 31-length victory at the Belmont Stakes—is still in the American vernacular. The movie based on his life brought in nearly $60 million in 2010. He's graced the covers of *Time*, *Newsweek*, and *Sports Illustrated*.

As interesting as Secretariat's story is, God doesn't delight in the strength of a horse, nor does He take pleasure in the legs of man—no matter how fast they can run or how much weight they can lift. Instead, He takes pleasure in those who fear Him and in those who hope in His mercy.

What might this look like? Albert Barnes, in his commentary, says you might find such reverential people "in the closet, when the devout child of God prays; in the family, when the group bend before Him in solemn devotion; in the assembly—quiet, serious, calm—when his friends are gathered together for prayer and praise; in the heart that truly loves, reverences, adores Him."

---

*Lord, I know that You take pleasure in those who fear You
while hoping in Your mercy. May I be quick to fall to my
knees in prayer and to lead my family into praising You.*

DAY 129
LOVING THE UNWORTHY

If your enemy is hungry, give him food to eat; if he is thirsty,
give him water to drink. In doing this, you will heap burning
coals on his head, and the LORD will reward you.
PROVERBS 25:21–22 NIV

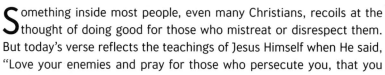

Something inside most people, even many Christians, recoils at the thought of doing good for those who mistreat or disrespect them. But today's verse reflects the teachings of Jesus Himself when He said, "Love your enemies and pray for those who persecute you, that you may be children of your Father in heaven. . . . If you love those who love you, what reward will you get?" (Matthew 5:44–46 NIV).

The answer to the question Jesus poses here, of course, is "none," and that's because God calls you to a higher life than those who don't know Him.

This is a question of trust, for it requires you to believe God when He says that He will set things right and that He will reward you for acts of kindness toward the undeserving.

Do you trust God enough to respond with love and compassion to those who mistreat you or speak ill of you? When you respond to the "unlovable" that way, you can trust God for the rewards that come with doing what makes no human sense.

Lord, remind me today that You call me to trust You enough to
love everyone equally—even those who hate me or mistreat me.

DAY 130
EYES ON HIM

*The king trusts in the LORD; through the unfailing
love of the Most High he will not be shaken.*

PSALM 21:7 NIV

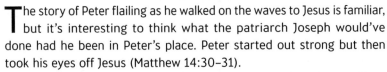

The story of Peter flailing as he walked on the waves to Jesus is familiar, but it's interesting to think what the patriarch Joseph would've done had he been in Peter's place. Peter started out strong but then took his eyes off Jesus (Matthew 14:30–31).

It's hard to imagine Joseph doing anything other than walking straight to Jesus. No doubt he had his down moments over the years, but his reconciling words to his brothers show his constant focus on God: "You meant evil against me; but God meant it for good. . .to save many people alive" (Genesis 50:20 NKJV).

To be sure, Joseph's situations gave him little choice other than to trust God. It was either sink or swim, so he kept paddling. Peter demonstrated a greater fear of his circumstances than of disappointing God, and he sank. Similarly, when Pharaoh ordered the Hebrew midwives to kill any male babies, they refused, trusting God, who "dealt well" with them (Exodus 1:20 NKJV).

Fearing God more than men, even when your life is at stake, results in blessing, so take the long view on God's promises. He's with you in every challenge, so keep your eyes on Him.

*God, thank You for the times You paint me into
a corner, forcing me to lay hold on You or sink.*

THE PLEASURES OF FOLLY

Then I saw that even [human] wisdom [that brings sorrow] is better than [the pleasures of] folly as far as light is better than darkness.
ECCLESIASTES 2:13 AMPC

In Ecclesiastes 2, Solomon chronicled his many attempts to find meaning in pleasure. He tried wine; built houses; planted vineyards, gardens, orchards, and fruit trees; bought servants; possessed many herds and flocks, as well as silver and gold; brought in singers to entertain him; and had many concubines. But all of it was vanity.

Ultimately, he found that wisdom, even if it brings sorrow, is better than the pleasures of folly. And that is still true today. What are you doing to gain wisdom? Of course, wisdom starts with the scriptures, so a steady diet of God's Word is important. But what else are you doing? Are you reading books that stretch you? Are you surrounding yourself with wise people who can speak into your life on a regular basis?

"Low culture" is usually referred to as pop culture, and it tends to engage the sense of pleasure. "High culture" focuses on art, literature, and scholarship, and it tends to engage the mind. Of course, there is some crossover, but the intentions are different. Solomon would say not to neglect high culture.

Father, I too have tried pleasure and found it lacking. Help me to develop a desire for Your high culture that will help me understand You and others better.

DAY 132
THERE'S HOPE

*May the God of hope fill you with all joy and
peace as you trust in him, so that you may overflow
with hope by the power of the Holy Spirit.*
ROMANS 15:13 NIV

What does it mean to "overflow with hope by the power of the Holy Spirit"? You might think it means to talk a lot. Then again, David Sanford's book *Loving Your Neighbor: Surprise! It's Not What You Think* includes this story:

While on business in Orlando I met a man named Leonard who poured out his heart to me. I didn't say a word. I just kept listening intently. When he was done, I kept looking into Leonard's angry, deeply hurt eyes and didn't say anything.

After a minute, with deepest sadness he said, "All I needed was hope and mercy." What a profoundly haunting lament. Yet if I had started talking, I never would have heard what he needed.

After Leonard told me, "All I needed was hope and mercy," I remained quiet for another minute. I let my eyes do all the talking. His eyes and facial expressions began to soften and change. Only God's love can do that. Then Leonard told me, "And by listening to my story, you've given me both." After an hour, Leonard didn't know the other guy's [my] name, but he knew he wanted to come back to the Lord. And he did!

Maybe you're the silent type. Maybe that's a good thing.

Lord, use my ears. Do all the talking.

DAY 133
FAVOR WITH GOD

The angel went to [Mary] and said, "Greetings, you who are highly favored! The Lord is with you." Mary was greatly troubled at his words and wondered what kind of greeting this might be. But the angel said to her, "Do not be afraid, Mary; you have found favor with God."

LUKE 1:28–30 NIV

Finding favor in God's eyes isn't about earning His approval. He cannot become obligated to anyone through their works. The Greek word translated as "favor" is *charis*. It can also be translated as "grace." Strong's Concordance says it means "disposed to, inclined, favorable towards, leaning towards to share benefit."

God is always leaning toward people to make Himself known. This is why James and Peter both reference Proverbs 3:34: "God opposes the proud but shows favor to the humble" (James 4:6; 1 Peter 5:5 NIV). God opposes pride because it causes a person to pull back just as God wants to come closer.

God is leaning toward you in Christ, wanting a deeper relationship. Take advantage of His unearned favor. Paul admonished, " 'In the time of my favor I heard you, and in the day of salvation I helped you.' I tell you, now is the time of God's favor, now is the day of salvation" (2 Corinthians 6:2 NIV). Don't miss a single day of His love.

Father, Your favor is all I need for my new life in Christ. I want to grow in Your grace.

DAY 134
FOR GAINING WISDOM

The proverbs of Solomon son of David, king of Israel: for gaining
wisdom and instruction; for understanding words of insight.
PROVERBS 1:1–2 NIV

S olomon's wisdom was greater than the wisdom of all the people of
the East and greater than all the wisdom of Egypt (1 Kings 4:30).
He spoke some three thousand proverbs during his lifetime and wrote
more than one thousand songs (1 Kings 4:32). Here, at the beginning
of the book of Proverbs, the believer is told that Solomon recorded his
wisdom so that the people of God could have greater insight.

How many times have you worked your way through the book of
Proverbs? Can you cite its wisdom regarding topics such as pride, money,
discipline, hard work, prudence, inheritance, justice, bitterness, anger,
patience, the tongue, wine, purity, and nearly anything else you need
to know? If it's been a while since you've studied the book, this is the
perfect time to do so again.

As you begin working your way through Proverbs, ask the Lord each
day what He wants you to learn this time through. Take notes as you
go, and end each session with a prayer of dedication to follow through.

Father, I confess to often turning to other books and other sources
for wisdom when Your book of wisdom is always available. Speak
to me in a fresh way as I work my way back through Proverbs.

BOLD ENOUGH TO ASK

Two blind men were sitting by the roadside, and when
they heard that Jesus was going by, they shouted,
"Lord, Son of David, have mercy on us!"
MATTHEW 20:30 NIV

When life is good and problems are few, you might think there's less need for God. You might spiritualize your attitude by thinking you're relieving God of the burden of taking care of you. If you can meet your own needs, you might think God is simply an option for when things get tough.

Interestingly, the greater your need, the more likely you are to be bold enough to make requests when praying. There are times in everyone's journey of faith when they discover it's impossible to manage life alone.

This was the case with two blind men who encountered Jesus. They had heard the stories of healing, restoration, and forgiveness. These men made their audacious request to Jesus and trusted enough to ask for mercy. Their bold faith was rewarded. They started by hearing His voice, and they ended up seeing His face.

You must believe before you see God's plan. This was true for two blind men. It's equally true in your personal journey with Jesus.

Dear God, You want me to see life from Your perspective. I always
see more clearly when I trust in the truth that You've always been
for me. May I remember that You help those who ask for help.

DAY 136
GOOD FOR THE SOUL

How can I know all the sins lurking in my heart?
Cleanse me from these hidden faults. Keep your servant
from deliberate sins! Don't let them control me. Then
I will be free of guilt and innocent of great sin.

PSALM 19:12–13 NLT

Confession is typically something you save for moments when you've really messed up, because even though you know you're a sinner who needs a Savior, who wants to be reminded of his mistakes all the time?

But that's why the gospel is such good news—God doesn't want to recall your sins any more than you do. Jesus told Peter, "Once you've had a bath, your body is clean; you only need to wash your feet as you go from place to place" (paraphrase of John 13:10). That suggests that confession goes beyond the moment of salvation; it's part of your sanctification, a daily habit not so different from taking a shower each morning before you go to work.

Sometimes, of course, confession is much more difficult. But as hard as it is, it's the only way to bring healing to yourself and others. Trust that God has good things ahead, and when you keep a clean slate, you prepare your heart to receive and appreciate them.

Lord, I echo David's prayer: show me the things I need
to confess, especially the sins I'm not even conscious of.
I want to start my day on solid ground with You.

WHERE IS YOUR TRUST?

*"It's summer, as you well know, and the rainy season is
over. But I'm going to pray to GOD. He'll send thunder
and rain, a sign to convince you of the great wrong
you have done to GOD by asking for a king."*
1 SAMUEL 12:16–17 MSG

Desiring a king was not wrong in itself, but the Israelites had lost trust
in God and were seeking a visible human leader. Samuel wanted to
convince them they had done a wicked thing, so he called upon the Lord
to send a crop-flattening rainstorm in the middle of a bone-dry summer.
When God answered, the Israelites were afraid.

This passage shows the opposite ends of trusting in God. Samuel
trusted that God would answer his prayer, while God's people had
misplaced their trust in an earthly king.

Do you see yourself in either scenario? Has your trust in a worldly
process caused you to stray from God? Or does your trust in God allow
you to pray for Him to show up to meet desperate needs or to manifest
Himself to people who have forgotten Him? If you're like Samuel, never
lose heart. If you're like the Israelites, repent and find forgiveness in
God's arms.

---

*Lord, sometimes I'm like Samuel, and sometimes, I admit,
I'm more like Israel when it comes to trust. May I never
fail to look to You, whatever situation I find myself in.*

DAY 138

YOUR REDEMPTION DRAWS NEAR

*And then they will see the Son of Man coming in a cloud
with great (transcendent and overwhelming) power
and [all His kingly] glory (majesty and splendor).*
LUKE 21:27 AMPC

A time is coming when God's world will face intense hardship. In Luke 21:20–24, Jesus foretold a time when multitudes of armies would surround Jerusalem, and when the people of Judea would need to flee to the mountains. It will be a time of great distress. But Jesus didn't leave His audience in despair.

In addition to great hardship, God's people can anticipate and trust that the Son of Man—Jesus—will come in a cloud in all His kingly glory to redeem His saints. The Church has been looking forward to the Second Coming ever since Jesus first mentioned it.

How about you? When you endure great hardship in the form of a job loss or a cancer diagnosis, are you more focused on your circumstances or your future redemption? Deliverance will quickly follow the coming upheavals and dangers. What does such worry reveal about your trust in Christ's promise to return for you? If you find your trust wavering, take heart: your redemption draws near (Luke 21:28).

---

*Lord Jesus, I can look at world events and see hardship coming,
but I'm choosing not to fear such a time. Yes, my family may
endure turmoil, but we will do so expecting Your return.*

HERE I STAND

*"Whoever believes in me, as Scripture has said,
rivers of living water will flow from within them."*
JOHN 7:38 NIV

Jesus attended the Festival of Tabernacles in secret (John 7:10), knowing that the Jewish leaders were watching for Him. Eventually, He entered the temple and began teaching, saying that His teaching came from God (John 7:16). This led to His proclamation that whoever believed in Him would have rivers of living water flowing from within them. He was talking about the Holy Spirit.

That promise changed your life. You trusted in Christ's sacrifice on the cross and passed from death to life the moment you believed. And every time you witness for Him, it's further evidence that living water is flowing within you.

Note that Jesus made this amazing proclamation in a hostile environment. The Jewish leaders wanted to silence Him and sought to arrest Him as He was speaking (John 7:32). Has this promise so revolutionized your life that you'd be willing to endure persecution, imprisonment, or worse for daring to speak it among people who don't want to hear it?

---

*Lord Jesus, thank You for the promise in today's verse.
Thank You for dying for my sin. Infuse me, through the power
of the Holy Spirit, with the same boldness that You had as
You proclaimed the truth in hostile territory. May I be willing
to suffer for doing so in unfriendly environments today.*

DAY 140
A SECOND CHANCE

*The LORD will save me, and we will sing with stringed
instruments all the days of our lives in the temple of the LORD.*
ISAIAH 38:20 NIV

Hezekiah certainly had reason to celebrate. After falling ill, the prophet Isaiah told him that he was supposed to put his house in order because he was going to die (Isaiah 38:1). He cried out to God and the Lord added fifteen years to his life (Isaiah 38:2–5). Why fifteen years?

The Bible doesn't say, but imagine thinking you're going to die at the age of seventy but learning you would get to live until you are eighty-five. How might you live those final fifteen years differently than your first seventy? Surely some of that time would be spent in praise and worship of the Lord.

Maybe God has already granted you a second chance by sparing your life in a car accident, in an extended illness, or in some other way as you prayed for a miracle. How are you using the extra time? He's given you a gift in response to your trust in Him. Put it to good use.

*Father, I know that I've had several near-death encounters
and maybe many more that I'm unaware of. Thank
You for responding to my prayers for an extended stay
on earth. I will praise You my remaining days.*

DAY 141
WITHIN THE BORDERS

The LORD said to Moses, "Come up to me on the mountain and stay here, and I will give you the tablets of stone with the law and commandments I have written for their instruction."
EXODUS 24:12 NIV

Moses was asked to meet God on the mountain. Moses was asked to refuse the impulse to run away. He was offered an incredible opportunity to trust God.

God wrote His heart for mankind on tablets of stone. Each command pointed to the one thing most important to God—love. If the people really chose to love, they wouldn't take things that didn't belong to them. If they chose to love people, they'd do the things that pleased God. Real love wants the best for others.

God wants you to trust that His commands are borders that keep you close to His best. If you go beyond His borders, you'll hurt others. And you will hurt yourself.

Your connection with God is just as real as the mountaintop experience was for Moses. And know this: God has something to tell you. Decide that you'll believe He has something better for you when you live within the boundaries He's designed for your benefit.

Lord, help me remember Your commands are for my protection and not because You want to keep me from things I want. Help me trust that Your best plan requires that I respect boundaries.

DAY 142
CONFIDENT REQUESTS

This is the confidence we have in approaching God:
that if we ask anything according to his will, he hears us.
And if we know that he hears us—whatever we ask—
we know that we have what we asked of him.
1 JOHN 5:14–15 NIV

Jesus once told His followers, "I will do whatever you ask in my name, so that the Father may be glorified in the Son. You may ask me for anything in my name, and I will do it" (John 14:13–14 NIV).

That's an amazing promise. However, it's important to understand that it's like most promises in the Bible in that it's conditional. You see, God isn't some kind of heavenly genie, just waiting on people and granting them whatever they wish for. No, when you ask God for something, you can expect Him to do it for you but only if that something is in line with His will.

When you know that what you're praying for in Jesus' name is God's will for you, you can approach Him and ask Him for it with confidence, knowing that He wants to do it for you. But how can you know what His will is? By asking Him and by going to His written Word to find out.

Thank You, Lord, for giving me Your Word so
that I can pray according to Your will.

DAY 143
MY SONG, MY STRENGTH

*But as for me, I will sing about your power. Each morning
I will sing with joy about your unfailing love. For you have
been my refuge, a place of safety when I am in distress.
O my Strength, to you I sing praises, for you, O God,
are my refuge, the God who shows me unfailing love.*
PSALM 59:16–17 NLT

The first song recorded in scripture is the song of Moses and Miriam in Exodus 1. It was a song of praise and thanks to God for rescuing the Israelites from the Egyptian army. The entire assembly sang it together. Many years later in the Promised Land, Judges 5 records the song of another duo, Deborah and Barak. They praised God for His power and faithfulness after defeating a Canaanite king.

Then, of course, there's King David, whose musical talents are on record in the book of Psalms. And though we don't have them today, according to 1 Kings 4:32, David's son Solomon wrote 1,005 songs.

Paul admonishes you to "be filled with the Spirit, speaking to one another with psalms, hymns, and songs from the Spirit. Sing and make music from your heart" (Ephesians 5:18–19 NIV). Don't worry how you sound. Embrace the power of singing praises to the one who loves to listen.

*Lord, You are my song and my strength! You are worthy
to be praised! I will sing of Your love and faithfulness!*

DAY 144
HUMILITY AND UNITY

Behold, how good and how pleasant it is for
brethren to dwell together in unity!
PSALM 133:1 NKJV

In the very middle of his letter to the Ephesian church, Paul told them to be humble and diligent to preserve the unity of the church (Ephesians 4:2–3). Unity of heart and mind among Christians is based on Christlike humility (Philippians 2:1–11).

When Christians argue and bicker and fight, what's the problem? Pride. One of the expressions of pride is contempt. "I'm right. You're wrong." Such men pour out their contempt on others.

Respect is the opposite of contempt. Respect embraces the truth that everyone is made in the image of God. Brothers in Christ are to be loved and respected. And your church's leaders deserve the highest respect. Great authority comes from great humility.

Another expression of pride is being judgmental and overly critical, as if you somehow know the motives of someone else's heart.

Being nonjudgmental, in contrast, means you assume the best about the other person.

What is the difference between criticism and exhortation? When you speak into difficult situations, you restore others gently (Galatians 6:1–5). Exhortation comes from a heart of love with a desire to help the other person and walk alongside them awhile.

Humility is healing. It alone releases the power and blessing of God among believers.

Lord, I want unity. You have commanded me to
humble myself before You. I do so now.

DAY 145
DREAM IN PEACE

"Walk with me and work with me—watch how I do it. Learn the unforced rhythms of grace. I won't lay anything heavy or ill-fitting on you. Keep company with me and you'll learn to live freely and lightly."

MATTHEW 11:29–30 MSG

H as God given you a dream—a vision of the man He wants you to be, or something He wants you to accomplish? If He hasn't, ask Him for one. If He has, trust Him with it.

God gave Joseph dreams, but to his brothers, they seemed like a brat's fantasies (Genesis 37:8). What if, instead, you saw him as the dreamer God wants *you* to be, someone attuned to His Word and His will in such a way that He gives you regular downloads that direct your steps and guide your plans?

Start by clearing away thoughts and habits that create doubt. You're not doubting yourself when you doubt. You're doubting God, who gave you the dream. When Jesus spoke of living a burden-free life, He didn't refer to freedom from hardship or challenges, but liberation from your own limitations.

To live like that is to echo David's song: "I keep my eyes always on the LORD. With him at my right hand, I will not be shaken" (Psalm 16:8 NIV).

Lord, let my dreams be Your dreams, my plans Your plans. Fill my heart with Your peace as I seek to honor You with all I have and am.

DAY 146
EXPECT GOD

Be brave. Be strong. Don't give up. Expect GOD to get here soon.
PSALM 31:24 MSG

God is never late. He isn't slow. He doesn't tease you by dangling a spiritual carrot of hope with no intention of actually providing help. God asks for patience and perseverance, however. He wants you to be courageous. God will show up. You'll discover your trust in Him is never misplaced.

God doesn't hide from those who stumble and make mistakes. His love was ensured when Jesus arrived with a rescue plan for all who wanted rescue. His actions are designed to bring you closer to Him.

Why would He ever push you away? His connection with you is lasting. Jesus died to create an uninhibited connection between His Father and mankind. Virtually everything He does is an introduction of, invitation to, or enhancement of that friendship.

When you're weary, weak, or wandering, remember that the God of rescue never leaves you. If you've been waiting for His arrival, don't worry. He will get here soon. The truth is He's already here.

Dear God, there's nothing I can offer to make You love me, but You do. There's nothing I can do to make You fulfill my wish list, but You give me life. There's nothing I can do to change my past, but You can change my future. Help me be courageous while waiting for You. I'm grateful You keep Your promises.

DAY 147
LIVE IN PEACE

Finally, brethren, farewell. Become complete.
Be of good comfort, be of one mind, live in peace;
and the God of love and peace will be with you.
2 CORINTHIANS 13:11 NKJV

Paul adds several bits of advice to the Corinthian church at the end of his second letter to them. In saying he wanted them to "become complete," he was saying he wanted them to "aspire to the highest degree of holiness," as John Wesley put it in his commentary, as they labored in unity for the advancement of the gospel. In so doing, the God of love and peace would be with them.

Putting aside personal and theological differences for the sake of the gospel isn't easy. No doubt, you've bumped heads with someone, or several people, from church or other Christian groups over the years—even though you both presumably had the best of intentions. Sometimes, when the friction is great, it's best to part ways, like Paul and Barnabas did (Acts 15:36–41), rather than arguing about your differences. But often, that isn't necessary. In such instances, seek peace. As you do, you can trust that God will be with you.

Father, You've made every person unique. As such,
we have different perspectives. Remind me of this the next
time I butt heads with a fellow believer over an issue that
really is of no consequence in Your eternal kingdom.

DAY 148

THE HOLY SPIRIT IS PROMISED TO YOU

"If you love me, obey my commandments. And I will ask the Father, and he will give you another Advocate, who will never leave you."
JOHN 14:15–16 NLT

The obedient receive the Holy Spirit because of Jesus' advocacy, and this changes everything. The Spirit is "another" advocate—in addition to Jesus—for disciples. After receiving the Spirit, Jesus assured His disciples that the Spirit would *remain* in them and guide them into all truth.

After reading about these striking promises for the disciples, perhaps you've felt that this doesn't reflect your Christian experience. Have you felt distant from God, prone to error, or uncertain about the Holy Spirit's influence in your life?

According to Jesus, the place to begin is with a simple act of faith that's the same for you as it was for the first followers of Jesus. Do you doubt that the Spirit is present in you? This promise has been extended to *all* of Jesus' followers, and if you receive it, you can participate in it by responding to Christ with love and obedience.

This gift of the Spirit's advocacy is something no one can earn, but it's one that Jesus graciously extends to His followers. Those who seek will find.

Jesus, help me to participate in Your promised Spirit today.

DAY 149

WHEN EXHAUSTION BECOMES FAITH

*Hear my cry, O God; attend to my prayer. From the end of
the earth I will cry to You, when my heart is overwhelmed;
lead me to the rock that is higher than I. For You have been
a shelter for me, a strong tower from the enemy. I will abide in
Your tabernacle forever; I will trust in the shelter of Your wings.*

PSALM 61:1–4 NKJV

In certain psalms, David holds nothing back. He was a man after God's own heart (Acts 13:22), yet put every fear, complaint, and disappointment into writing.

Despite his devotion to God, David was sometimes overwhelmed. The unique thing about him was that his utter exhaustion drove him *toward* God's mercy. He cried out for his Savior—the "rock that is higher than I." He longed for God to be his refuge in the midst of his turmoil.

The tabernacle (tent) he referred to was the place where God's presence had abided since the days of Moses, where the ark of the covenant resided, and where the wings of the cherubim covered the mercy seat. Those are the "wings" David trusted in for shelter.

When life becomes overwhelming, let it drive you to the Rock, to the shelter of God's mercy. When your heart is near breaking, don't pull away from the only one who can be your strong tower.

---

*Father, I cry out to You! Keep me close,
and lift me up. You are my refuge!*

DAY 150
NOT ALWAYS REWARDED IMMEDIATELY

"I am blameless before God; I have kept myself from sin. The LORD rewarded me for doing right. He has seen my innocence."
2 SAMUEL 22:24–25 NLT

David faced adversity that few can imagine. He didn't just fight in battles and bear the weight of being king; he also lived years of his life as a fugitive, hunted by King Saul. If David had judged his circumstances on the run as the reward for his faithfulness, few could have blamed him for giving up on God. However, David remained blameless because he believed God would reward him for his faithfulness.

Is there an area of your life where you have to trust in God's faithfulness? Are there promises that you need to desperately hold on to? While you may know how David's story ends and can see how his trust in God won out, no one has that assurance while going through the fire. Faith must fill this uncertainty gap.

Where is your hope today?

It's tempting to place your hope in the things you can control and predict. Placing yourself in God's care is hardly an assurance of an easy, conflict-free life. The promise of God is that your love and obedience are always seen and always rewarded—even if that reward comes in the future.

Today's faithfulness will pay off. Your obedience today that leads to a perceived loss will one day return to you as a blessing.

Lord, I place today's challenges in Your loving care.

DAY 151
BEWARE THE WARNING SIGNS

*Solomon made an alliance with Pharaoh, the king of Egypt,
and married one of his daughters. He brought her to live in
the City of David until he could finish building his palace and
the Temple of the LORD and the wall around the city.*

1 KINGS 3:1 NLT

Solomon was praised as an obedient and wise king who loved the Lord. However, by allying himself with Pharaoh and marrying his daughter, Solomon violated God's commands and sowed the seeds of his future downfall into sin.

Are there warning signs that you've been ignoring today that could spell trouble in the future? Perhaps your faith is wavering in a key area of your life or you simply can't trust God to provide for your needs.

If a man with Solomon's wisdom couldn't spot serious warning signs, it's likely that, at times, you too may need a spiritual reminder from God and need to wake up and take immediate action. Perhaps Solomon's sin also came about because he relied too heavily on his *own* wisdom.

A life of faith will have many ups and downs, and the best defense against falling into sin isn't your own wisdom. Every believer, no matter how wise, needs the support of friends and guides, much like the Old Testament prophets, who can speak—what are to you—revelations and show the path away from sin.

Lord, help me to remain vigilant against sin in my life today.

WHO HAS GOD ENTRUSTED TO YOU?

*It was soon evident that God had entrusted me with the same
message to the non-Jews as Peter had been preaching to the Jews.*
GALATIANS 2:7 MSG

When Paul realized that God had entrusted him with reaching the Gentiles, it couldn't have been easy for him. He expressed his feelings in Romans 9:2–5. His heart was with the Jews. "If there were any way I could be cursed by the Messiah so they could be blessed by him, I'd do it in a minute," he wrote in verse 3 (MSG). "They're my family. I grew up with them."

Who has God entrusted to you? Are you open to the possibility that He might lead you to reach people who don't look like you, talk like you, or think like you—no matter how burdened you might be for those who do?

Galatians 2:8 (NIV) explains why Paul came to the conclusion that he did: "For God, who was at work in Peter as an apostle to the circumcised, was also at work in me as an apostle to the Gentiles." How is God at work in you? Who is He reaching through you?

*Father, make it clear to me whom You want me to reach.
Of course, I want to be available to all, but I know that
You often equip us to reach a specific people group.*

DAY 153
A RETURN TO CLARITY

And [Jacob] built an altar there and called the
place El Bethel, because there God appeared to him
when he fled from the face of his brother.
GENESIS 35:7 NKJV

After a disastrous episode in his life where God seemed far away and he didn't seek Him (Genesis 34), Jacob was in dire need of clarity. He returned to Bethel, the place where God had revealed He was with him, where Jacob had come alive spiritually and God reminded him of His protection and provision (Genesis 35:7–14).

To be fully available to God, you must get to a place where you truly recognize your need and His presence in your life. To have a Bethel moment, clear away the cobwebs of cluttered thinking (and schedules). Remind yourself of what you know to be true about God. Make time to worship, thanking and honoring Him with your words and actions.

David wrote a primer on drawing close to God: "Walk straight, act right, tell the truth. Don't hurt your friend, don't blame your neighbor; despise the despicable. Keep your word even when it costs you, make an honest living, never take a bribe. You'll never get blacklisted if you live like this" (Psalm 15:2–5 MSG).

I want to get back to basics, God, focusing on godly
behavior as a response to You and Your faithfulness, goodness,
and mercies. Help me to see You on the path ahead of me.

WHO ARE YOU TRYING TO PLEASE?

*Then Pilate tried to release him, but the Jewish leaders shouted,
"If you release this man, you are no 'friend of Caesar.' Anyone
who declares himself a king is a rebel against Caesar."*

JOHN 19:12 NLT

Pilate faced the unenviable situation of judging an innocent man before an angry crowd that threatened to destroy his reputation and career. He sought to do the right thing by releasing Jesus, but the threats of the crowd proved too much. He found himself at the mercy of the mob. He was too busy looking at the shouting mass of people in front of him that he overlooked the words of Jesus: God had handed over the power of life and death in that moment to him.

It's easy to lose sight of what God has entrusted into your care in the moment of a difficult decision or a challenging conflict. Disastrous decisions can result from trying to protect yourself from the anger of others. A moral compromise that appears to be for the greater good today can have disastrous consequences in the future.

Oftentimes doing the right thing requires a leap of faith, trusting that the truth will win out eventually and God will recognize your faithfulness.

---

*Lord, I surrender my reputation and my future into Your
hands. Give me the courage to trust You even when
doing the right thing causes others to despise me.*

DAY 155
PHARISEE IN TRAINING?

*No one could answer him. And after that, no one
dared to ask him any more questions.*
MATTHEW 22:46 NLT

———

The Pharisees were religious leaders. They asked Jesus questions—lots of questions. They asked questions they hoped would trap Him. They hoped to expose Him as a fraud. They tried. They failed.

What was proven was that Jesus was faithful and the Pharisees weren't to be trusted. However, before criticizing the Pharisees, remember they weren't the only untrustworthy people in the Bible. Because mankind sins, no human is completely trustworthy.

Love is the only remedy for this lack of trust. Love allows trust in others to grow. This is true even when you're fully aware of times when they haven't been dependable. You can interact with others knowing they'll let you down at some point. Other people can interact with you knowing you'll fall short on promises made.

Jesus came for those who'd been faithless. He said that when His people show they can be trusted in small things, He would trust them with bigger responsibilities.

Lord, it's easy to look at the failings of others and think I've done better. Help me remember You're the only fully trustworthy one I'll ever encounter. May I be faithful in the things You ask that seem small, so I'll have a chance to be trustworthy in bigger things.

GOD WON'T ABANDON HIS PEOPLE

*"May your eyes be open to my requests and to the
requests of your people Israel. May you hear and
answer them whenever they cry out to you."*

1 KINGS 8:52 NLT

A s Solomon dedicated the newly constructed temple to the Lord, he recounted all that could be expected to happen to the people of Israel and the ways they could trust in God. This was a great moment of hope and optimism, as the people had just witnessed God's presence settle in the temple. What other people on earth had ever seen such a powerful display of divine power in their place of worship?

In the midst of this celebration, Solomon was well aware that hard times might be ahead. As he prayed, he recounted the ways that Israel could fail. He encouraged the people to repent and asked God to hear their prayers. His prayer was a foreshadowing of the coming years of Jewish unfaithfulness and exile.

The unfaithfulness of God's people is nothing new. However, Solomon's prayer offers hope for today because God remains willing to forgive His people. No matter how far you've fallen or what you've done—or will do—there's a promise of God's forgiveness and attentiveness. By trusting that God's eyes and ears are always open and then humbling yourself before Him, you too can experience His faithful presence today.

Lord, I surrender my failures to You and trust in Your faithfulness.

DAY 157
DESPAIR GIVES WAY TO FAITH

Then the disciple who had reached the tomb first also went in, and he saw and believed—for until then they still hadn't understood the Scriptures that said Jesus must rise from the dead.

JOHN 20:8–9 NLT

At the height of their grief and confusion, Peter and John learned that the body of Jesus was no longer in the tomb. The women had at first suspected that it was stolen, but as Peter and John ran to the tomb, the teachings of Jesus finally made sense. As they saw the empty tomb with their own eyes, they realized that Jesus had told them all along that He would rise from the dead. In a moment, their despair shifted to hope.

There may be difficult circumstances in your life today—or in the future—that leave you in pain and confusion. Sometimes the relevance or trustworthiness of scripture may prove hard to apply in those circumstances. However, even the disciples of Jesus, who had the benefit of sitting at His feet, reached rock bottom at some points. It took the most unlikely and unexpected shift in events for them to finally believe.

You may not see that change coming. It will most likely surprise you. God's power may show up and bring renewed hope and restoration when you least expect it.

---

*Lord, I trust in Your power and care even
when my life doesn't make sense.*

DAY 158
WISDOM FROM AGRICULTURE

Sow for yourselves righteousness; reap in mercy;
break up your fallow ground, for it is time to seek the
LORD, till He comes and rains righteousness on you.
HOSEA 10:12 NKJV

In Old Testament times, many of the Jewish people were either farmers or familiar with the practices in agriculture. In today's verse, the prophet Hosea uses word pictures the people of that time and place would have understood to give them specific instruction as to how they were to prepare themselves to approach the God they had neglected for so long.

While far fewer people today know much about the world of agriculture, Hosea's message is still important. It simply means that all believers should take the time to earnestly seek God and ask Him to reveal to them any areas of their lives where they've neglected Him.

There's not a man of God alive who doesn't have some area of his life in Christ that needs growth. The good news is that God has promised to make that growth happen if you simply prepare your heart to receive what He has for you. You must also seek Him in prayer and Bible reading until He shows you what area He wants to grow in you.

Father in heaven, thank You for faithfully hearing me when I ask
You to show me any area of my life in which I've neglected You.

SEDUCED BY SUCCESS

"But woe to you who are rich, for you have already received your comfort. Woe to you who are well fed now, for you will go hungry. Woe to you who laugh now, for you will mourn and weep. Woe to you when everyone speaks well of you, for that is how their ancestors treated the false prophets."

LUKE 6:24–26 NIV

Woe to you" is not a phrase used much today. It literally means *grief upon you*. Jesus used the term to warn people who had become seduced by success. The apostle John offers a parallel warning: "Do not love the world or anything in the world. If anyone loves the world, love for the Father is not in them" (1 John 2:15 NIV).

It would be hard to find any society in history that didn't value the four things Jesus points out in these verses—particularly ours today.

So, does Jesus condemn those things in and of themselves? Should we pursue poverty, starvation, sorrow, and contempt to be more "spiritual"? Of course not. But just as it's better to pluck out an eye if it causes you to sin (Mark 9:47), it would be better to be an abject failure by this world's standards than to be seduced by the false salvation it offers.

Father, show me where I might be headed for "woe" in my own life. Help me to use all that I have and succeed for Your kingdom.

DAY 160
NO FEAR

*Have no fear of sudden disaster or of the ruin that
overtakes the wicked, for the LORD will be at your
side and will keep your foot from being snared.*
PROVERBS 3:25–26 NIV

Solomon wanted his readers to be tuned in to the Lord's wisdom,
understanding, and knowledge (Proverbs 3:20–21). Those who are
will walk in safety (v. 23) and they will lie down at night unafraid, with
no fear of disaster because the Lord is on their side. That's not to say
that disaster can't strike the life of the believer. The Bible is full of such
examples. But resting in the Lord brings peace.

Do these admonitions and subsequent results describe you? Or are
you fearful of sudden disaster, always wondering when the other shoe
might drop? Seek the Lord's wisdom, understanding, and knowledge.
It is readily available in scripture, through the promptings of the Holy
Spirit, godly people whom God has placed around you, and the many
Christian resources you have at your fingertips.

Once you find security in God's hands, your soul will find peace—no
matter the circumstance—and you'll be a beacon of gospel hope for
those around you.

---

*Father, I earnestly desire the peace that comes from having
You by my side. I've spent enough time seeking the world's
wisdom, understanding, and knowledge. Now I want to
immerse myself in everything You have to say and offer.*

DAY 161
ABSOLUTE COMMITMENT

*"He who does not take his cross and follow after Me is
not worthy of Me. He who finds his life will lose it,
and he who loses his life for My sake will find it."*
MATTHEW 10:38–39 NKJV

You've heard people say they have a "cross to bear." They're usually referring to some burden they must endure—a hard relationship, a chronic disease, an addiction. But the cross really means only one thing: suffering and death. Jesus' call to take up your cross is about dying to self, letting go of your plans and desires, and letting God replace them with His.

This is especially difficult for those who think they're doing God a favor by receiving Christ: *Imagine God using my talents and connections for the good of the kingdom!* But if they had anything to offer God, would the cross have been necessary?

In Christ, you're reborn spiritually, but you'll bear the burdens of the flesh until either you die or Jesus comes back. However, you'll share in the suffering that Christ endured, and because you belong to Him, God can redeem all your mistakes and hardships, self-made or not. He can turn them into bridges to others' pain. It's not easy to love people the way Jesus loves you, but it's worth it.

---

*God, strengthen me for the journey ahead. I willingly
share in Your suffering, knowing that You will be with
me and that the reward is worth the pain.*

DAY 162
DEEPEN YOUR FAITH NOW

Job Trusts in His Redeemer
JOB 19 HEADLINE NKJV

———————

I magine your life is a book. The title is your name. Inside, it has dozens of chapters. What would you guess is the title of this particular chapter of your life?

The New King James Version captions Job 19 with "Job Trusts in His Redeemer." In the midst of his nightmare, while enduring the rebukes of three otherwise wise friends, Job affirms his belief, faith, and trust in the Lord, Creator of heaven and earth. True, Job didn't know exactly what God would orchestrate after his own death, but he expressed his abiding, almost unshakable trust in his Redeemer.

While writing this and other devotionals, this author learned about his own mortality. His lung disease, sarcoidosis, already had cut many years off his projected life span. A few days ago, he learned the disease had infiltrated his heart. His cardiac sarcoidosis could stay status quo for many years. If it progressed to stage three, however, he would have a 50 percent chance of dying within a year. In other words, he would have one or two or maybe three more years before dying (likely from sudden cardiac death).

Such news pushes everything else off the table for a few days and you quickly learn whether you fully trust your Redeemer.

Lord, right now, in the midst of this life chapter, I want to deepen my faith. How good that You are so trustworthy!

DAY 163

NO ONE ABANDONS GOD
IN A SINGLE DAY

*The LORD had clearly instructed the people of Israel,
"You must not marry them, because they will turn your
hearts to their gods." Yet Solomon insisted on loving them
anyway. He had 700 wives of royal birth and 300 concubines.
And in fact, they did turn his heart away from the LORD.*

1 KINGS 11:2–3 NLT

Solomon knew the boundaries that God had established for his family and for his devotion, but he decided to venture beyond them to his great detriment and that of his kingdom. It's likely that Solomon moved in this direction slowly, marrying a foreign wife, observing a ceremony of worship for a false god, and gradually shifting in his thinking and commitments. For all of the wisdom he had for ruling his kingdom, he failed to discern the shift in his own heart.

While no one today can relate to Solomon's precise circumstances, you may be able to relate to his divided heart and the temptations he faced. One wrong decision can lead to another. You may feel the pull toward indulging your desires as a means of escape. Or you may trust in something other than God for your peace and security. One step away from Him can quickly lead to ten steps from Him.

---

*Lord, reveal the compromises I've made,
and restore my heart today.*

DAY 164
ASTOUNDED

Good people, cheer GOD! Right-living people sound
best when praising. Use guitars to reinforce your
Hallelujahs! Play his praise on a grand piano! Compose your
own new song to him; give him a trumpet fanfare.
PSALM 33:1–3 MSG

God prepares, protects, and provides. He does what you can't. He just wants you to follow His lead. So cheer God, and give Him a trumpet fanfare. But remember, the only way to legitimately offer Him praise is to trust that He's the author of life.

If Christians sound best when praising, then there should be more praise. If you're astounded by God's trustworthiness, then your life should be a long and sincere hallelujah. God makes a difference, and it should change your outlook. That outlook should make a difference for everyone you encounter.

Live your life like you're in a parade honoring the God who brings hope to the despairing. Remember how despair once felt?

Trust has always been essential to understanding the value of God—not that anyone has ever been able to estimate it. Trust in a big God and you'll be filled with hope and joy to overflowing. The hope He gives will change your life for the better.

Dear God, focus my spiritual vision so that I can see
You as mighty to save, worthy of trust, and the author
of life. May my life be lived in an attitude of praise to
You as You control what I can't. Thank You.

DO YOU LOVE THOSE JESUS LOVES?

A third time he asked him, "Simon son of John, do you love me?" Peter was hurt that Jesus asked the question a third time. He said, "Lord, you know everything. You know that I love you." Jesus said, "Then feed my sheep."

JOHN 21:17 NLT

Peter committed an act of self-preservation that left him ashamed and in deep despair. Facing the prospect of torture and death alongside Jesus, he denied even knowing Him. How could he ever recover? Well, Jesus restored him by offering him chances to affirm his love. Then He instructed him to care for His followers. If Peter truly loved his Lord, he had to shift from self-preservation to the preservation of others.

Are there people around you today whom you need to notice and serve in some way? Whether or not you've failed in the past, Jesus is inviting you to daily reaffirm your love for and commitment to Him.

There may be sacrifices or changes that you need to make today in order to serve others. Most importantly, you need to ask how to routinely look beyond your own well-being in order to care for the people Jesus loves. As often as you care for one of the least of these, you will have done the same to Jesus Himself.

Lord, open my eyes to the ways I can use my time and talents to serve others.

DAY 166
DELAYED WRATH

"For my own name's sake I delay my wrath; for the
sake of my praise I hold it back from you,
so as not to destroy you completely."

ISAIAH 48:9 NIV

Today's verse is a sober one. God held numerous things against Israel. They invoked the name of God but didn't walk in righteousness (Isaiah 48:1). God knew them to be a stubborn people (48:4), who were rebels from birth (48:8). They were deserving of His wrath, but for His own name's sake, He delayed it.

God's name is holy. He's a jealous God who is unwilling to share His glory with anyone else. Does this make you uncomfortable when you think about your own behavior? You were born a rebel, deserving of God's wrath. You invoke His name but don't walk in righteousness—at least not perfectly, sometimes not even well.

But thanks be to God, you can trust in the fact that He paid the price for you, for His name's sake, in the person of Jesus. You've been set free from the penalty of sin. Now walk in newness of life in a way that is honoring to Him.

Father, I'm so thankful that You paid a debt I could
never pay. I know it cost You dearly, so I want to live
in a way that honors You and Your name.

DAY 167
ALL IN

*I've already run for dear life straight to the arms
of GOD. So why would I run away now when you say,
"Run to the mountains. . . . The bottom's dropped out
of the country; good people don't have a chance"?*
PSALM 11:1–3 MSG

Much more than the ongoing misadventures of a slick trickster, Jacob's life is the story of the faithful God who stuck with him even when he messed up. And when he feared the consequences of his past the most, God didn't chew him out. Instead, He told him, "I am with you, and I will protect you wherever you go. . . . I will not leave you until I have finished giving you everything I have promised you" (Genesis 28:15 NLT).

Jacob realized that God was there *with* him and—even more amazingly—*for* him! He then committed wholeheartedly to God for the first time in his life—all his provision, resources, and plans—and left the rest up to God.

All your mistakes, all the things that haunt your memories, God knows all of it and still gave Himself for you. Let that sink in. When it does, you'll see that the only reasonable response is gratitude, and then commitment. There's nothing you can do to earn God's grace, but you can respond to it by giving all of yourself to Him.

---

*God, there's no turning back. I trust that You are
here with me, now and always. I'm all in.*

DAY 168

RESPONDING TO GOD, OUR SHEPHERD

*Come, let us worship and bow down. Let us kneel
before the LORD our maker, for he is our God. We are
the people he watches over, the flock under his care.*

PSALM 95:6–7 NLT

The people of Israel recognized that there was only one appropriate response when they clearly saw God as the Creator of the world—they were to bow down in worship. Those who fear God recognize that they are His creation and owe everything they have to Him.

The good news of the scriptures is that God depicts Himself as a shepherd who cares for His flock and wants to see it flourish. The trouble is when the sheep believe they know better than the shepherd and deserve better things than He provides.

Are there times when you've either expected better or become too distracted to recognize God's love and care? This psalm can serve as an invitation to remember that you're deeply loved by God because you're His creation. Today is as good a time as any to bow down before God, knowing that He has your best interests in mind.

Lord, I trust that You're loving and worthy of following.

NO ONE CAN CHANGE GOD'S PEOPLE

The LORD will not reject his people; he will not abandon his special possession. Judgment will again be founded on justice, and those with virtuous hearts will pursue it.

PSALM 94:14–15 NLT

A fter all the ways the people of Israel failed to remain faithful to their Lord, they were still described as His special possession. God can't abandon His own, even if they abandon Him. This grace and mercy from God works to restore people to a right relationship with Him and to restore justice in the world. Restoration in the land of Israel came through the transformation of the Israelites, renewing their hearts as God's own people who learned to love justice.

There's no hope apart from the love of God. If you believe that you have been rejected by God, you're believing that the impossible has happened to you. God's own people can't change who they are at their core.

Whatever you have done against God or others, that only obscures the truth about you. You may fear being found out for something you've done, but the truth is that you still can't undo what God has said about you.

Lord, I accept the truth of Your love for me today.

DAY 170
LIVING THE CHRISTIAN LIFE

*I have no greater joy than to hear that
my children are walking in the truth.*

3 JOHN 4 NIV

If you're a Bible-believing, Jesus-following Christian, you can be sure that people will say you are "different." They may mean that as a compliment, or they may be mocking you, but when you have God's Spirit inside you, your words and actions *will* be noticeably different from those of men who don't know Jesus.

Today's verse is part of a letter from the apostle John to a man named Gaius, a member of an unnamed church John apparently oversaw. In this deeply personal letter, John tells Gaius that his greatest joy was hearing that the believers in this church were "walking in the truth."

The phrase "walking in the truth" has simple but profound meaning. It speaks of believers who live and think according to the ways of the faith as God has revealed them in the Bible. It means, as the apostle Paul wrote, that a man of God does "not conform to the pattern of this world, but [is] transformed by the renewing of [his] mind" (Romans 12:2 NIV).

Do you trust God enough to walk daily with Him and His ways, to allow Him to continually transform you into the man He intends you to be?

*Lord, thank You for revealing to me Your truth through Your
Word and for empowering me to live daily in that truth.*

FORGIVE AND FORGET

*LORD, if you kept a record of our sins, who, O Lord,
could ever survive? But you offer forgiveness,
that we might learn to fear you.*
PSALM 130:3–4 NLT

Toward the end of summer break, a college student in Chicagoland joined his parents on the deck of their home and handed them a four-page handwritten letter. In the letter, he detailed all of the ways he had sinned against the Lord and his parents.

When they finished reading the letter, the father stood up, walked over to the propane barbeque grill, put the letter inside, lit the fire, and erased all record of his son's wrongdoings. Then he and his wife hugged their son and shed tears of grief and joy. Beyond words, the college student knew all was forgiven.

Years later, that same father wrote a one-page letter to his wife. In it, he confessed that he had looked at online pornographic videos for less than ten minutes. After his wife read the letter, she walked onto the deck, sent it up in smoke, embraced her husband, and said how proud she was that he was a godly man.

It doesn't have to involve a gas barbeque grill and fire, but what is your family's way of offering forgiveness when a spouse, child, or parent confesses his or her sins?

*Lord, thank You for how completely You forgive my sins. May I fear
You even more and extend godly forgiveness to my loved ones.*

DAY 172
FIRST THINGS FIRST

Jesus [said,] "First things first. Your business
is life, not death. Follow me. Pursue life."
MATTHEW 8:22 MSG

Part of being a responsible adult is making plans and following through on commitments. Take a moment to think of all the things you've done in the past week and all the things on tap for this week. When your head stops spinning, think of how often you deliberately brought God into those plans. You've probably brought Him into a *lot* of what's going on—maybe *all* of it—and that's good.

But is it God's best for you? Why do I ask that? Well, trusting God includes trusting His timing. Life is just plain busy, and with work and family appointments and church activities, it's easy to reach not just a level of spiritual exhaustion but unrealistic expectation—that just because you're doing the best you can, God's schedule is going to fit into yours. Stay focused on God, not the tyranny of the urgent.

Are you willing to let God interrupt your plans? Part of being His son means being willing to slow down, ask Him for perspective, and trust that His interruptions are for your ultimate benefit.

Father, Your business is my business. Help me to make sure
what I'm doing is what You want me to be doing. If it's not,
help me to shift the focus to You and Your priorities.

BAD LIFE MOMENTS

"If those days had not been cut short, no one would survive,
but for the sake of the elect those days will be shortened."
MATTHEW 24:22 NIV

This passage of scripture is dedicated to prophecy, but it offers hope for *every* dark day you encounter. There will be times when God allows bad days. They are often allowed to refine character, instill trust, and offer a greater reason to accept God's help.

Bad days can cause you to think there's no hope. You might even entertain the idea that God has abandoned you and left you stuck in darkness. Yet God has promised that He will never leave or forsake you. This verse suggests He will intervene and shorten the duration of your struggle.

As with everything you've been reading in this book, the bold question you must answer in these moments is "Do I trust God to lead me through?" If you believe, then you must let Him lead—and you must follow.

God has promised that there will be days of trouble, but they won't last forever. Trust the one who knows the way out.

Dear God, thanks for caring enough about me to walk
with me through the pain, anger, and stress of living life
with fallen people. Thanks for shortening the duration
as I trust that You will get me through this.

DAY 174
CRUSHED—BROKEN—RESTORED

The LORD is close to the brokenhearted
and saves those who are crushed in spirit.
PSALM 34:18 NIV

You've had bad days, lived through moments marked by heartbreak and soul-crushing circumstances. You didn't enjoy it, sought a way out, and would have welcomed relief.

God is in the business of spiritual pain relief. He's been waiting for your call. God's ability to rescue isn't influenced by things like an attractive financial portfolio, your willingness to "owe Him one," or whether you think you deserve His help.

God has always done what you can't. He paid your sin debt, made you part of His family, forgave you, fixed your broken heart, and restored your crushed spirit. You could try doing everything on your own, but if you've tried that before, you know the results are less than ideal. Let God do what He does best.

Godly wisdom recognizes who does the work—and lets Him. The God who heals loves to stand with those who need healing. He doesn't look down on those who hurt. This could be a new experience for you, because while mankind values perceived perfection, God desires honesty. Transparency with God is the best way to access His help.

Bad things happen. Wounds will be inflicted. Hearts are subject to breaking. Admit the hurt and God will step in. Accept the help and let the healing begin.

When life's troubles are too much to bear,
remind me to count on You for comfort and restoration.

DAY 175
HONESTY WITH GOD

"I do believe; help me overcome my unbelief!"
MARK 9:24 NIV

The words spoken in today's verse came from the mouth of a man who was out of options. He wanted Jesus to heal his demon-possessed son, and he had no doubt heard of this Man who had healed many sick, lame, and demoniacs. But still, he doubted.

At first glance, you may wonder how a man who had heard so much about Jesus could possibly doubt Him. And you may even look at his words as a contradiction. But maybe you shouldn't see his words as a contradiction at all. And maybe you shouldn't assume that he had a hard time believing Jesus could heal people. Maybe you should look at his words as an admission that he wondered if Jesus could and would help *him*.

The thought of speaking to God with this kind of honesty scares many men. There are things, after all, you wish you could hide from Him, things you don't even want to admit to yourself. But when you come to the end of yourself and still need God to do something great *for* you and *within* you, it's just the kind of honesty He wants from you.

Do you sometimes find yourself doubting that God wants to do a miracle for *you*? If so, then confess your doubt to Him. He can handle it, and He can also open your heart and mind to what He has planned for you.

Lord, thank You that I can be honest with You when I feel doubtful. I bring my doubts to You and ask that You help me to rest in who You are.

DAY 176
CHAIN OF COMMAND

The centurion answered and said, "Lord, I am not
worthy that You should come under my roof. But only
speak a word, and my servant will be healed. For I also am
a man under authority, having soldiers under me."
MATTHEW 8:8–9 NKJV

Jesus praised this Roman for his faith, which came because, as a soldier, he recognized what it meant for men to obey his authority. The centurion was the forerunner of all those who would come to faith in Jesus even though they hadn't grown up as Jews. He saw the bigger picture.

Isaac, for example, wouldn't see the fulfillment of God's promise to him and his ancestors in his lifetime, but when God told him to stay in the Promised Land, he obeyed (Genesis 26:2–5). Just so, each believer has to trust God to keep His promises of sanctification and ultimate glorification—that, as crummy as things get in this life, God is working it all for good.

How often do you sow in fields from which you won't reap? God can bless both you where you are and others down the road because of your faithfulness. When you honor God with your commitment to follow Him, you're participating in a chain of command that serves God's bigger picture, the results of which will eventually be His glory and your blessing.

Lord, I make myself available today for Your purposes.
Give me the wisdom to be a conduit of blessing.

DAY 177
NO MATTER WHAT

"Though He slay me, yet will I trust Him."
JOB 13:15 NKJV

I f you love missions, you probably have heard about famed twentieth-century martyr Jim Elliot thanks to *Life* magazine, Elisabeth Elliot's books, stage dramatizations, the movie *End of the Spear*, and much more.

Then again, you probably haven't heard about Jim Elliot's older brother, Herbert Elliot. Bert and his wife, Colleen, left for South America before Jim and Elisabeth and faithfully served the Lord as missionaries all across the northern half of Peru for sixty-two years. They finally passed away and went to glory fifty-six years after Jim's martyrdom.

No one was more surprised than Bert himself. While walking in a remote area of the Amazon jungles in 1985, near an area where he used to evangelize, disciple, and then "kidnap" the slaves of drug lords, Bert told a reporter that he fully expected to leave Peru with a bullet in his head.

Except for Saturday nights, when the local bar's music blared the loudest and longest, Bert and Colleen both slept soundly. Their secret? Fully trusting in God's sovereignty and providence. They just didn't plan to do so well into their eighties.

Do you ever fear dying before your time? If so, you're like other men. The challenge? To trust God no matter what.

---

*Lord, You knew the day of my birth and the day of
my death before the days of creation. So I fully trust
Your greatness and goodness. Guide me aright.*

DAY 178
BUILDING A LIFE

"These words I speak to you are not incidental additions to your life, homeowner improvements to your standard of living. They are foundational words, words to build a life on."
MATTHEW 7:24 MSG

Imagine everything you've worked for in life—your education or career or even family—crumbling under the assault of a natural disaster. Now imagine that instead of an earthquake, flood, or fire, *you're* to blame. Jesus said, "Knowing the correct password—saying 'Master, Master,' for instance—isn't going to get you anywhere with me. What is required is serious obedience—*doing* what my Father wills" (Matthew 7:21 MSG).

It's just as big a disaster to call yourself a Christian and not live by what the Bible says as it is to never receive Him at all. That doesn't mean you must be perfect—in fact, that's the whole point. Rather than trying to be something you're not and never could be, embrace God's grace fully. Trust that He loves you just as you are and that nothing could ever make Him love you less.

He just wants an honest day's work from you—living out His will for your life, letting His words be your guide. "Those who know your name trust in you, for you, LORD, have never forsaken those who seek you" (Psalm 9:10 NIV).

Lord God, let my actions match Your words. May I never pretend to be something You haven't made me to be.

DAY 179
WORK OUT YOUR OWN SALVATION

But the path of the just is as the shining light, that shineth more and more unto the perfect day. The way of the wicked is as darkness: they know not at what they stumble.

PROVERBS 4:18–19 KJV

Solomon offered a stark contrast in today's verses. The path of the wicked is fraught with danger. Those who take it stumble but aren't even sure what tripped them up. The person who walks the path of the just leaves darkness behind. The farther he goes down the right path, the brighter his path becomes since God's grace completely illuminates it.

The apostle Paul offered a similar message: "Wherefore, my beloved, as ye have always obeyed, not as in my presence only, but now much more in my absence, work out your own salvation with fear and trembling" (Philippians 2:12 KJV). We work while trusting God with the results.

What does working out your own salvation look like in your life? What specifically are you doing to flee the way of the wicked in favor of the path of the just? Are you taking responsibility for feeding yourself spiritually? Are you gathering with other believers? Are you staying steadfast in prayer?

Father, I see two paths in front of me. May I walk the path of the just today and every day, forsaking my former ways in favor of obeying and honoring You.

DAY 180
THE HAND OF RESCUE

Is anyone crying for help? GOD is listening, ready to rescue you.
PSALM 34:17 MSG

A man dangles from a tree root just over the cliff's edge. He shouts for help. If he falls, he'll be injured or killed. He needs to be rescued. Another man hears his cries and makes his way to the edge of the cliff. He offers a hand and pulls the first man to safety.

It seems like a simple exchange, but there were decisions to be made. The first man had to recognize his situation and ask for help. The second man had to come close enough to offer help. The first man also had to decide whether to trust that the second man could help him.

You're the first man and Jesus is the second. He can rescue if you cry for help—and if you accept His help. As you learn more about the Lord who reached down and drew you to safety, you'll find a richer and deeper sense of gratitude. The one who rescued you was the only one who could answer your call.

Cry out for help. The Lord is listening.

Lord, I can't rescue myself from wrong thinking and bad decision-making. Time and again, You've rescued me from spiritual cliffs. May I always accept Your hand of rescue. Teach me how to avoid the cliffs, and help me to remember the mercy I have found in You.

DAY 181
WHO'S YOUR ENEMY?

*Be alert and of sober mind. Your enemy the devil prowls
around like a roaring lion looking for someone to devour.*

1 PETER 5:8 NIV

If someone were to ask you who or what is the greatest enemy of the church today, how would you answer? Some would answer that the biggest enemy is government institutions, which in many ways are becoming more hostile toward the Christian faith. Others might say that other human institutions seem to work tirelessly to oppose the preaching of the gospel.

While there's no doubt that some worldly and human institutions want to keep Christianity in a corner, Christian men need to understand that they're in a spiritual battle, not a political or physical one. The apostle Paul put it like this: "Our struggle is not against flesh and blood, but against the rulers, against the authorities, against the powers of this dark world and against the spiritual forces of evil in the heavenly realms" (Ephesians 6:12 NIV).

Yes, you should stand against evil in the secular world today and contend for what is right in God's eyes. But you should never forget that your ultimate enemy is the devil, not the lost and misguided people who oppose God.

And above all, you need to remember to put on the full armor of God (Ephesians 6:10–18) as you do battle against the devil and his minions.

*All-powerful God, I have a spiritual enemy who knows
my weaknesses and has the ability to throw me off track.
Thank You that You have ultimate power over him.*

DAY 182
SEEING GOD AS HE IS

*Return to the LORD your God, for he is gracious
and compassionate, slow to anger and abounding
in love, and he relents from sending calamity.*

JOEL 2:13 NIV

M any earthly fathers aren't exactly living pictures of graciousness and patience. There are exceptions, to be sure, but many fathers have the rules and punishment thing down with little focus on the fatherly compassion and the patience children need.

Your Father in heaven has mastered that balance perfectly. The Bible contains many accounts of God dealing harshly with people's sin. But on every such occasion, He persistently, patiently, and lovingly reached out to His people, calling them to repentance—back to Himself. And when they repented, He was right there, speaking words of love and comfort and restoring them to Himself.

This is a question of balance between the fear of God and the love of God. You may already understand God as a holy and righteous punisher of sin, and that He most certainly is. But you should temper that understanding of Him with the equally true picture of a heavenly Father who extends His compassion and patience to *you*.

Even if your earthly father lacked compassion and patience, you can still learn to relate to God as the loving, patient, compassionate heavenly Father He truly is.

*Lord, let me see You as You are: as a holy and righteous God but
also as my gracious, compassionate, loving heavenly Father.*

DAY 183
GOD'S DELIGHT

*Since the world in all its fancy wisdom never had a clue when
it came to knowing God, God in his wisdom took delight in
using what the world considered stupid—preaching, of all things!—
to bring those who trust him into the way of salvation.*

1 CORINTHIANS 1:21 MSG

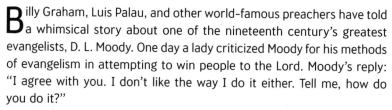

Billy Graham, Luis Palau, and other world-famous preachers have told a whimsical story about one of the nineteenth century's greatest evangelists, D. L. Moody. One day a lady criticized Moody for his methods of evangelism in attempting to win people to the Lord. Moody's reply: "I agree with you. I don't like the way I do it either. Tell me, how do you do it?"

The lady answered, "I don't do it."

Moody replied, "Well, then, I like my way of doing evangelism better than your way of not doing it."

True, public evangelism isn't solely locked into preaching. Still, at the end of the day, it's what God loves to use "to bring those who trust him into the way of salvation." Thankfully, there are 105 ways to do evangelism. So if you're not a public proclaimer, you still have plenty of options.

Just don't make the mistake of criticizing evangelists, pastors, and other public proclaimers of the life-changing gospel of Jesus Christ. After nearly two thousand years, God still loves to use preaching.

*Lord, You made me, You equipped me, and now You can use
me. Help me honor and support the preaching of the gospel.*

GOD'S PROVISION BLESSES MANY

Then the LORD said to Elijah, "Go and live in
the village of Zarephath, near the city of Sidon.
I have instructed a widow there to feed you."
1 KINGS 17:8–9 NLT

Elijah went from one impossible mission to another. When it appeared that everyone had abandoned God, the Lord instructed him to perform signs before the people in the hope of sparking a revival. When food became scarce, God chose a poor widow to provide for him.

This situation placed Elijah wholly at the mercy of God to care for himself, the widow, and her child. However, caught up in the blessing to Elijah were the widow and her son. His faithfulness to God's commands had a far-reaching impact on their lives as well.

When God calls you to take a leap of faith, it's likely that the resources and means will not be readily apparent. You may be called to undertake a project that appears next to impossible.

But if you remain faithful to God's calling, many others may benefit from your decision. From those impacted by your choices to those encouraged by the stories of God's provision, your decision to trust God today can have a significant impact in helping future generations believe in God.

Lord, I trust that You can provide for me
when the future appears uncertain.

CONTENT OR COMPLACENT?

*I have learned how to be content with whatever I have. I know
how to live on almost nothing or with everything. I have
learned the secret of living in every situation, whether it
is with a full stomach or empty, with plenty or little.*
PHILIPPIANS 4:11–12 NLT

What would make you content? You're probably thinking of things like money, a particular home, or maybe a certain vehicle. If you just had whatever you're thinking about right now, all would be perfect in your world and you'd discover ultimate contentment, right?

But every time you set your eyes on the next contentment-inducing object, the target shifts. When you have what you think you want, you discover something newer that promises greater contentment. Yet with each acquisition you schedule a new party for discontent.

The apostle Paul had almost nothing but knew contentment. He discovered contentment was the secret of living in varying circumstances. Contentment is being satisfied with where *God* places you. If He's with you, there's nothing to fear because you'll have exactly what you need.

Sometimes it's easy to exchange "contented" for "complacent." Someone who's satisfied in a circumstance he personally created is complacent. God can encourage him to move, but he doesn't want to take one step beyond the comfort zone he's made. Complacency is often found among those who've decided God can't be trusted to lead. With God in control, however, contentment can be found in multiple circumstances.

---

*Lord God, help me to focus completely on You and Your
goodness so that I can be content in every life situation.*

DAY 186
NOT A GAME

"Don't bargain with God. Be direct. Ask for what you need.
This isn't a cat-and-mouse, hide-and-seek game we're in."
MATTHEW 7:7–8 MSG

Life tests you. God allows it, to challenge you to learn and grow, but the lessons are almost always about learning to trust more in Him. God shows you who He is—His power and holiness but also His mercy and grace. The only way to pass such tests is to take God seriously.

When God told Abram to sacrifice his only son, Abram didn't hesitate to obey. He reasoned that if God was going to let him take Isaac's life, God would then have to raise Isaac from the dead to keep His promises (Hebrews 11:17–19). That's why he told his servants, "The lad and I will go yonder and worship, and we will come back to you" (Genesis 22:5 NKJV). Only faith prepares you for such a test, and only faith will help you pass it.

It's dangerous to play at following God. To act the Christian on Sundays and spend the rest of the week living how you want to is, as Charles Spurgeon put it, practical atheism. That reveals a man living in fear of other men instead of reverent fear of God. Worship isn't part of your Sunday face but is part of your life each day.

Father, I choose to recognize and honor You with
all I have and all I do, today and every day.

DAY 187
LIVING IN THE PAST

Do not say, "Why were the old days better than these?"
For it is not wise to ask such questions.
ECCLESIASTES 7:10 NIV

Have you ever gotten together with a group of old friends—maybe at some reunion—to catch up with one another and reminisce about your times together many years back? Those kinds of gatherings can be enjoyable because you get to see people you haven't seen in a long time and share laughter and memories.

But they can also be frustrating if they cause you to look at your current experiences through the lens of days gone by. As many have found out, that's not a good thing.

It can be easy sometimes to find yourself living in the past and longing for what you remember as "better times." That can be especially true when you feel dissatisfaction with the present or when you're going through difficult circumstances. In times like these, you may find yourself feeling a sense of ingratitude for what God is doing in your life at present.

There's nothing wrong with reminiscing, with thinking and talking about great times you've enjoyed in the past. You can remember those days fondly and even thank God for them. But you should never let your great memories of days gone by get in the way of living out what God has for you in the here and now.

Loving heavenly Father, thank You for the great memories
from my past. Help me never to simply live in those times but
instead to look forward to what You have for me today.

DAY 188
TRUST GOD'S THOUGHTS

"For my thoughts are not your thoughts,
neither are your ways my ways," declares the LORD.
ISAIAH 55:8 NIV

In Isaiah 55:7 (NIV), God tells the wicked to "forsake their ways and the unrighteous their thoughts." In verse 8 He explains, "For my thoughts are not your thoughts, neither are your ways my ways." Does that mean if you're saved and obeying Him, then your thoughts and ways are much closer to *God's* thoughts and ways? Absolutely!

Still, God is all-knowing and sees the end of all matters from their beginning and understands absolutely everything—things that you find incomprehensible. So it's still often a quantum leap to trust God's thoughts since what He says often flies in the face of human logic.

But you've already learned down through the years that people you didn't think knew what they were talking about actually *did*. A quote often attributed to Mark Twain says, "When I was a boy of fourteen, my father was so ignorant I could hardly stand to have the old man around. But when I got to be twenty-one, I was astonished at how much he had learned in seven years."

When you get to heaven, you'll have a good laugh about how you once thought you knew better than God.

Lord, You are the Almighty, from eternity to eternity, wiser
than any man. Nevertheless, help me begin to understand
Your ways and Your thoughts. In Jesus' name, I pray.

DAY 189
GIVE ME STRENGTH

I can do all things through Christ who strengthens me.
PHILIPPIANS 4:13 NKJV

The apostle Paul turned to Christianity after condemning and even murdering Christians. He eventually dedicated his life to serving Christ and his journey led him to abundant wealth, extreme poverty, and everything in between. He was imprisoned for several years but still wrote this joyful letter from prison. When Paul says he "can do all things through Christ," he's not talking about superhuman ability to accomplish goals that satisfy his selfish purpose. Paul learned to get by with whatever he had, whether it was little or nothing. He focused on what he should *do*—serve the Lord—instead of what he should have. Paul set his priorities in order and was grateful for all that God gave him. Paul faced many trials and tribulations, but he found joy in spreading God's Word and was not deterred by any trouble he encountered along the way.

You also "can do all things through Christ." You can accomplish any task, overcome any adversity, and survive any trouble if you come to the Lord and ask Him to strengthen you. He will not grant you the power to accomplish anything that does not serve His interests, but He will help you every step of the way as you build your faith and develop a relationship with Him.

Lord Jesus, without You I can't do anything of eternal importance. But I thank You that with Your strength, I can accomplish anything and everything You have for me to do.

LISTENING TO THE WISE

*So Mordecai went away and did
everything as Esther had ordered him.*
ESTHER 4:17 NLT

At the end of a daylong seminar on a biblical understanding of humility, two very elderly gentlemen asked to speak to the audience. The men had sat on opposite sides of the auditorium that day and hadn't conferred with each other. Yet what each said was haunting.

On the far left of the auditorium, one of the gentlemen said, "I've been married to a very wise woman all these years. Why, oh why, didn't I listen to her?" In the back on the right side, an even more elderly gentleman said, "I'm so ashamed. I married a wonderful woman of God. I can't believe it. Why didn't I listen to her?"

Nothing said that day had addressed this topic, but God had spoken in no uncertain terms to each gentleman.

Scripture portrays Wisdom as a godly woman, exalts her throughout the book of Proverbs, and celebrates her good husband's attitude toward her (Proverbs 31:10–31). This includes listening to her, heeding her advice, praising her to others, and allowing her to make important financial decisions pertaining to her household, her business ventures, and her favorite charitable concerns.

So it shouldn't surprise us that wise, learned, and older Mordecai—Esther's father figure—"did everything as Esther had ordered him."

*Lord, I want to be a strong, confident, and wise man who
listens to the wisdom of the godly women in my life.*

DAY 191
WALKING WITH GOD

The LORD has told you what is good, and this
is what he requires of you: to do what is right,
to love mercy, and to walk humbly with your God.
MICAH 6:8 NLT

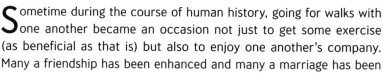

Sometime during the course of human history, going for walks with one another became an occasion not just to get some exercise (as beneficial as that is) but also to enjoy one another's company. Many a friendship has been enhanced and many a marriage has been strengthened just through going for walks—or for hikes in the case of the more athletic, more motivated crowd.

The Bible contains two examples of people who "walked with God," using those exact words: Enoch (Genesis 5:21–24) and Noah (Genesis 6:9). Of course, many other men "walked with God" in the sense that they remained in close relationship with Him and obeyed His commands.

But it's probably not much of a stretch to see the use of that exact phrase in reference to Enoch and Noah as a word picture of men who walked with God in the sense that they could fellowship with Him as closely as if they literally went for a stroll with Him, sharing their hearts with Him and allowing Him to share His heart with them.

What about you today? Maybe going for a walk and taking God with you through prayer—talking and listening to Him—could enhance and strengthen your relationship with Him.

Father God, help me to always walk with You in every
way. Help me to keep my relationship with You at the
very center of everything I do and everything I am.

DAY 192
REDEEMING THE PAST

*"So I will restore to you the years that the
swarming locust has eaten, the crawling locust,
the consuming locust, and the chewing locust."*
JOEL 2:25 NKJV

Regret is a terrible feeling for any man, including the man of God. Regret causes him to look back at past mistakes, indiscretions, and missed opportunities and think, *If I could only go back to that time in my life, I'd do so much differently. I'd make much better decisions.*

Nearly everyone has things in his past he's not proud of—things he knows God would not approve of if he did them in the present. But God promises to redeem your past mistakes, sins, and missteps and use them for His glory and your good.

That is partially what the apostle Paul meant when he wrote, "We know that in *all* things God works for the good of those who love him, who have been called according to his purpose" (Romans 8:28 NIV, emphasis added).

The past is just that—the past. And there is nothing you can do to change it. You can't undo the things you wish you hadn't done, and you can't redo the things you wish you had done. But when you bring your past to the Lord, He has a way of redeeming even your worst mistakes and using them to build something good.

---

*Lord, remind me always that You are my
Redeemer, including the redeemer of my past.*

NO BARRIER EQUALITY

*There is no longer Jew or Gentile, slave or free,
male and female. For you are all one in Christ Jesus.*
GALATIANS 3:28 NLT

Jesus came with a radical and unexpected message: God loved all mankind and didn't discriminate; women had equal standing in His plan, and the sick were never considered unacceptable.

A person's social status meant nothing to Jesus. Each person had a gift to share and a role in His plan. Where women and children were once treated as property to be discarded at will, men were told, "Love your wives and never treat them harshly" (Colossians 3:19 NLT). God also taught in Ephesians 6:4 (NLT), "Fathers, do not provoke your children to anger by the way you treat them. Rather, bring them up with the discipline and instruction that comes from the Lord."

Part of Jesus' plan was to equalize humanity. No one was less important to Him than another. He didn't come to save a few. His rescue plan was for all. His love was accessible to everyone.

Jesus introduced a new pledge, and He didn't change His mind. This generous pledge challenged popular thinking and created new opportunities. God doesn't erect barriers when it comes to a relationship with Him. Christian men should remove every barrier that makes it hard for others to meet Jesus or love people the way Jesus loves.

Jesus brought exceptionally good news. Share it. Live it.

---

*Jesus, thank You for bringing the good news of salvation
for all people through You. Help me to recognize the
opportunities You give me to share it with others.*

DAY 194
YOUR DEBT TO EVERY MAN

Don't run up debts, except for the huge debt of
love you owe each other. When you love others,
you complete what the law has been after all along.
ROMANS 13:8 MSG

Jesus wants you to be a nice, loving Christian neighbor, right? While "loving Christian" is essential, *nice* definitely isn't a big enough word for what the Lord has in mind.

The closest you get to the word *nice* in the Gospels? Away from the crowds, when confronted by the scribes and Pharisees, Jesus rails against their hypocrisies. The climax? He scorches them by saying, "You have a fine way of setting aside the commands of God in order to observe your own traditions!" (Mark 7:9 NIV). Major burn!

Jesus, of course, is never a hypocrite. One of the staggering implications? He loves every man He meets—even His fiercest critics. To Jesus the master conversationalist, relationship and meaning triumph over social norms. . .every time. He interrupts. He puzzles. He changes the subject. He provokes. He monologues. It's all fair game toward His overriding mission: to shake each man to the core of his being; to inflict many a sleepless night; to haunt him with statements he never wanted to hear; and, ultimately, to win his heart.

Yes, it's possible to be *too* nice. . .and still fail to love others. So love the Lord God with all your heart, soul, strength, and mind. And love your neighbor well.

Lord, give me Your love for every person I meet.

DON'T WASTE AN OPPORTUNITY

"The master was full of praise. 'Well done, my good and faithful servant. You have been faithful in handling this small amount, so now I will give you many more responsibilities.' "
MATTHEW 25:21 NLT

Jesus told parables to help people understand spiritual truths. Some understood. Some did not. This was a parable about investing. Three men were given money by their boss. He expected that while he was away they'd invest the money in a way that would provide a financial return. It would also allow him to see how they handled responsibility, and who could be trusted.

The first two men increased the funds they'd been given. The third simply buried the money in the ground and gave back the money when his employer returned. Sure, the boss got his money back, but he wasn't very impressed by the employee.

God has invested in your life, and He wants to see if He can trust you to do something with what He's given you. He may not give you more until He sees what you do with what He's already given. You need to do more than acknowledge the gift and then bury it.

God, it's an honor to know that I've been given something that You can use to help others. May I use that gift for Your benefit. Help me not to hide it and waste the opportunity.

BEGINNING AGAIN WITH REPENTANCE

Peter replied, "Each of you must repent of your sins and turn to God, and be baptized in the name of Jesus Christ for the forgiveness of your sins. Then you will receive the gift of the Holy Spirit."

ACTS 2:38 NLT

The people listening to Peter were truly interested in finding God as they came to Jerusalem for a religious festival, but Peter's sermon nudged them into unknown territory. They were asked to repent of their sins and turn to God as if they were starting over. After they humbled themselves before God, they were promised the gift of the Holy Spirit, uniting themselves with God in a way that was foretold by the prophets.

On the day of Pentecost, the apostles gave a starting point for every believer: repent and be filled with the Holy Spirit. If your faith feels unsteady or you're struggling to believe today, perhaps the place to begin is to repent and surrender to God.

As you open your heart to God and come clean with your need for forgiveness, a need all people have, you remove all obstacles to the Spirit's cleansing power and restoration. If you feel like you're starting over, you're in good company.

*Lord, I repent of choosing my own ways
and thank You for the gift of the Holy Spirit.*

PUT FAITH FIRST

*"But seek first his kingdom and his righteousness,
and all these things will be given to you as well."*
MATTHEW 6:33 NIV

F ollowing Christ means trusting Him to keep this promise. You understand that He will, because of who He is and all He has done for you, but when it comes down to brass tacks—unpaid debt, piles of bills, joblessness, illness—part of you wonders, *I know He can, but will He?*

Even Abram found this difficult. He had God's promise of blessing— of guidance, presence, descendants, and land—and yet he fled the Promised Land and lied about his wife out of fear and uncertainty. That led to situations like the Philistine Abimelech chastising him for his dishonesty and lack of integrity. When unbelievers are calling out believers, it's *not* good.

Small faith fails to put God and His priorities first, but a little faith gets you back on track. How big is God? Let David remind you: "GOD, brilliant Lord, yours is a household name. . . . I look up at your macro-skies, dark and enormous, your handmade sky-jewelry, moon and stars mounted in their settings. Then I look at my micro-self and wonder, Why do you bother with us?" (Psalm 8:1, 3–4 MSG). He's the mighty Creator, but He's also your loving Father.

---

*Lord, You put humanity at the pinnacle of creation.
Help me to embrace the provision You've given
me in Christ and trust You for every need.*

OUTWARD ACTS OF REPENTANCE MATTER

*But when Ahab heard this message, he tore his
clothing, dressed in burlap, and fasted. He even slept
in burlap and went about in deep mourning.*

1 KINGS 21:27 NLT

King Ahab is remembered as one of the worst, wickedest kings of Israel, but even he found God's mercy and forgiveness when he repented of his sins. When Ahab learned that his kingdom would fall and his family would be destroyed, he responded with great grief and mourning. He didn't seek ways to hide or numb his pain. His repentance for his well-known sins was public and sincere.

Torn clothing and burlap sheets are hardly standard for expressing sorrow and repentance today, but they serve as helpful pictures of sincere repentance. You may not opt for those practices when confessing your sins to God, but the symbols you use and the actions you take can help communicate the sincerity of your heart.

It's true that anyone can fake their spirituality or their repentance, but when your actions and your heart are united in the same direction, you can effectively express your remorse and take a step toward obedience.

*Lord, search my heart today for anything
that is counter to Your will.*

DAY 199
ASK

*Wise words bring approval, but fools are
destroyed by their own words.*
ECCLESIASTES 10:12 NLT

Wisdom recognizes the importance of every decision. Wisdom understands time should be used well. It seeks advice, makes a house a home, and softens the hardest disposition.

Wisdom knows that personal opinion is less important than God's truth. Wisdom is simply knowledge until it's filtered through God's truth. Get wisdom and find that it guards you. Seek wisdom and discover it in the pages of God's Word. Follow wisdom and meet the Lord. Wisdom has rewards that exceed the possession of gold or silver. The greatest wisdom of man is foolishness when compared to the wisdom of God.

Everything you just read was paraphrased from God's Word. If you want to become a man dedicated to wisdom, you will need to return often to wise words in the book that God wrote. It's an instruction manual and book of encouragement, filled with words of grace, and it's offered to enhance life, improve marriage, and deliver wisdom.

The wisdom you'll discover will bring light to dark places, hope to desperate situations, and a way forward when the way seems blocked.

Make wisdom your pursuit; know and stop guessing; seek God's heart and find that doing His will is the pinnacle of your life purpose. God promised to give wisdom to all who ask, so if what you've read sounds good, ask.

---

*Father in heaven, thank You for giving me Your written Word so
that I can know Your heart and learn Your kind of wisdom.*

DAY 200
SWEETER THAN HONEY

How sweet are Your words to my taste,
sweeter than honey to my mouth!
PSALM 119:103 NKJV

While excavating ancient Egyptian tombs, archaeologists often find pots of honey. Remove the seal and the golden honey looks brand-new. Dip in a spoon and it tastes absolutely fresh. And it is. The Smithsonian says sealed pure honey has an "eternal shelf-life."

So it's apropos that scripture compares God's words to honey: pure, sealed, desirable, and absolutely fresh despite the millennia.

What else the Bible tells us:

- *God's Word is to be desired more than anything else you could delight in (Psalm 19:10).*
- *Besides the immediate joy of studying God's Word, there are lasting and eternal benefits (Proverbs 24:13–14).*
- *A personal relationship with God is prerequisite before digesting His Word (Jeremiah 15:16).*
- *God's Word is to be digested, not just observed or read. It is to fill your life (Ezekiel 2:8–3:3).*
- *Digesting requires attentiveness to God's Word and obedience (Ezekiel 2:8–3:3).*
- *God's Word always tastes sweeter than honey, yet words of judgment can turn one's stomach sour (Revelation 10:8–11).*
- *You don't want to settle for less than God's words (Psalm 119:103).*
Hungry? Eat!

Lord, I know You, I read the Bible, and I desire to taste more of Your sweeter-than-honey Word. Always keep me hungry for more.

DAY 201
REAL RICHES

*Better is the poor who walks in his integrity
than one perverse in his ways, though he be rich.*
PROVERBS 28:6 NKJV

F ar too often in our culture, the measure of a man is stated in terms of what he earns or what he possesses. Those with the biggest bank accounts or the most and best "toys" are the ones many see as the most admirable, as those we should emulate.

Your Father in heaven, however, applies no such measure to men. He sees men's hearts and is concerned above all that your thoughts and behavior reflect the standards He's given in His written Word.

Integrity, which can be defined as living and thinking in a way that matches one's profession of what he believes, is of the highest importance to God. He's not so concerned with what you accomplish here on earth as He is with you living a life of integrity.

Whether you're rich or poor by worldly standards, God calls you to let your thoughts and actions align themselves with your verbal profession of faith. A man who does that, whether he's filthy rich or dirt poor, is rich indeed.

Thank You, Father, that You don't measure me in terms of what I earn, what I own, or what I've accomplished. Instead, You measure me in terms of the integrity You've instilled in me.

SHARING BLESSINGS
THROUGH COMMUNITIES

*Elisha said, "Borrow as many empty jars as you can from
your friends and neighbors. Then go into your house with your
sons and shut the door behind you. Pour olive oil from your
flask into the jars, setting each one aside when it is filled."*
2 KINGS 4:3–4 NLT

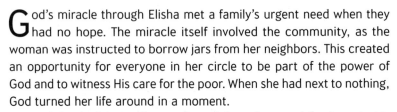

God's miracle through Elisha met a family's urgent need when they had no hope. The miracle itself involved the community, as the woman was instructed to borrow jars from her neighbors. This created an opportunity for everyone in her circle to be part of the power of God and to witness His care for the poor. When she had next to nothing, God turned her life around in a moment.

Today, whether you have a financial need or a spiritual need, this story may offer a way forward. You don't have to suffer your lack of resources on your own. Make your needs known to God and to the community around you. Give God a chance to provide what you need, and then invite others to become a part of God's work.

God is deeply concerned about you and your needs, and those who are tuned in to God's heart will be able to help meet your needs as well. Or perhaps God wants to use you to help meet others' needs.

God, help me to join You in blessing others today.

DAY 203
CLOUD AND FIRE TRAINING

*The cloud of the LORD was over the tabernacle
by day, and fire was in the cloud by night, in the
sight of all the Israelites during all their travels.*
EXODUS 40:38 NIV

Moses spoke to the miracle-performing God. He heard God answer in return. God offered to give the people the land He'd promised at the start of their journey. Their refusal to accept it meant that more than a million people would live as nomads for four decades.

They were disobedient, but God invited them back to a place of trust. If they wouldn't trust that He could give them the land He'd promised, then maybe they'd learn to trust when God led them using a cloud by day and a pillar of fire by night.

For forty years the Israelites watched the cloud and pillar of fire. When they moved, the people moved. They learned to trust God and follow Him.

Maybe you're in the middle of your journey. You might feel that you've blown the early opportunities God had for you. But He's still leading. Each new day brings an opportunity to follow Him. Your real destination has always been toward His plan. You're closer today than you think.

Lord, I once refused to follow You. Thanks for encouraging me to return from my disobedience. Thanks for considering my life worth the effort. May each decision I make help me follow Your plan.

DAY 204
DIFFERENT KINDS OF TRUTH

We have different gifts, according to the grace
given to each of us. If your gift is prophesying,
then prophesy in accordance with your faith.
ROMANS 12:6 NIV

Not all truths are created equal. Scripture accurately records Satan's outright lies (see Genesis 3:6), straightforward historical facts (2:14), insights about how life works (1:30), and divinely revealed truths (4:7). The Bible places the most value on the latter.

Among divinely revealed truths, only a small number form the core of orthodoxy. The rest are secondary points of doctrine. They're worth studying and discussing, of course, but not worth arguing or fighting over.

Divinely revealed truths consistently display these five hallmarks:

1. *Each truth is stated in clear, plain, straightforward language.*
2. *Each truth is stated in at least three verses, and usually many more.*
3. *Each truth typically is found or foreshadowed in the Old Testament, which the apostles searched diligently. Paul didn't invent "the wages of sin is death." This truth appears nearly a dozen times in the ancient Hebrew scriptures.*
4. *Each truth is found in the Gospels. Yes, Peter, Paul, James, John, and Jude indirectly quote Jesus a lot. James does so 31 times in 108 verses.*
5. *Each passage shines light on a particular facet of an even more important truth.*

Lord, I will strive to agree with You.

JUSTIFICATION ACCEPTED

Since we have been justified through faith,
we have peace with God through our Lord Jesus Christ.
ROMANS 5:1 NIV

The word *justification* isn't commonly used outside a courtroom, but it's a great concept. To be justified means God views you as guilt-free. Justification doesn't require any extra work on your part, you don't have to argue your case, and infractions are removed from your *sin ledger*.

Justification is difficult to understand when you're convinced you need to work to pay for every sin. Justification is foreign to social norms. People are conditioned to believe that if you want something, you work for it. But God offers a real-life benefits package as a gift. If you could pay for it, you'd have to call it something else. Gifts can't be earned. God did what you could never do, and He simply asks you to accept it.

Romans 5 says you can have peace with God because by accepting what's already been done you can stand confident, clean, and forgiven before God. The resulting experience is a restored relationship.

Justification makes the unacceptable acceptable, the impure pure, and the stained spotless. It accepts the sacrifice of Jesus as payment for your sin. Justification restores what was lost, broken, and disbelieving. It softens hearts and changes minds. Justification is a perfect gift and the only solution for the charge of *lawbreaker*.

Father in heaven, I first came to You as a sinner
who had nothing to offer You. Thank You for
receiving me and making me just before You.

THE HEART OF GOD

*"If you forgive those who sin against you, your heavenly
Father will forgive you. But if you refuse to forgive
others, your Father will not forgive your sins."*
MATTHEW 6:14–15 NLT

Forgiveness is closely related to trust. God knows it's your greatest need and so provided a Savior for you. In return, you choose to respond to Him in faith, trusting Him to save you. Then you're to extend forgiveness to others—both the news of God's forgiveness in Christ and forgiveness to those who have wronged you personally.

Saying "I'm sorry" is a start, but it can only express your regrets. To ask someone to forgive you is to put the power in their hands—to say, "In order to make this right, I need you to let go of the wrong I've done you." It's a gift to forgive and be forgiven.

When Abram interceded on Sodom's behalf, he asked, "Should not the Judge of all the earth do what is right?" (Genesis 18:25 NLT). He believed that God would forgive any who repented and sought His forgiveness. That's God's heart.

God loves to turn your mistakes into blessings, but forgiveness is key to that. When you take refuge in and put your trust in God (Psalm 7:1), He will help you deal with the consequences of all the things that need to be forgiven.

---

*God, I trust You to turn mistakes into blessings.
Help me to forgive and to seek forgiveness from others.*

DAY 207
ACT LIKE MEN

Watch ye, stand fast in the faith, quit you like men, be strong.
1 CORINTHIANS 16:13 KJV

I n his first letter to the Corinthian church, the apostle Paul tells them he plans to pass through Macedonia before visiting Corinth for the winter (1 Corinthians 16:5), if the Lord allows. Until he gets there, he has several messages for them. He wants them to take a collection for poor Christians (vv. 1–4), to take good care of Timothy when he visits (vv. 10–11), and to be on the lookout for a possible visit from Apollos.

Then he adds the admonition in verse 13 that you see above. They were to stand fast in the faith and to "quit you like men." This phrase was used in the English-speaking world at the time the King James Version was translated, and it is the equivalent of our modern phrase "act like men." In other words, Paul was telling them to hold fast until learned believers could arrive to encourage them in the faith.

Here's how Bible commentator Matthew Henry describes this phrase in his *Commentary on the Whole Bible*: "Act the manly, firm, and resolved part: behave strenuously, in opposition to the bad men who would divide and corrupt you, those who would split you into factions or seduce you from the faith: be not terrified nor inveigled by them; but show yourselves men in Christ, by your steadiness, by your sound judgment and firm resolution."

Take inventory of the worldly men around you. Are they seeking to corrupt you? Stand firm against them—resolved to stay true to the faith.

My Lord in heaven, give me the strength and wisdom
to stand against those who would try to move me
away from Your truth and Your standards.

DAY 208
STANDING IN THE GAP

*"So I sought for a man among them who would make
a wall, and stand in the gap before Me on behalf of the
land, that I should not destroy it; but I found no one."*
EZEKIEL 22:30 NKJV

When God commissions the prophet Ezekiel to chronicle a long list of sins committed by Jerusalem, Ezekiel covers all his bases: murder, idolatry, mistreatment of parents, oppression of strangers, mistreatment of the fatherless and the widow, profaning of the Sabbath, acts of lewdness, bribery, and extortion, as well as her priests' violation of God's law. In every sense, Jerusalem had become a den of iniquity.

And yet, in the midst of such wickedness, God was looking for a man who would make a wall and stand in the gap before Him on behalf of the land, that He would not destroy it. But sadly, He found no one. As Bible commentators point out, not every man was caught up in debauchery. But one of the few who wasn't—Jeremiah—was forbidden to pray for the city (Jeremiah 11:14). Apparently, the city had crossed the point of no return with God. The righteous had abandoned the gates, His judgment certain.

Nations fall as the righteous stop practicing righteousness. Before you know it, you have lost your house, and then your city. If God were to look for a man to stand in the gap today, would He find you there?

*Righteous God, I look around me and see a world desperately
in need of miracles on Your part. Please allow me to
"stand in the gap" for people I know, for my community,
and for my nation. . .in any way You choose.*

DAY 209
EXPERIENCE GOD'S LOVE ANEW

*Those who trust God's action in them find that God's
Spirit is in them—living and breathing God! Obsession
with self in these matters is a dead end; attention to God
leads us out into the open, into a spacious, free life.*

ROMANS 8:5–6 MSG

Slow down and take a minute to carefully reread the scripture verses above. Isn't that the kind of life *you* want to experience?

Sadly, many men think God doesn't look on them with love, favor, or delight—let alone desire to fill every fiber of their being. In their heart of hearts, they feel God is angry with them. . .or, at best, distant and uncaring. They certainly don't trust what He does in their lives. This is the great disconnect that the Father wants to deal with in your heart today.

When you trust and embrace God's deep love for you, you become better able to love others in return. Loving what God loves is the key—and yes, He absolutely loves you. Both Jesus and the apostles affirm this truth repeatedly.

One pastor told his church congregation that he knew God loved him but that the past week, for the very first time, he had experienced a profound revelation of "Jesus loves me, this I know" deep within his heart. He was completely transformed by this experience.

Lord, I want to experience Your love anew. Transform me, I pray.

DAY 210
WORTHY OF YOUR TRUST

I know whom I have believed and am persuaded that He is
able to keep what I have committed to Him until that Day.
2 TIMOTHY 1:12 NKJV

Paul had committed his eternal spirit and his earthly suffering to God, and the reason he could do so was because he trusted Him. Paul was convinced that God would guard what he'd entrusted to Him. Paul knew he could count on God to reward him for his sacrifices and suffering. He trusted God because he knew Him.

The Lord is completely dependable. The Bible assures you: "God is not a man, that He should lie. . . . Has He said, and will He not do? Or has He spoken, and will He not make it good?" (Numbers 23:19 NKJV). And Jesus promised, "In My Father's house are many mansions; if it were not so, I would have told you" (John 14:2 NKJV).

Like Paul, you believe in God and trust Him for good reason. Looking around, it often appears that worldly people are way ahead in the game of life and that you're losing out by playing a clean game and making sacrifices for others. But the reality is quite different. God is on your side, and when His kingdom has come, you'll be way, way out ahead.

Lord, help me to trust You completely
with my future, my dreams, my concerns,
my sacrifices, and my suffering. I love You, Lord.

DAY 211
WISE WORDS

"Let your 'Yes' be 'Yes,' and your 'No,' 'No.'
For whatever is more than these is from the evil one."
MATTHEW 5:37 NKJV

Part of being trustworthy is being a man of your word. It's a lost value in an age where almost everyone feels like they have to lie at least a little bit just to get by. And in a broken world, you must look to God as your anchor for what is true and right. To be a man of your word, first you must be a man of God's Word.

God's living Word cuts through the shifting morality and offers clarity (Hebrews 4:12). Even when an issue isn't specifically addressed, the Bible directs you to timeless principles that not only guide you but offer you a brighter path forward (even if in the world's eyes, it's a narrower, more challenging road).

James wrote, "Do not merely listen to the word, and so deceive yourselves. Do what it says" (James 1:22 NIV). A man for whom God's Word is his bond will stand out. When people ask you why you're like you are, you can tell them it's because you're trusting your words to God, who has called you to a higher standard and helps you live up to it.

Father, help me to believe what I say I believe,
trusting that Your unchanging principles and eternal
Word will help me to speak and act in wisdom.

DAY 212
DRINK FROM THE FOUNTAIN

How exquisite your love, O God! How eager we are to run
under your wings, to eat our fill at the banquet you spread
as you fill our tankards with Eden spring water. You're a
fountain of cascading light, and you open our eyes to light.

PSALM 36:7–9 MSG

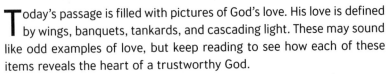

Today's passage is filled with pictures of God's love. His love is defined by wings, banquets, tankards, and cascading light. These may sound like odd examples of love, but keep reading to see how each of these items reveals the heart of a trustworthy God.

Wings—The psalmist shows a God who shields, shades, and protects. You're always safe when you accept the security of His wings.

Banquet—God wants to be clear. His love chooses to meet your needs. He loves you, and your needs are important to Him.

Water—You can't live without water. Like water, love offers refreshment and clear thinking.

Light—Light doesn't just eliminate darkness. It also allows you to discover things that were hidden in the shadows.

Love God enough to trust Him and gain access to protection, compassion, refreshment, and wisdom.

Lord, You chose to love me. I can't offer You anything but my heart.
You demonstrate love in so many ways that when I accept it I begin
to understand the value of Your protection, care, and wisdom.
Help me trust You so I can learn more about Your heart.

DAY 213
THE COMPANION

*[Jesus said,] "The Helper, the Holy Spirit, whom the Father
will send in My name, He will teach you all things, and bring
to your remembrance all things that I said to you."*
JOHN 14:26 NKJV

Friends are important. Life can be lonely without them. Proverbs 27:17 (NLT) says, "As iron sharpens iron, so a friend sharpens a friend." Your best friends help keep you focused, honest, and inspired. These traits are also found in the Holy Spirit, the least-discussed member of the Trinity. He takes up residence in the core of who you are.

Every temptation you face can be endured with the help of this friend. Jesus sent the Spirit as a personal companion to help you when you need help. Listen closely and learn what God wants from you. The Spirit can speak to your inner man and remind you of things God has already said. He's the companion, the one sent to walk beside you, the one who teaches, and the one who helps God's character grow in your heart, mind, and soul.

Saying that the Holy Spirit and your conscience are the same thing doesn't take into account all the things God's Holy Spirit can do. He can and does remind you when you're heading in the wrong direction. He can point you in the right direction. And, if allowed, He can teach, train, and transform you into the man He wants you to be.

*Lord Jesus, thank You for sending me Your Holy Spirit so that I
can overcome temptation, so that I can face any obstacle, and
so that I can do what it takes to help expand Your kingdom.*

DAY 214
DISCIPLINE FROM A LOVING FATHER

"As many as I love, I rebuke and chasten.
Therefore be zealous and repent."
REVELATION 3:19 NKJV

A lot of things go into being a good father, and one of them is discipline. The Bible goes so far as to say that a father who doesn't correct his children doesn't actually love them as he should (see Proverbs 13:24).

God is more than a good Father; He's a *perfect* Father. He's perfect in His holiness and perfect in His love, and that's why He disciplines every man He calls His son. The writer of the epistle to the Hebrews echoed today's verse when he wrote, "My son, do not make light of the Lord's discipline, and do not lose heart when he rebukes you, because the Lord disciplines the one he loves, and he chastens everyone he accepts as his son" (12:5–6 NIV).

When God's hand of discipline is upon you—and it can be difficult and unpleasant when it happens—you can be grateful, for it reminds you to trust in God and in His intense love for you. And it also encourages you to zealously examine your heart attitudes and your actions to make sure they're pleasing to Him.

Father in heaven, I may not enjoy those times when You
send discipline my way, but I thank You for them because
they're yet another demonstration of Your love for me.

DAY 215
A WELL-VERSED MAN

*This Ezra was a scribe who was well versed in the Law of
Moses, which the LORD, the God of Israel, had given to the
people of Israel. He came up to Jerusalem from Babylon,
and the king gave him everything he asked for, because
the gracious hand of the LORD his God was on him.*

EZRA 7:6 NLT

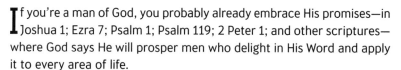

I f you're a man of God, you probably already embrace His promises—in
Joshua 1; Ezra 7; Psalm 1; Psalm 119; 2 Peter 1; and other scriptures—
where God says He will prosper men who delight in His Word and apply
it to every area of life.

As you read the Bible, you probably say "Yes!" to its declarations
about God, creation, the fall, God's chosen people, and His love for the
whole world; about Jesus' life, ministry, teachings, miracles, betrayal,
passion, death, burial, and resurrection; about the Church's miraculous
birth, expansion, teachings, and blessed hope.

As you read, you probably wince at the biblical scoundrels
(1 Corinthians 10:1–13) and cheer the stories of the great heroes of
the faith (Hebrews 11:4–12:1). And you probably affirm its clear-cut
commands for believers today.

Whether you are focusing on the Psalms, Proverbs, a Gospel, an
epistle, or Revelation, may you be led by God's Spirit into all truth.

---

*Lord, I want to be a dedicated student of a
specific Bible book, and of the entire Bible.*

HEARING WITH SPIRITUAL EARS, SEEING WITH SPIRITUAL EYES

*Those who passed by hurled insults at him, shaking their heads and
saying, "So! You who are going to destroy the temple and build
it in three days, come down from the cross and save yourself!"
In the same way the chief priests and the teachers of the law
mocked him among themselves. "He saved others," they said,
"but he can't save himself! Let this Messiah, this king of Israel,
come down now from the cross, that we may see and believe."*

MARK 15:29–32 NIV

J esus made some outrageous claims—at least to those who weren't
listening with spiritual ears or seeing with spiritual eyes. His claim
that He could rebuild the temple in three days referred to His death and
resurrection (John 2:20–22)—which was happening right before their
very eyes. But they couldn't see it.

Likewise, those who taught scripture for a living couldn't see that
"this Messiah" was indeed going to come down from the cross, but in
a way that brought salvation. They were "blind guides" (Matthew 15:14
NIV) even as they watched scripture being fulfilled.

In your life, is it possible that there's a promise of God being fulfilled
in a way you just aren't seeing? If so, open your spiritual eyes and ears,
and ask Him to let you see the spiritual reality.

*God, open my spiritual eyes. I don't want to miss
what You're doing right in front of me.*

DAY 217
WORK IN PROGRESS

Clothe yourselves with tenderhearted mercy, kindness, humility,
gentleness, and patience. Make allowance for each other's faults,
and forgive anyone who offends you. Remember, the Lord forgave
you, so you must forgive others. Above all, clothe yourselves
with love, which binds us all together in perfect harmony.
COLOSSIANS 3:12–14 NLT

True humility allows you to recognize you're a sinner saved by God's grace and no better than other human beings. You're a co-recipient of God's grace, forgiveness, and love. You have fallen short of God's perfect standard (see Romans 6:23), yet God did the remarkable and offered a rescue plan so comprehensive it made you part of His family. He orchestrated His plan to encompass a restored relationship between a perfect God and imperfect people.

Humility takes the clothing of sober judgment and offers others tenderhearted mercy, kindness, humility, gentleness, patience, forgiveness, and love. You're asked to model the behavior of your Father, God. He offers all of these things to you, so He's not interested in seeing you treat others in a way that's inferior to the way He treats them.

Christians are bound together by love, and it's the choice to love that inspires harmony between God's people. God didn't love you because you deserved it. He loved you—period. The same should be said of you. Love others because you see people differently, not as wretched and unredeemable, but as loved by God and as works in progress. Just like you.

God, help me to love others, to see them as Your creations whom
You loved enough to send Jesus to rescue. . .just like You did me.

FORGIVE ME, FATHER

*Restore to me the joy of your salvation, and make
me willing to obey you. Then I will teach your
ways to rebels, and they will return to you.*
PSALM 51:12–13 NLT

Have you ever felt disconnected from God because of your sin? Perhaps you are so embarrassed by your actions that you feel unworthy of being in the Lord's presence at church. David felt this way when he sinned with Bathsheba. In this prayer, he cries out to God: "Restore to me the joy of your salvation." David truly repented of his sin and asked for forgiveness.

God wants you to be close to Him, but sin drives a wedge between you and Him. Unconfessed sin pushes you further away from God, and it can separate you entirely from Him if you don't confront it, beg Him for forgiveness, and learn to obey Him. You may end up suffering earthly consequences for your sin. For example, adultery may lead to divorce. Fraud may lead to imprisonment. But God's forgiveness gives you the joy of a relationship with Him.

Once you experience that joy, like David, you will want to share it with others. David wanted to teach "rebels" and help them "return" to the Lord. You can help your friends and relatives by telling them about the joy of God's forgiveness and your fellowship with Him.

Father God, I don't like feeling distant from You because I've gone off track in some area of my life. Help me to quickly recognize when I've blown it. . .and then to come to You seeking restoration.

A BIBLICAL ANATOMY LESSON

*Just as a body, though one, has many parts, but all
its many parts form one body, so it is with Christ.*
1 CORINTHIANS 12:12 NIV

In 1 Corinthians 12, the apostle Paul likens the church (not the building but the believers who gather there to worship God and fellowship with one another) to the human body, which consists of many individual parts that work wonderfully together for one purpose: to keep you alive and moving.

Paul wanted the believers in Corinth to understand that they all had a role to play within the local church—some bigger and others smaller, some more up front and others more behind the scenes—but all important to the church as a whole. "Now you are the body of Christ, and each one of you is a part of it," he wrote (v. 27 NIV).

If Paul were writing to the different church bodies today, he'd tell them the same thing. Each member has a part to play for the greater good of the church.

God doesn't intend for you to attend church services every week just to warm a pew. On the contrary, He has given you special gifts and abilities so that you can serve this wonderful organism called the body of Christ. Your part in this bargain is to seek out and discover your gifts so that you can begin serving.

*Father God, I want to be a servant to my brothers
and sisters in You. Show me daily how I can use
the gifts You've given me to do just that.*

DAY 220
DON'T TRUST CASH

*Teach those who are rich in this world. . .not to trust in their
money, which is so unreliable. Their trust should be in God,
who richly gives us all we need for our enjoyment.*
1 TIMOTHY 6:17 NLT

It's easy to default to trusting in money. After all, it seems to solve
problems, resolve anxieties, create friends, and generally make people
happy. But there's a harsh reality behind this rosy picture.

Paul taught that money is *unreliable*. You might not have chosen that
word, but think about it. Recent recessions wiped out billions of dollars of
savings overnight. Banks collapsed. Financial institutions folded. Solomon
warned, "Riches disappear in the blink of an eye; wealth sprouts wings
and flies off into the wild blue yonder" (Proverbs 23:5 MSG).

If you have money, good for you. Chances are good you worked
hard or smart (or both) to earn it. But you still shouldn't put too much
trust in it. That's tantamount to trusting in yourself, and Deuteronomy
8:18 (NKJV) says that "you shall remember the LORD your God, for it is
He who gives you power to get wealth." God is a surer foundation than
wealth. He supplies everything you need, including love, faith, peace,
and assurance before Him.

---

*God, I trust You above all things. Thank You for the wealth
You've enabled me to earn. May I invest wisely, spend thriftily,
give generously, and—above all—trust in You.*

DAY 221
TRUST, NOT CERTAINTY

In peace I will lie down and sleep, for you alone,
O LORD, will keep me safe.
PSALM 4:8 NLT

Even as a committed follower of Christ, it's tempting to turn to success in the world for comfort. When Satan tempted Jesus in the wilderness, he hit Him with the big three: material needs, physical comfort, and financial success. You need all three to survive in this world, but all three can come and go. And if they do, what's left? *Without* God, nothing. *With* Him, all you'll ever need.

Jesus gave the template for resisting the temptation to rely on man's strength instead of God's: "Away with you, Satan! For it is written, 'You shall worship the LORD your God, and Him only you shall serve' " (Matthew 4:10 NKJV). Stick to God's Word. Even the most familiar verses have power and meaning to help you live the life God has called you to.

To do that, you must trust God more than your own ability to provide. When you're set apart for God, He will answer when you call on Him (Psalm 4:3). Faith is a matter of trust, not certainty, and you can rest assured in what the Bible tells you about God. You can call on Him for help and vindication because you know you belong to Him.

God, I am set apart for Your purposes, and I can face any challenge,
even my prideful tendencies, knowing that You are with me.

DAY 222

NO MORE ROAMING—
NEVER ABANDONED

*I once was young, now I'm a graybeard—not once have I seen
an abandoned believer, or his kids out roaming the streets. Every
day he's out giving and lending, his children making him proud.*

PSALM 37:25–26 MSG

It's one thing to recognize God as trustworthy in your own circumstances, but this is enhanced when you recognize God's faithful footsteps leading others over the years.

This psalm by King David reflects a life filled with years of perspective. What did David reflect on? Was it his strength as a warrior? Perhaps his time as a fugitive, running from Saul? No. His recollections were centered around other people. He saw that even in the most difficult times believers weren't abandoned, God's children had purpose, and God's generosity couldn't be questioned.

Not only was David convinced that God was trustworthy, but he saw that He wasn't selective in compassion and mercy.

Perhaps God directed David to write these words so when you go through hard times, this man who had a passion for God can remind you that whatever bad days you face, you'll never be beyond God's compassion.

---

*Lord, help me look for Your faithfulness in the praises of Your
people. You're good. I want to pay attention to how You help
others, knowing You don't exist just for my benefit. May I discover
reasons to worship by rejoicing with others in Your compassion.*

DAY 223
STANDING IN THE WAY

*Not that we are sufficient of ourselves to think of anything
as being from ourselves, but our sufficiency is from God.*
2 CORINTHIANS 3:5 NKJV

The problem with self-sufficiency is *self*. This one little word makes the assumption that each individual can find a sense of completeness by simply following his own abilities, decision-making, and strengths. It also assumes that every individual has a complete understanding of what sufficiency means, looks like, and how to know when he's obtained it.

God made relationship a priority with and for mankind. Relationship is always improved when someone meets a need. Marriage meets many needs, but not all. Friendships meet needs, but not all. There's always something missing until you accept friendship with Jesus. You have needs that only God can meet. If you could meet all your own needs, there'd be no need for God.

You'll only be sufficient when you make room for God to begin His good work in you. He will complete it, and you'll find rescue, restoration, and purpose. Wholeness can only truly be achieved when you accept friendship with the God who actually knows where you're going and how to get you there.

When you're tired of trying to do life alone only to discover failure, it's time to remove *self* from sufficiency. Wholeness is available. Don't stand in the way.

---

*Lord, thank You that You've made me so dependent on You.
Help me never to forget that You alone are sufficient for me.*

HUMBLE BEGINNINGS

*"The LORD took me as I followed the flock, and the
LORD said to me, 'Go, prophesy to My people Israel.' "*
AMOS 7:15 NKJV

Humanly speaking, Amos doesn't look like the kind of man God would send to preach to the eighth-century BC nation of Israel. He was a simple shepherd when God called him to prophesy to His people. Yet God used him in powerful ways.

In reality, Amos fit the profile of just the kind of man God so often called to serve Him and to make a difference in the world. Moses was also a shepherd, Amos was a fig farmer, Joseph (Jesus' earthly father) was a carpenter, and the apostles Peter, James, and John were fishermen—to name a few.

God doesn't always use the highly educated or the credentialed to accomplish His purposes. On the contrary, He uses the humble, the willing, and those who have the courage and faith to say, "I'm here and available, Lord. Use me!"

If you feel unworthy or unprepared, it may just be that God has you right where He wants you. Your part in that equation is to say to Him, "I'm willing. Use me as You will."

*Lord, You've used men with little education or credentials to
do great things for Your kingdom. Though I may not have an
impressive background, I know You can do the same with me.*

DAY 225
THE BEST MEMORIES

*I have rejoiced in the way of Your testimonies, as
much as in all riches. I will meditate on Your precepts,
and contemplate Your ways. I will delight myself in
Your statutes; I will not forget Your word.*

PSALM 119:14–16 NKJV

What are some of your favorite memories?

Some favorite memories may be mosaics. They may be montages of watching stunning sunrises and sunsets with loved ones and friends. They may be panoramas of the most picturesque scenery you've seen while driving long distances. They may be kaleidoscopes of some of your favorite sports and concert experiences.

Then again, some of your favorite memories may be snapshots. They may be specific moments like the time you knelt down and your girlfriend said "yes," your huge smile when she started walking down the aisle, and the joy of holding your first child moments after his or her birth.

Now, imagine including God's inspired Word among your favorite memories. That's what the verses quoted at the top of this page are describing.

Your favorite scripture memories may be the stories of specific Bible heroes or villains, kaleidoscopes of God's amazing miracles, or panoramas of Christ's public ministry on earth. Then again, your favorite memories may be specific Bible passages or verses. The more you remember them, the happier you'll be.

Lord, please bring favorite scripture memories to my mind often.

DAY 226
KEEP A CLEAR CONSCIENCE

Cling to your faith in Christ, and keep your conscience clear.
For some people have deliberately violated their consciences;
as a result, their faith has been shipwrecked.

1 TIMOTHY 1:19 NLT

John 3:36 (NKJV) says, "He who believes in the Son has everlasting life," so you clearly need faith in Jesus. But if you lack love for God and your fellow man, and don't have a clear conscience, these can badly injure and/or shake your faith.

If you willfully disobey God then refuse to repent and accept His forgiveness, you violate your conscience. You won't necessarily lose your connection with Christ but will likely live in defeat and condemnation, not enjoying the freedom and assurance that are your rights in Him.

If you've sinned, repent today and trust that God will forgive you. What gives you the right to trust that He will do that? His Word promises: "If we confess our sins, He is faithful and just to forgive us our sins and to cleanse us from all unrighteousness" (1 John 1:9 NKJV). "He who covers his sins will not prosper, but whoever confesses and forsakes them will have mercy" (Proverbs 28:13 NKJV).

God longs to forgive you and set you free. He wants to restore your ability to live an overcoming, victorious life by His Spirit.

Lord, I confess my sins to You, and I forsake them.
Help me to accept Your forgiveness and make
things right with others, if possible.

DAY 227
SET APART FOR THE LORD

All the Israelites twenty years old or more who were able to
serve in Israel's army were counted according to their families.
The total number was 603,550. The ancestral tribe of the
Levites, however, was not counted along with the others.

NUMBERS 1:45–47 NIV

A s the people of Israel were preparing to enter the Promised Land,
God commanded a census be taken so that a standing army could
be assembled. But the Levites were left out. Why? Because they were
to be a priesthood for the tabernacle, set apart to the Lord for His use.

They were in place of all the "firstborns" that the Lord had already
said were His. More than forty years earlier, before they crossed the Red
Sea, God said, "Take the Levites for me in place of all the firstborn of
the Israelites" (Numbers 3:41 NIV).

Peter declared to believers, "You are a chosen people, a *royal*
priesthood, a holy nation, God's special possession, that you may declare
the praises of him who called you out of darkness into his wonderful
light" (1 Peter 2:9 NIV, emphasis added). He was telling you that you're
His *firstborn*, with all the privileges and responsibilities that accom-
pany that. You're allowed to bear His name in this world because you
are set apart in Jesus.

Father, You have included me in Christ as a firstborn.
Help me to honor You by living a holy life.

DAY 228
IRRITATING THE LORD

People were bringing little children to Jesus for him to place his hands on them, but the disciples rebuked them. When Jesus saw this, he was indignant. He said to them, "Let the little children come to me. . .for the kingdom of God belongs to such as these. Truly I tell you, anyone who will not receive the kingdom of God like a little child will never enter it."

MARK 10:13–15 NIV

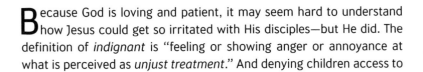

B ecause God is loving and patient, it may seem hard to understand how Jesus could get so irritated with His disciples—but He did. The definition of *indignant* is "feeling or showing anger or annoyance at what is perceived as *unjust treatment.*" And denying children access to the Messiah was about as unjust as it got. It was completely contrary to Jesus' heart for people.

The surest way to irritate the Lord is to stand in the way of people coming to Him. He reserved His harshest criticism for those who interfered with salvation, saying, "Woe to you, teachers of the law and Pharisees, you hypocrites! You shut the door of the kingdom of heaven in people's faces. You yourselves do not enter, nor will you let those enter who are trying to" (Matthew 23:13 NIV).

True believers should be indignant like He was when the way to God is blocked by religious systems and prejudices.

O Lord, let me always make the way open
for those who are seeking You.

DAY 229
UNSTOPPABLE

"I will put enmity between you and the woman,
and between your seed and her Seed; He shall
bruise your head, and you shall bruise His heel."
GENESIS 3:15 NKJV

Nothing is beyond God's control. Even at the fall, when His brand-new creation was ruined by the serpent's deception and His children's disobedience, God immediately announced His prophetic plan to redeem His people—the Seed who would crush the serpent and release mankind from sin and death. Nothing catches God off guard.

Satan's whole game plan is predicated on disrupting God's redemptive plan. Time and time again, he failed—going back as far as Cain killing Abel. Other examples are when Pharaoh and later Herod committed infanticide. And when Jesus allowed His hands to be nailed to the cross, Satan thought he had won, but "the one who rules in heaven laughs. . . . For the Lord declares, 'I have placed my chosen king on the throne' " (Psalm 2:4, 6 NLT).

Adam and Eve fell because they didn't trust God. They saw in the serpent's questions a reason to doubt that God was looking out for them. They fell for what today is a common malady—the fear of missing out. God doesn't promise you everything that is good, but He freely gave you His very best in Jesus Christ.

Even in the worst times, God, You are still sovereign,
and Your Word is still being fulfilled. No enemy can
thwart Your plans for the world or for my life.

DAY 230
WITH YOU ALWAYS

"Go and make disciples of all nations, baptizing them in the name of the Father and of the Son and of the Holy Spirit, and teaching them to obey everything I have commanded you. And surely I am with you always, to the very end of the age."
MATTHEW 28:19–20 NIV

Jesus made it clear to His disciples that instead of returning to their old jobs they would be world changers. They weren't to stay home. They were to bring the good news they'd heard to people of every nation. Just as they were discipled by Jesus, they were to disciple others. They were to lead by example. They had marching orders and the world was their mission field.

If the disciples had any qualms as to the sanity of this new venture, they nonetheless were to step forth in courage after Jesus left. The trust they had in Him would enable them to do great things.

You've also been given a big job. Learn, then share what you've learned. Obey, then encourage others to obey. Identify with Jesus, then invite others to trust. The benefit? Jesus said, "I am with you always, to the very end of the age."

Dear God, help me to remember that every generation needs to hear Your message and every generation needs ambassadors to share that message. May I use my voice, actions, and life to share the truth that even today You are with Your children.

WISDOM, POWER, COUNSEL, AND UNDERSTANDING

*"Is not wisdom found among the aged? Does not long
life bring understanding? To God belong wisdom
and power; counsel and understanding are his."*

JOB 12:12–13 NIV

Who do you listen to when you need advice? Is it someone who doesn't have a fully formed picture of life? Or is it someone who's spent time in life's trenches and has lived to gain understanding? There's a reason you might seek the advice of your father or other mature men. Their life experience may help you learn what to avoid and what to pursue.

This idea is linked to finding a mentor or becoming a disciple. You'll need to admit you don't know everything in order to learn something. If it's true that you'll likely seek older men with more life experience to draw from, then shouldn't it be true that you become doggedly determined to follow the God who possesses *complete* wisdom, power, counsel, and understanding?

God wants you to pay attention and make choices as to whose voice you allow into your thinking. If you're careful whom you listen to among your sphere of friendships, shouldn't the voice of God and the wisdom He's given in His Word take first place as your source of counsel for today's tough choices? And tomorrow's?

"Come near to God and he will come near to you" (James 4:8 NIV).

*God of wisdom, give me the wisdom to know that I need
to hear and obey Your voice before any other.*

DAY 232
"FRIEND OF GOD"

So now we can rejoice in our wonderful new relationship with
God because our Lord Jesus Christ has made us friends of God.
ROMANS 5:11 NLT

Have you ever thought of yourself as a friend of God? If so, have you ever said it aloud?

True, the Bible doesn't talk often about this. Mostly, it's reserved for the great patriarch Abraham, who is called the "friend of God" in 2 Chronicles 20:7; Isaiah 41:8; and James 2:23. Another important early patriarch of the faith, Job, talks about his friendship with God in Job 29:4.

Then again, James 4:4 and Romans 5:11 make it clear that *any* man can be a friend of God if he repents, trusts Jesus Christ, and loves the Lord wholeheartedly. This isn't "friend" in the Facebook sense. Instead, the apostle Paul describes it as "our wonderful new relationship with God."

By now, you may be thinking, *That's right. That makes me a friend of God.* Do you believe it enough to say it aloud? Say it first in prayer to God. Then mention it in a conversation with your spouse, child, friend, colleague, or neighbor.

Lord, "friend of God" seems like such a lofty title for me.
Yet I believe what Romans 5:11 says. I want to enjoy a
wonderful relationship with You. Please draw me closer to
Your heart. And give me the courage to talk about my
friendship with You to another person before day's end.

WHY ARE YOU AFRAID?

When Jesus woke up, he rebuked the wind and said to
the waves, "Silence! Be still!" Suddenly the wind stopped,
and there was a great calm. Then he asked them,
"Why are you afraid? Do you still have no faith?"

MARK 4:39–40 NLT

One day, Jesus and His disciples were on a boat heading to the other side of the lake. Then a storm came up. Jesus was so secure He'd fallen asleep. The disciples weren't feeling very secure, however. They tried to be brave, but things were getting out of hand—even for those among Jesus' disciples who had made their living on boats. Finally, they woke Jesus and He calmed the storm.

Jesus was speaking to His disciples, but He was also speaking to you when He asked, "Why are you afraid? Do you still have no faith?" Trust is a primary component of faith, but too often fear is a first response, not faith. Burdens become personal, not shared. Outcomes include best efforts, not God's help.

When the storm was the worst for the disciples, Jesus was with them. And when He spoke, things immediately became calm.

Lord, You want me to replace fear with faith and anxiety with trust.
You give examples of what that looks like, and I'm left to remember
that even mighty men and women of the Bible struggled with trust.
Help me learn what they learned and, in doing so, trust You.

DISHONORED

[Jesus] began teaching in the synagogue, and many who heard him were amazed. They asked, "Where did he get all this wisdom and the power to perform such miracles?"

MARK 6:2 NLT

The people of Nazareth knew Jesus as the son of Mary. They couldn't see Him as the Messiah. Hadn't He been a playmate for their children? How could this former village boy have the power to heal? And where did He discover such wisdom?

The phrase "You can never go home again" suggests that when you leave home and return wiser and more skilled, there'll be those who only connect their memories to someone younger and less wise. The people of Nazareth struggled with that about Jesus.

His former neighbors speculated about Him. You can almost hear them whispering words behind their hands that betrayed envy, malice, and gossip. Jesus was aware that He had no honor in His hometown nor His childhood home.

Jesus faced criticism, so He understands the way you feel when you're criticized. He knows what goes through your mind. So when you feel left out, gossiped about, or belittled for following God's plan for you, remember that you face each trouble with Jesus.

God, forgive me when I think You could never understand the things I face. Your Son suffered, so He knows what I'm suffering. Thank You for taking action to connect my pain with Your comfort.

SHOW AND SAY

*How can they call on him to save them unless they believe in him?
And how can they believe in him if they have never heard about
him? And how can they hear about him unless someone tells them?*

ROMANS 10:14 NLT

I t's claimed that Saint Francis of Assisi said each man should always preach Christ and if necessary use words. The problem is no one can actually find these words (or anything similar) in his writings. Whether true or embellished, people have gripped this idea with a strong hand. Artwork has been made featuring these words. The quote has been shared in many small groups and Bible classes.

Nevertheless, the idea of letting your life convince others that you're different comes straight from the Bible. First Peter 2:9 (NLT) says, "You are a chosen people. . .God's very own possession. As a result, you can show others the goodness of God, for he called you out of the darkness into his wonderful light."

Your life *can* show there is a difference among those who follow Jesus, but some people will never ask why you're different. Perhaps that's why the apostle Paul said so dramatically in today's verse that people need to actually hear you *talk* about Jesus and what He's done. If they won't ask and you don't tell them, they miss opportunities to believe in the one who rescued you.

Let your life point to your faith. . .and let your mouth share what you believe.

Lord, make my life a shining beacon that may point people to You.

THE PERIL OF GREED

*The greedy stir up conflict, but those
who trust in the LORD will prosper.*
PROVERBS 28:25 NIV

T*he greedy stir up conflict.* It shouldn't surprise any believer when real life reflects the truths of scripture. But probably no starker example of this is the conflict the sin of greed so often causes. Think of Bernie Madoff, Joseph Nacchio, Bernard Ebbers, and a host of others. Each of these men's crimes resulted in billions of dollars in losses to those they defrauded. . .and also landed them in prison.

The apostle Paul uses the phrase "the love of money" to describe greed. And he warns that those who engage in that sin do so at the risk of their eternal souls (see 1 Timothy 6:9–10).

Today's verse contrasts two different heart attitudes: that of greed, and that of trust in God. It's not a stretch, then, to infer from this verse that greed and trust in God cannot dwell within the same heart and mind. In other words, if you trust in God, then there is no place in your heart for greed.

Do you want to guard your heart against the sin of greed? Then devote yourself to trusting in God to care for you and provide for you.

---

*Father, You are my protector and provider,
and I ask You to teach me to trust in You and not
in financial riches, lest I fall into the sin of greed.*

BEYOND PEAK EXPERIENCES

Thou art my God, and I will praise thee:
thou art my God, I will exalt thee.
PSALM 118:28 KJV

What are your favorite college and professional sports teams? Can you remember scenes from some of their most famous victories? And have any of your favorite teams ever won a national championship? If so, how did you feel? Elated? Electrified? Ecstatic? Enthusiastic beyond words?

Who are your favorite musicians and music groups? Can you remember specific songs from some of their concerts? And have they ever had a #1 hit? If so, how did you feel when you heard it for the first time?

The funny thing about peak experiences is they never last. That's not just true in sports and music but also true in every other sphere of life. Sadly, some peak experiences end up leaving a bitter taste in your mouth. That team isn't so special anymore. That #1 hit song now just gets on your nerves.

How good that you can thank the Lord every day for who He is and what He means to you! As you read His Word, be sure to look for "peak" reasons to keep praising God.

Lord, You are my God, and I want to honor and praise You
every day of my life. Help me notice and remember scores
of reasons why. You are worthy beyond measure!

DAY 238
WHAT GOD REQUIRES

The whole point of what we're urging is simply love—love uncontaminated by self-interest and counterfeit faith, a life open to God.
1 TIMOTHY 1:5 MSG

Living an authentic Christian faith isn't easy. It can be difficult— sometimes very difficult. To live as Jesus' disciple, you must have the love of God motivating you in all you do. That's because Jesus commands that you love others, and while this can be relatively easy when you're in a good mood, much of the time it goes against your natural instincts.

You really have to believe that Jesus was right about this "love your neighbor as yourself" thing, and that it's worth it. Of course, the person on the receiving end is convinced that it's a good thing, but when you're on the giving end where the price tag is attached, it's not always so clear.

In the New International Version, 1 Timothy 1:5 says, "The goal of this command is love, which comes from a pure heart. . .and a sincere faith." You not only need to have a pure heart free of selfish motivations, but—to get over the hump and *keep* on loving others when the warm emotions dissipate—you also need faith. You must believe that it's the right thing.

God, motivate me by Your love. Help me believe deep down in the core of my being that loving others is what You genuinely desire me to do. In Jesus' name, I pray.

GET HERE SOON

Come quickly to help me, O Lord my savior.
PSALM 38:22 NLT

When someone lets you down, you lose trust in their willingness or ability to help. When trouble returns, there may be one less name on your contact list. You've encountered people who promised help but failed to deliver. In moments when you feel dejected and find yourself taking on a jaded perspective, pay attention to nine words written by King David: "Come quickly to help me, O Lord my savior."

David asked God for help because he knew He would actually help. David stressed the urgency of his need by asking God to come quickly. He also spoke of his allegiance to God by calling Him "Lord." Finally, David recognized that God's help would be the only thing that would save him.

A king who had an army at his disposal still recognized that the help he really needed could only come from God. The only one David could trust with his life was God.

David wasn't just saying he was having a bad day. David was saying he trusted God enough to see Him as his best source for help. You can too.

Lord, You're my best source of help. I can trust You with every difficulty that comes my way. I don't need to wonder if You care. You've never left me, and You never will leave me. I'm overwhelmed by Your faithfulness.

MAKING HIS WAYS YOUR ROUTINE

And his master saw that the Lord was with him and that the Lord made all that he did to flourish and succeed in his hand.
GENESIS 39:3 AMPC

Joseph's story is a classic riches-to-rags-to-riches tale, but the most remarkable thing about him—his greatest trait—was that God was with him. That fact explains his survival and his successes—and the wise and compassionate character he consistently showed.

Is God the core of *your* daily routine? It takes discipline not to take God for granted, to seek Him when things are going well, not just when they aren't. Joseph's consistency made him a model employee—the best worker his bosses had, a conduit of God's blessings to them. It had nothing to do with Joseph's education or accomplishments but everything to do with his trust in God.

God is faithful even when you're not. That's not a guilt trip but a get-out-of-jail card—a gift that can't be earned, only received, and one that changes everything. And you can tell that you have received it, not because all the storms in your life suddenly cease, but because you suddenly have a remarkable sense of peace and freedom as you face them.

Father, "I'm not trying to get my way in the world's way. I'm trying to get your way, your Word's way. I'm staying on your trail; I'm putting one foot in front of the other. I'm not giving up" (Psalm 17:4–5 MSG).

DAY 241
IMPRACTICAL PRIDE

A man's pride will bring him low,
but the humble in spirit will retain honor.
PROVERBS 29:23 NKJV

Sometimes God's plan doesn't make sense, but there are practical reasons for His commands. Pride is a good example. God says He resists the proud (James 4:6). Other people recognize pride and turn away. God says pride leads to self-deception (Galatians 6:3). Other people believe those with blatant pride are delusional. God says pride leads to destruction (Proverbs 16:18). Proud but broken people make the news every day.

Pride causes an inflated view of yourself. It favorably compares personal accomplishments with others' and believes itself to be superior. Pride pays attention to personal success while minimizing personal failure. Pride has no place in God's plan because comparing personal skills and accomplishments with others is not the comparison God uses. He compares you with His Son, Jesus—and the comparison isn't in your favor.

By God's grace you're made acceptable (not superior) to God and others. He wants to use you, not to elevate you, but to advance His plan.

Proverbs 27:2 (NIV) says, "Let someone else praise you, and not your own mouth; an outsider, and not your own lips." Pride always has a motive for its actions. It demands to be noticed and is never really satisfied with each new accomplishment.

Honor is always a by-product of thinking more of others and less of self (see John 3:30).

Father God, teach me to be a humble man, a man
who sees myself as no better than any other person.

TAKING GOD SERIOUSLY

When the disciples had Jesus off to themselves,
they asked, "Why couldn't we throw it out?" "Because
you're not yet taking God seriously," said Jesus.
MATTHEW 17:19–20 MSG

People make time for the things that matter most to them. It's one thing to say something is important, but another entirely to internalize it, spend time on it, and act because of it. This happens even with Christians who understand that Jesus is preeminent (Colossians 1:15–20) but put getting to know Him better behind more urgent things like work, family, or hobbies.

Good intentions aren't enough to walk fruitfully with Jesus. The disciples discovered this when they failed to cast out a demon. Jesus told them, "The simple truth is that if you had a mere kernel of faith, a poppy seed, say, you would tell this mountain, 'Move!' and it would move. There is nothing you wouldn't be able to tackle" (Matthew 17:20 MSG).

Don't let that discourage you, though. David tells how to take God seriously: "Unto You, O Lord, do I bring my life. O my God, I trust, lean on, rely on, and am confident in You. Let me not be put to shame or [my hope in You] be disappointed; let not my enemies triumph over me" (Psalm 25:1–2 AMPC).

Jesus, make me aware of anything that is coming
between me and You. I want to put You first in everything,
knowing You'll take care of my every need.

READY, WILLING, AND ABLE

He said, "Then you see how every student well-trained in God's kingdom is like the owner of a general store who can put his hands on anything you need, old or new, exactly when you need it."
MATTHEW 13:52 MSG

God does things in unexpected ways, at unexpected times, and through unexpected people. He tends to turn conventions upside down, doing things in what seems to us like the most difficult and convoluted ways. God uses the least likely people to do the least likely things, all so He gets His rightful glory even as He blesses His people.

You won't always know how God is going to work, but you know the ultimate result: "The LORD gives victory to his anointed. . . . Some trust in chariots and some in horses, but we trust in the name of the LORD our God" (Psalm 20:6–7 NIV).

The key to working with an unpredictable but always victorious God (instead of against Him) is to make yourself available. Then, as Matthew 13:52 suggests, you have to stock your shelves with the right supplies, and the Bible is your chief supplier. It's so important to be filled with His Word daily so you'll be topped up and available for His purposes at any given time.

Father, teach me more about You and Your ways through Your Word so that I can know You more and be useful to You in any situation You put me in.

DAY 244
SIMPLE, PROFOUND, AND WISE

Fear God and keep his commandments,
for this is the duty of all mankind.
ECCLESIASTES 12:13 NIV

If the God who made everything had a plan for your life, would you follow it? If the God who knew your name before you were born gave you a purpose, would it change how you live? If the God who's making a place for you in His future called you to active duty in your faith, would you do everything you could to follow the Leader? Well, He does have a plan, He's given you a purpose, and He calls you to active duty.

Today's verse is simple and profound. It contains impressive wisdom and a divine directive. It contains the core of God's will for you.

While there's a *fear of God* that's connected to pending judgment (think Noah), the use of the term in this verse is positively reinforcing the view that God is awe-inspiring and worthy of the highest priority in your thinking and actions.

Keeping His commands points to your willingness to follow His leadership. By agreeing to follow, you're saying you believe He holds the key to truth and correct thinking.

By saying that *this is the duty of all mankind*, you can begin to see that even before the Bible said, "God so loved the world" (John 3:16), He had a plan for every woman, child, and man. The question isn't whether God has a plan; it's whether you'll follow.

Almighty God, teach me what it really means to fear You,
and remind me often that it is my duty to obey Your commands.

DAY 245
ALWAYS TRUST THE LORD

It is better to take refuge in the LORD
than to trust in humans. It is better to take
refuge in the LORD than to trust in princes.
PSALM 118:8–9 NIV

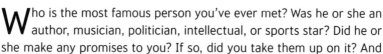

Who is the most famous person you've ever met? Was he or she an author, musician, politician, intellectual, or sports star? Did he or she make any promises to you? If so, did you take them up on it? And did they keep their promise?

Conversely, who is the least famous person you have ever met? Maybe he or she is an elderly relative, neighbor, or church member. Did he or she ever tell you something meaningful? If so, did you believe them? And were they telling the truth?

When it comes to trusting other people, the old adage is apropos: "Consider the source." It doesn't matter if the person is famous or obscure. The key question is this: Are they trustworthy? While you may sometimes have a hard time judging the trustworthiness of others, the Bible, Church history, modern biography, and contemporary experience constantly reaffirm the Lord's absolute trustworthiness.

Granted, God gets blamed for a lot He didn't actually do or say. Still, if you take Him at His Word, as stated repeatedly in the scriptures (not half a verse here and there ripped out of context), you can sleep well at night.

Lord, thank You that You are the same yesterday,
today, and forever. I trust You always.

DAY 246
DEFEATING THE DEVIL

But the Lord is faithful, and he will strengthen
you and protect you from the evil one.
2 THESSALONIANS 3:3 NIV

There will be times when you'll be under intense attack by the devil. Why then and not some other time? Probably it's because the devil—like a shark drawn by blood—senses when you're weak and most susceptible to temptation. Luke 4:13 (NIV) says that after tempting Jesus, "he left him until an opportune time." He wasn't getting anywhere, so he retreated and waited for a future opportunity.

The Lord will not only strengthen you to enable you to withstand the enemy, but He Himself will protect you from his protracted attacks. You may wonder why God doesn't immediately dispose of the devil but allows a lengthy battle, but this is often to toughen you and allow you to demonstrate your resolve. You may not understand why God permits it, but you must trust Him just the same.

One of the most oft-quoted promises states, "Resist the devil, and he will flee from you" (James 4:7 NIV). But he won't necessarily flee immediately. Often you will be required to take a stand, defend your ground, and continue resisting the evil one. Finally, when he can't stand it anymore, he will suddenly turn and flee.

Lord Jesus, I pray You strengthen me and protect
me from the enemy. Don't allow him to get the
victory in any area of my life, I pray.

DAY 247
DIFFERENCE MAKING

*For I have kept the ways of the Lord and
have not wickedly departed from my God.*
PSALM 18:21 AMPC

Martin Luther King Jr. dreamed of a day when people would be judged not by their skin color but by their character. This isn't an excuse to ignore the impact of people's ethnicity and experiences, but a reminder that, in God's eyes, all people are on the same footing. God, being just, sees and condemns sin, but God, being merciful, provides a Savior who unites all people as His children, regardless of background or politics or any other worldly division.

As a Christian, you're in a unique position to move beyond dreaming of a better day to actually making one happen. It happens one heart at a time, as people realize their brokenness and need while grasping that God is throwing them a life preserver.

While you might not have treated differences with prejudice and injustice, others have, and you need to represent God's compassion as you listen to their stories, sharing His truth as you emphasize the equality of all people before God. Everyone you meet matters to God, and everything they've experienced is preparing them to meet Him. You can make the introduction that makes the difference.

*Lord, help me to walk before You in a way that honors the
value of each person I meet. Give me the opportunity to
point them to You and support them in their seeking.*

CONVINCED AND HOPEFUL

That evening, after the sun was down, they brought sick and evil-afflicted people to [Jesus], the whole city lined up at his door!

MARK 1:32–33 MSG

G od's Word describes hope as the anchor of the soul (see Hebrews 6:19). This hope is trusting that something you believe is true will actually come true. To hope means to be convinced. There's no wishful thinking involved.

Jesus was bringing hope to the people of the first century. People had this convincing hope that if they could meet Jesus they would be healed. In the middle of this hope the entire city came to see what would happen at the finish line of trust. They believed the reports of His ability to heal. They came believing He could heal them. They came without hesitation.

Today it may be a lack of trust that leaves people unconvinced that God is really that good, loving, or merciful. You might believe today's verse is simply a piece of history and things like that could never happen today.

God never promised He would heal everyone in every situation. But He welcomes the worship offered by those who believe He can.

Dear God, my hope in You leaves me convinced You're good and Your plans are best. May the trust I have in You never limit You from doing miracles. Help me to be convinced of Your power.

DAY 249
WISDOM'S ROAD MAP

Be careful how you live. Don't live like fools, but like those who are
wise. Make the most of every opportunity in these evil days. Don't
act thoughtlessly, but understand what the Lord wants you to do.
EPHESIANS 5:15–17 NLT

The pursuit of wisdom requires intentional decision-making. The choices you make impact personal wisdom. God's Word says it's better to follow the wise than lament your own poor choices. You've probably heard, "You'll learn from your mistakes." While that may be true, God places a great emphasis on obedience.

Because God wants you to have a good reputation, He says, "Be careful how you live." Because you're to reflect God's character, He says, "Don't live like fools." Because He built you for positive relationships, He says, "Make the most of every opportunity." Because He wants you to love others, He says, "Don't act thoughtlessly."

So what is godly wisdom? Making an intentional choice to pursue, knowing God will help you "understand what [He] wants you to do." Wisdom isn't available in any store, can't be inherited, and is nontransferable. God can make you wise as you learn what He's said and do what He's asked.

You'll make mistakes. Sin will inevitably be part of your life experience. Wisdom understands that God gave you a choice and the help you'd need to keep your distance from decisions that keep you at arm's length from the one who loves you most (see 1 Corinthians 10:13).

Lord, remind me often how important it is to You
that I make wise decisions and avoid unwise choices.

SAVED TO SERVE

The righteous care about justice for the poor,
but the wicked have no such concern.
PROVERBS 29:7 NIV

O ver the past few decades, a movement within Christianity has arisen teaching that the Christian faith should be defined by acts of compassion, by a new focus on "social justice." However, this line of thinking, as well intentioned as it might be, is exactly backward because it places works of compassion ahead of the biblical teaching of salvation by faith alone.

The Bible consistently and explicitly teaches that salvation can't be "earned," that it comes as a result of faith in the work of Jesus Christ on the cross. But it also teaches that true saving faith will result in a heart of compassion for those Jesus called "the least of these." That is what James meant when he wrote, "Faith without works is dead" (see James 2:17).

Your concern for the plight of those less fortunate than yourself won't save you, and neither will any amount of humanitarian or charity work. Rather, your concern for others in all situations will be visible evidence that you are a true follower of Christ.

Trust God for your salvation though. When you do, God will motivate you and empower you to serve others by doing justice for the poor.

Lord, help me to be ever mindful of believers in difficult life
situations—and alert for opportunities to serve those in need.

DAY 251
THE TRUTH ABOUT GOD

They exchanged the truth about God for a lie,
and worshiped and served created things rather
than the Creator—who is forever praised. Amen.
ROMANS 1:25 NIV

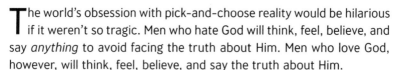

The world's obsession with pick-and-choose reality would be hilarious if it weren't so tragic. Men who hate God will think, feel, believe, and say *anything* to avoid facing the truth about Him. Men who love God, however, will think, feel, believe, and say the truth about Him.

Here's a quick overview of that truth:

- *God is almighty. He is everywhere. He knows everything. Nothing is outside His infinite sovereignty.*
- *God is the creator and sustainer of all that exists, temporal and eternal. He knows and controls every subatomic particle in the universe.*
- *God is love, and all people benefit from His goodness.*
- *God is absolutely just, pure, and holy. He's perfect in every way. Everything He says is true. Everything He does is best.*
- *God is a triune being: God the Father, God the Son, and God the Holy Spirit.*
- *God desires that none perish but that all repent, turn to Him, trust Him, and receive all that faith in Jesus offers.*
- *God is mystery. God has infinite knowledge, insight, and understanding. His ways are far higher than man's ways.*

Lord, I love the truth about who You are. I will worship and serve You, my Creator. You alone are worthy of eternal praise.

DAY 252
A SHINING LIGHT

Jesus replied, "My light will shine for you just a little longer.
Walk in the light while you can, so the darkness will not overtake
you. Those who walk in the darkness cannot see where they
are going. Put your trust in the light while there is still time;
then you will become children of the light." After saying these
things, Jesus went away and was hidden from them.
JOHN 12:35–36 NLT

Jesus was speaking to a crowd of people in Jerusalem when they asked Him how the Son of God could possibly die. He explained to them He would only be with them in person for a short time and urged them to take advantage of His presence on earth. He was the light of the world, trying to show them how to walk out of darkness. If they followed Him, they would enjoy eternal salvation with His Father in heaven.

As a Christian, you are called to bear Christ's light to the world. God wants you to let your light shine for others to see. Can those around you see Christ in you? Is your light shining brightly? Or has it dimmed? Today, get up and go out there and spread the Word of the Lord. Be a shining light for someone else to see. Be a blessing to someone. Inspire someone to come to the Lord by illuminating your light to the world around you.

Lord Jesus, I want more than anything for people
to see You first when they see me. Make me the kind
of man who shines Your light in all situations.

MONDAY MORNING IS A GIFT

If you are a thief, quit stealing. Instead, use your hands for
good hard work, and then give generously to others in need.
EPHESIANS 4:28 NLT

Work is God's idea. We may be anxious for the weekend, but God's work idea has a purpose.

While God could speak the world into existence, man would need to use his hands and skills to keep things in good shape. While God has a pretty good handle on how to manage the world, He made mankind so that they must use their minds to complete a job.

When we work, we keep ourselves from considering theft as a means of meeting our needs. When we work, we can use some of the money we earn to help those who can't work.

Work provides finances for meeting the needs of our family, offers a sense of purpose, initiates ideas that help others, and gives a sense of satisfaction to the end of our day.

If we think of work as a drudgery to endure, we miss the point. Work of any kind (even volunteerism) gives us a means of helping others with something God has entrusted us with.

Your perspective of your work (and even of Monday mornings) will change when you view work as a *gift* that has the ability to bless others, honor God, and keep your mind focused.

Lord, thank You for the gift of work. Remind me often to
express my gratitude for the work You've given me to do.

CAUTION: THINKING AHEAD

You'll do best by filling your minds and meditating on things true, noble, reputable, authentic, compelling, gracious—the best, not the worst; the beautiful, not the ugly; things to praise, not things to curse.

PHILIPPIANS 4:8 MSG

There's a children's song that says, "Be careful, little eyes, what you see." The song continues by urging us to be careful with what our ears hear, where our feet go, what our hands do, and what our mouth says.

If we think about things that are off-limits for too long, we will see, hear, do, and say the wrong thing. When bad ideas gain a foothold, we'll go to the wrong places as well. It seems that this song for children is just as applicable to grown men.

We almost always become trapped when we give bad ideas too much time in our mental Crock-Pot. Bits and pieces of wrong thinking combine for a potent stew that leaves us confused and unfocused. And in those vulnerable moments, our greatest adversary, the devil, makes sure we have everything we need to tempt us to try the life that God has always warned us against.

God knows that the battles we most often lose start in the mind. Getting our thinking straight can help keep our decisions honorable.

Deciding beforehand how you'll respond to sin-influenced ideas will go a long way in helping you make the best decision when it's easier to move in the wrong direction.

My Father in heaven, help me to focus my mind on the things that please You and help me to live as You've called me to live.

DAY 255
HOLINESS

God's will is for you to be holy, so stay away from all sexual sin.
1 THESSALONIANS 4:3 NLT

To be holy means to be set aside for special use, to be dedicated and blessed. It's a big deal. *Holy* is a term that easily applies to God, but it's a bit harder to embrace it for yourself. After all, you sin, go your own way, and are easily distracted (see Romans 3:23; Isaiah 53:6; 1 Corinthians 7:35).

When the term *God's will* is applied to biblical thought, it's part of His plan. In this case, God wants *you* to be holy. It's the next part of the verse that can seem troubling. How does sexual purity connect with God's will for personal holiness?

If you're set apart for God's use, then your greatest relationship will need to be with God. While God established sexual relationships within marriage, men sometimes take what He meant for their benefit and turn it into something that taints and subverts His plan. It doesn't show genuine love to the other person because it's mere physical desire. And it doesn't honor God's plan because it replaces an enduring expression of intimacy and love with the momentary satisfaction of lust.

It's not always easy to resist sexual temptation. But it's well worth the cost of refraining from sin to enjoy an unbroken spiritual relationship with God and a truly intimate, faithful relationship with your wife.

Holy God, some of the most persistent temptations that come my way have to do with sexual sin. Help me to keep my body and my mind from that type of unholiness.

HOPE IS THE RESULT OF SELF-SACRIFICE

"Those who love their life in this world will lose it. Those who care nothing for their life in this world will keep it for eternity."
JOHN 12:25 NLT

Jesus asked His followers to do what appeared to be impossible, following His example of self-sacrifice—and even death—with the hope of God's new life expanding to many. Could they ever hope to see the fruit of their sacrifices? What benefit could they ever see from this counterintuitive selflessness?

The only guarantees offered—to them and to you—are the example of Jesus and His promise that you can't protect your life. The only way you can save your life is to surrender it to God. The only path to eternal life is through Jesus' promise of the resurrection.

There is nothing in this world that you can protect. There is ultimately nothing to gain by serving yourself. True security and hope for the future come through surrender to God and a daily trust in the life and message of Jesus.

Is there an area of your life that needs to be surrendered to God? The harvest that Jesus spoke of extended beyond the disciples and even impacts future generations. There may be people among your family, friends, and coworkers who will be inspired to seek God tomorrow because of the sacrifices you make today.

Lord, I trust You to use my life to bless others.

DAY 257
TRY HARDER?

You are not controlled by your sinful nature. You are controlled by the Spirit if you have the Spirit of God living in you. (And remember that those who do not have the Spirit of Christ living in them do not belong to him at all.)

ROMANS 8:9 NLT

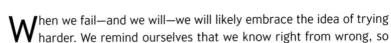

When we fail—and we will—we will likely embrace the idea of trying harder. We remind ourselves that we know right from wrong, so all we need to do is police ourselves and double our efforts. After all, God gave us His laws, so shouldn't it be easy to obey them?

Who are we kidding? We tag an extra five miles per hour onto the speed limit and somehow feel law enforcement should allow a little discretion. We've become masters at riding the edge of sin and hoping we don't fall off the edge.

All the self-discipline, extra effort, and good intentions have never been 100 percent successful in keeping us away from sin, because those things have never been enough.

God sent a helper called the Holy Spirit to be both a spiritual companion and a living guide. We tend to ignore His influence and grow deaf to His advice. God wants to help us avoid sin, but we need to be willing to accept the help. Ask for God to open your heart to the Spirit's leading, and ask the Spirit Himself what He would show you today.

Father in heaven, on my own I am defenseless against the temptation to sin in many ways. Thank You that Your Holy Spirit lives in me, helping me to say no to temptation.

DAY 258
JOYFULLY MERCIFUL

Who is a God like You, pardoning iniquity and passing over
the transgression of the remnant of His heritage? He does
not retain His anger forever, because He delights in mercy.
MICAH 7:18 NKJV

If you've ever spent much time in the company of a perpetually angry man, you know he's no joy to be around. He hangs on to wrongs done against him as if they were his life preserver as he tries to keep from drowning.

The Bible says, however, that God can actually become angry, even at those He calls His own people. He became angry with Moses, and of course His anger burned against the people of Israel on numerous occasions. And Jesus Himself sometimes spoke well-timed words of anger to His disciples.

But God isn't like the man who won't let go of his anger. In fact, today's verse says, "He does not retain His anger forever, because He delights in mercy." Another way to say this is that God not only lets go of His anger and grants mercy to those in need of it, but actually takes joy in doing so.

That's an important part of God's character to remember when (that's *when*, not *if*) you mess up and sin against Him. When you approach Him seeking forgiveness, you can trust Him to joyfully show you mercy.

Gracious Father, thank You for loving me. . .
and for joyfully showing me mercy when I sin against You.

DAY 259
ONLY ONE

*Oh, the joys of those who trust the LORD, who have no
confidence in the proud or in those who worship idols.*

PSALM 40:4 NLT

When you get married, you might think you've married your *soul mate* or the one who *completes* you. The Bible teaches that you should never place someone on such a high pedestal that they take God's place.

This is true for sports figures, actors, business leaders, friends, and spouses. Yes, marriage provides opportunity for sharing vulnerabilities and building trust, but even as close as marriage is, it was never intended to replace the only perfect trust you'll ever find—trust in God.

When pride is evident in yourself or someone you know, there has been a shift in focus from God to self. When anyone chooses a new object of affection, can they be trusted to understand what's truly important in life?

God repairs the brokenness that comes with being human. Those closest to you are also human, so they need the same grace of God that you do. Consider them partners in the journey while trusting the one who repairs broken people.

---

*Lord, help me accept the love others offer but to trust
the faithfulness You offered before I was even born.*

DAY 260
PROUD OF THE GOOD NEWS

*For I am not ashamed of the gospel, because it is the power
of God that brings salvation to everyone who believes: first to
the Jew, then to the Gentile. For in the gospel the righteousness
of God is revealed—a righteousness that is by faith from first
to last, just as it is written: "The righteous will live by faith."*

ROMANS 1:16–17 NIV

The apostle Paul was a master communicator and made frequent use of literary devices. That's especially true when he uses the phrase "not ashamed." What he's really saying is he's "proud" of the life-changing gospel of Jesus Christ.

Ironically, when you hem and haw, when you cop out, when you never say anything, people are disappointed. Sometimes they're outright offended that you don't stand up for the gospel. They want to know what you believe—and expect that you believe it wholeheartedly. And when you boldly but graciously and courageously talk about your relationship with the Lord, they're often interested—even thankful.

True, on the list of seven things God hates is *bad* pride (focused on *I*, *me*, and *my*). Thankfully, there is also *good* pride (focused on God at work in and through you). That's the kind of pride Paul has in view here. You really have only three choices: Embarrassed. Apathetic. Or proud.

Which will you choose?

---

*Lord, I'm proud of the gospel of Jesus Christ.
Fill me with grace and boldness, I pray.*

DAY 261
WORKING HIS PURPOSES

*We ought always to thank God for you. . .because
your faith is growing more and more, and the love
all of you have for one another is increasing.*
2 THESSALONIANS 1:3 NIV

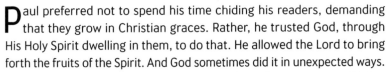

Paul preferred not to spend his time chiding his readers, demanding that they grow in Christian graces. Rather, he trusted God, through His Holy Spirit dwelling in them, to do that. He allowed the Lord to bring forth the fruits of the Spirit. And God sometimes did it in unexpected ways.

At the time Paul wrote this letter, the Thessalonians were suffering persecution. Jesus warned that often during such suffering, "the love of many will grow cold" (Matthew 24:12 NKJV). It also causes believers to betray one another (v. 10). But this wasn't happening in Thessalonica. Instead, persecution was causing the Christians to love each other even more.

Paul was so struck by this beautiful fact that he mentioned it in the very opening of his epistle. As bad as it seems, therefore, persecution is actually good for the Church. It can take great faith to trust that God is working things for good in such situations, but that's exactly what He's doing (see Romans 8:28).

You may not be suffering persecution, but you might be suffering in other ways. Trust God to see you through.

*Father, help me to trust You when things are dark and
trouble is all around, to trust that You're still working
out Your purposes somehow through it all.*

DAY 262
HEART PROTECTION

How can a young person stay pure? By obeying your word. I have tried hard to find you—don't let me wander from your commands. I have hidden your word in my heart, that I might not sin against you.

PSALM 119:9–11 NLT

G loves protect our hands. Shoes protect our feet. Safety goggles protect our eyes. What protects our hearts?

Hearts are where spiritual decisions are made. The heart remains unprotected when we don't know which rules to follow. Accurate spiritual decisions can't be made when we have no idea what God has to say about important life issues.

When we argue that we have no time to read God's Word, we shouldn't be surprised when we break God's law. Christian men lead their families by example. Consuming God's Word is essential to demonstrating how to live a godly life.

Our decisions cannot be made simply because we feel like it's a good decision or because the majority of people we talk to have a strong opinion about it.

The integrity of the heart and the decisions it makes will always be based on the connection between consulting God's Word and being willing to obey what we read. When we fail in either area, we resemble the heart in Jeremiah 17:9 (NLT), which reads, "The human heart is the most deceitful of all things, and desperately wicked. Who really knows how bad it is?"

Thank You, Father in heaven, for the protection Your Word provides for me in overcoming sin and temptation.

DAY 263
GOD HONORS HARD WORK

A sluggard's appetite is never filled, but the
desires of the diligent are fully satisfied.
PROVERBS 13:4 NIV

It might be hard at times to believe it (especially when it's time to get up each Monday morning), but from the very beginning, God intended for man to work. His first assignment for Adam was to live in the Garden of Eden and "to work it and take care of it" (Genesis 2:15 NIV). Sadly, when Adam and Eve sinned, work turned into toil—and it has been that way ever since (see Genesis 3).

But the fact still remains that it is God's will that each man work and produce. Not only that, He warns against laziness in today's scripture and encourages us to work hard and with diligence. He tells us that laziness leads to poverty and that those who demonstrate diligence in their work will find that their needs are met.

So work hard. Approach what you do for a living with commitment and passion. And as you work so you can provide well for yourself and your family, don't forget Paul's words: "So whether you eat or drink or whatever you do, do it all for the glory of God" (1 Corinthians 10:31 NIV).

Thank You, Creator God, for the gift of work. May I
always work hard, knowing that it leads to financial
blessing. . .and knowing that it honors You.

DAY 264

WHERE TO TURN WHEN TIMES ARE TOUGH

The LORD is good, a refuge in times of trouble.
He cares for those who trust in him.

NAHUM 1:7 NIV

On their road to spiritual maturity, some Christians find themselves disappointed—sometimes bitterly so—that their life in Christ isn't the rose garden they thought it would be. Those who have walked with Him over a long period of time, however, understand that God never promised those who trust in Him that life would be easy. On the contrary, Jesus Himself taught, "In this world you will have trouble" (John 16:33 NIV).

But you can find comfort in the second half of Jesus' statement about troubles in this world: "But take heart! I have overcome the world." That's an important promise to remember when you're up against problems you can't solve on your own.

Remember also that the Bible promises "that in all things God works for the good of those who love him, who have been called according to his purpose" (Romans 8:28 NIV). *Even this mess?* you might be thinking. Yes, even this mess!

When you're going through difficult times, you can believe that God cares for you and is fully aware of your stress and your suffering. Not only that, you can count on Him to bring something good out of what you're enduring.

Lord, help me to trust in You at all times,
especially when I'm enduring difficulty in this life.

DAY 265
SHOWING RESPECT

Show proper respect to everyone, love the family
of believers, fear God, honor the emperor.
1 PETER 2:17 NIV

Today's culture puts great value on respect. But while not everyone practices respect for their fellow human beings, nearly everyone feels entitled to it.

It may come as a surprise to many Christian men, but all people feel an innate need for respect. Even more surprising to some is that God calls each of His people to show respect for others, no matter their beliefs or lifestyles. It's not always easy to show proper respect to others, and it's especially difficult with people whose attitudes and actions show disregard for the truths revealed in God's Word. But the actions and words of others who don't know God don't relieve those who *do* know Him of the responsibility to treat them with respect.

Respect doesn't mean giving approval or acceptance to lifestyles and actions you know God disapproves of. It means simply seeing and treating those you meet—no matter how much you disagree with their views and lifestyle choices—as valued creations made in the image of God.

Your role as a Christian living in a fallen world full of imperfect people is to be an example of God's love and grace. You move yourself closer to that goal when you show love and respect for others, both in how you speak to them and in how you treat them.

Lord, help me always to honor You by paying proper respect to all people, whether or not I agree with what they think or how they live.

DAY 266
DEVOTED WORDS

The plan seemed good to Pharaoh and to all his officials.
So Pharaoh asked them, "Can we find anyone like
this man, one in whom is the spirit of God?"
GENESIS 41:37–38 NIV

Pharaoh recognized that Joseph was different, that he had something most men didn't—the Spirit of God in him. The Holy Spirit indwells every believer at salvation, but most don't fully grasp who He is or what He does. He's the third person of the Godhead, present at creation and salvation, and He empowers leaders, convicts unbelievers, and guides and intercedes for believers, achieving what "might" and "power" can't.

Joseph's heart reflected the work of God's Spirit in and around him, something Jesus touched on when He said, "For whatever is in your heart determines what you say" (Matthew 12:34 NLT). If what's stored in your heart is good, good things will come out. If not, bad things will. And you'll be held accountable for all of them (v. 36). Is God's Spirit evident in your words?

David gave the key to cultivating a relationship with God, which is made possible through His Spirit: "I love You fervently and devotedly, O Lord. . .my keen and firm Strength in Whom I will trust and take refuge" (Psalm 18:1–2 AMPC). When God's words fill your heart, His love and wisdom follow, and people will recognize the overflow and glorify God.

Lord, You are my rock, my fortress, and my deliverer.
Fill me with Your Spirit so I can bring glory to Your name today.

DAY 267
INSTINCTIVE TRUST

Whenever we're sick and in bed, GOD becomes
our nurse, nurses us back to health.
PSALM 41:3 MSG

If there's a fire in your home, you put your trust in a fireman. If your electricity is out, you'll trust the linemen. If you're sick, you trust a nurse to help you feel better.

You might remember a parent or grandparent who took care of you when you were sick. Maybe they offered medicine, cough syrup, or chicken soup. They wiped your nose or made sure you had enough tissues. David may have had something similar in mind when he referred to God as a nurse who stayed with him when he was sick. God is compassionate, understands what you need, and can be trusted to make sure everything turns out right.

Maybe you've thought of God as regal and king-like (and He is), but that mental image can make it hard to see Him as having the tenderness to take care of you better than the most compassionate caregiver.

Seeing God as compassionate can help you trust Him to be with you in the struggles you face. You could have a health issue. You could be facing a job loss. Or you might need the care God provides for those in the midst of broken relationships.

Dear God, knowing You can provide such tender care is welcome
news. I'm grateful for the help You provide, because I need it.

DAY 268
TEMPORARY HOUSING

Friends, this world is not your home, so don't make yourselves
cozy in it. Don't indulge your ego at the expense of your soul.
1 PETER 2:11 MSG

You live in a town or maybe the country. The road outside can be identified by those who visit. You have items in your home that may be heirlooms passed on by loved relatives. You can trace your history for generations. You might have children, guaranteeing that your family name will live on.

Sometimes these facts cause us to forget our lives here are little more than a vacation on our way *home*. If you think you're here for a long time, you begin to trust your temporary home as the sum total of your existence. When you think of "home," is it a house on the road with your stuff inside?

God wants heaven to be the place you think of when you think of home. Someday God will bring His family home, and then you'll understand why making yourself cozy here was a shortsighted decision. Trust that heaven is your home. Trust that the best you'll find here is temporary housing.

Dear God, there are days when I think I'd like to stay here. You've
created some absolutely beautiful places to visit. I can only imagine
what my real home looks like. Keep me focused on Your forever
dwelling, as well as the plans You have for me in the here and now.

DAY 269
LONE RANGER CHRISTIANITY

*All the believers devoted themselves to the apostles'
teaching, and to fellowship, and to sharing in meals
(including the Lord's Supper), and to prayer.*

ACTS 2:42 NLT

In several polls in recent years, more and more people—including many professing Christians—say they don't go to church services regularly, if at all.

One of the most common alibis for consistently skipping church is "I don't have to go to church to be a Christian." While it may technically be true that you don't have to attend church to be a believer, it's also true that in order to *grow* in your faith, you need the teaching and fellowship you receive when you gather for worship and Bible study.

You receive these things when you attend services at church. That's why the writer of Hebrews admonishes followers of Jesus Christ not to neglect "meeting together, as some are in the habit of doing" (Hebrews 10:25 NIV).

Today's verse gives a list of great reasons to attend church regularly, starting with receiving sound biblical teaching. It's also at church that you fellowship with other Christians, which the Bible teaches is important for your spiritual growth.

God never intended for you to be a Lone Ranger Christian. He established the church to provide believers a means to receive teaching and fellowship. That's why it's a good plan for you to find a church that provides sound teaching and then commit yourself to going there on a regular basis.

---

*Lord, never let me forget the importance of regular
fellowship with my local body of believers.*

DAY 270

TRUST THE LORD FOR VICTORY

O Israel, trust in the LORD;
He is their help and their shield.
PSALM 115:9 NKJV

In Psalm 115:1–10, the writer exalts the Lord (vv. 1–3), ridicules idols and idol-worshippers (vv. 4–8), and calls on God's people to trust in the Lord (vv. 9–10).

Just for fun, you may want to read Isaiah 44:9–20, where the prophet's all-out satire inoculates God's people against ever turning back to idol worship. Then again, the psalmist who wrote Psalm 115 does a great job mocking idols and idol-worshippers. His closing zinger: "Those who make them will be like them, and so will all who trust in them" (v. 8 NIV).

In contrast, believers throughout the ages have worshipped the Lord, maker of heaven and earth, who has infinite power to do as He pleases. He alone is God, and that makes Him the ultimate source of life and meaning. And the wonderful thing is He's your very own Father and delights to call you His son.

You have every reason to hold your head high as a believer. You have put your trust in the Creator of temporal and eternal realities.

So. . .always, *always* be proud of who you worship!

Lord, I am proud to worship You. Please help me to
grow ever more thankful for who You are.

DAY 271
TRUST GOD FOR THE FUTURE

"For I know the plans I have for you," says the LORD.
"They are plans for good and not for disaster,
to give you a future and a hope."
JEREMIAH 29:11 NLT

—

C an you trust that God has wonderful plans for you—that He desires to give you a future and a hope? It would seem that *everyone* would embrace such a promise, but many find it difficult to do so. They're focused on the world's problems—pollution, poverty, economic crises, and weather gone wild—and think it's too late for hope.

If you read only the dismal headlines, it's easy to get a negative mindset. Things *are* becoming more difficult. But in the midst of all this, God holds out a promise of hope. . .if you have the faith to receive it. He also says, "These things I have spoken unto you, that in me ye might have peace. In the world ye shall have tribulation: but be of good cheer; I have overcome the world" (John 16:33 KJV).

When Jeremiah prophesied hope, the Jews also had little reason to have any. God was still punishing them for their sins. But He wanted His people to look beyond the present and trust Him for a wonderful future. He wants you to do the same.

Lord, the days ahead look bleak now, but help me to trust that
You have a wonderful future planned for me and my family.

DAY 272
FORGIVE YOURSELF!

Therefore, there is now no condemnation
for those who are in Christ Jesus.
ROMANS 8:1 NIV

Some Christian men haven't quite mastered what it takes to let go of the past. They walk around filled with regret and guilt, believing deep down that even though they've given themselves over to Jesus Christ, God still intends to lower the boom on them for the terrible things they've done.

The Bible calls our spiritual enemy, Satan, the "accuser of our brothers and sisters" (Revelation 12:10 NIV) and a "liar" (John 8:44 NIV), and he loves few things more than tormenting believers with reminders of their sinful pasts. But the Bible also tells us that there is no condemnation for those of us who belong to Jesus and that our sins are forgiven and buried in a sea of divine forgetfulness (see Micah 7:19).

So no matter what you've done in your past, no matter how awful a sinner you believe you were before Jesus found you, forgave you, and cleansed you, forgive yourself. Let go of your sinful past (God already has) and move on into the wonderful, full life God has given you through the sacrifice of His Son.

God of righteousness, I sometimes find it easy to condemn
myself when I mess up. Help me to remember that You don't
condemn me but instead draw me ever closer to You.

DAY 273
WHEN GOD IS SILENT

How long, LORD, must I call for help, but you do not listen?
Or cry out to you, "Violence!" but you do not save?
HABAKKUK 1:2 NIV

There's an old saying—a cliché, really—about how God answers the prayers of His people. It goes something like this: God answers in three ways: "Yes," "No," and "Not yet."

But what about those times when you've prayed fervently, consistently, and persistently over some important issue in your life, and all you hear in return is. . .silence? Does that mean God has forgotten you? Or that He isn't concerned about the issue that has your gut in a knot? Or that there is some hidden sin in your life that renders your prayers ineffective?

We mere humans will never fully understand the mind of God, and that includes why He chooses to wait before answering our prayers. We only know that He does sometimes wait, and it can lead us to frustration and despair.

There may be times in your walk with the Lord when it seems like your prayers are bouncing off the ceiling, like God just isn't listening. But He has promised to hear the prayers of His people. So even when it seems like God isn't listening to you, trust His promises to hear you and to act.

Lord, help me to continue trusting You and calling
out to You, even when it seems You're silent.

LIFE IS SHORT—CHOOSE GOD

*Your life is like the morning fog—
it's here a little while, then it's gone.*
JAMES 4:14 NLT

At the end of your life you don't get a mulligan, a do-over, or a divine reset in an attempt to get it right. You have one life to make the decisions you need to make to determine your place in eternity. Your time on earth isn't an endgame; it's a potent beginning. If you only live for what you can get here, you're missing out on the preparation for what's to come.

Life is like grass—here for a season and gone. Life is like fog—visible and impacting for a short period of time. Life is shorter than you realize, yet long enough that you're sometimes convinced to put off making the kind of decisions that must be made *today*.

You can choose to do things your own way or you can find out what God wants you to do. You can determine your own truth or you can consult the God of *all* truth. You can live as though this life is all there is or you can discover this life is a small step into forever.

The only redeemable promises and guarantees you have in life are *God-made*. He promises to be with you. He guarantees Christians an eternal home with Him. There's no good reason to intentionally separate yourself from God. Life is short, so choose Him.

*Eternal God, life here on earth is short. So help me to make
choices that reflect my hope of eternity with You.*

DAY 275

CONFIDENCE, STEADFASTNESS, AND TRUST

*They will have no fear of bad news; their hearts
are steadfast, trusting in the LORD.*
PSALM 112:7 NIV

In Journalism 101, students are told there is no such thing as "good news." Instead, there are only occasional "brights" to slip into the midst of all the bad news of the day.

Terrorist attack. Stock market down. Rape in local park. "Bright." Fortune 500 corporate merger proposed. Grisly triple homicide. University assistant coach accused of sexual assault. "Bright." Amazon CEO holds press conference. State SAT scores down for sixth year. Historic department store closes its doors for the last time. "Bright."

The reality is that no "bright" can change the reality of the bad news that precedes it.

It's enough to make you discouraged, distressed, even depressed . . .that is, unless your heart is steadfast, trusting in the Lord.

Whatever else Psalm 112:1–9 tells us about godly men, it makes it clear they don't fear or lose sleep over bad news. It's not a matter of denying the reality of daily life "in the midst of a crooked and perverse nation" (Philippians 2:15 KJV). Instead, it's a matter of trusting the one who's so much bigger than society at large. His infinite power, wisdom, holiness, and love keep you strong and steady, no matter what.

*Lord, my focus isn't on the news. It's on You—always You.
Your infinite greatness gives me so much joy and peace.*

DAY 276
REDISCOVERED PRAISE

*Why are you down in the dumps, dear soul? Why are
you crying the blues? Fix my eyes on God—soon I'll be
praising again. He puts a smile on my face. He's my God.*
PSALM 42:5 MSG

It's easy to think God has abandoned you when facing disappointment, distress, and discomfort. You can assume you've been abandoned and forsaken. In those moments, you might conclude that you're on your own.

When you're in the middle of personal pain, God wants you to remember the story isn't finished. You haven't seen His rescue. You can't understand the plot twists that will be revealed in the next chapter of your story.

It's easy to trust God when everything you want is coming true. But it's easy to abandon trust when struggles drop by like an overdue bill.

The psalmist suggests that instead of throwing a pity party on the bad days, you should change what you're looking at. When you focus on God's goodness, praise is the result of your redirect in thinking. Remembering God's past faithfulness reminds you that since God never fails or forsakes His people, then your present crisis is no match for His ongoing faithfulness. Believe it, and rediscover worship.

*Dear God, I don't know why I'm so easily distracted. I don't know
why I can't remember that You're bigger than my worst moments.
Help me focus on who You are. Help me recall all You do.*

TRUSTING GOD TO DO IT

*We are not trying to please people
but God, who tests our hearts.*
1 THESSALONIANS 2:4 NIV

Paul commended the Christians of Thessalonica because when they received the gospel he'd preached to them, they accepted it not merely as a human message but as the powerful Word of God (1 Thessalonians 2:13). Paul explained, "My speech and my preaching was not with enticing words of man's wisdom, but in demonstration of the Spirit and of power" (1 Corinthians 2:4 KJV).

Paul kept his message simple and unadorned. He had a broad and deep knowledge of scripture, as well as of Greek and Jewish cultures, but he said, "I determined not to know any thing among you, save Jesus Christ, and him crucified" (1 Corinthians 2:2 KJV). He didn't need to resort to fancy oratory, flattery, or trickery to win his listeners over (1 Thessalonians 2:3, 5).

When you share about Christ, let it be not just words but "in demonstration of the Spirit and of power"—by the profound changes God has made in you by the power of the Holy Spirit, by the simple wisdom with which you speak, by the love that permeates your life. Then trust God that your simple, uncomplicated message will speak to your listeners' hearts.

---

*God, please help me to keep things simple—to not try
to impress people with knowledge or speaking skills,
but to trust Your Spirit to convince them.*

DAY 278

A MIGHTY, AFFECTIONATE GOD

"The LORD your God is with you, the Mighty Warrior who saves. He will take great delight in you; in his love he will no longer rebuke you, but will rejoice over you with singing."
ZEPHANIAH 3:17 NIV

Kids living in complete families have a way of almost deifying their fathers. In their young minds, Dad is strong enough to move mountains—or at least fix the chain on their bicycles. And they really hit the jackpot if their he-man daddy also regularly speaks words of love and affection.

While it's sadly true that not all fathers are like the one above, there is one perfect Father who embodies everything His child could ever need or want. Today's verse represents a God who is mightily able to do what no man can do—save! And it's a picture of an affectionate heavenly Father whose deep love for His people moves Him to joyful singing.

God isn't just your heavenly Father—He's your *perfect* heavenly Father. He's infinitely strong and mighty, yet tender and affectionate in His love. And while you may at times feel unworthy of that kind of love, today's verse can be your source of assurance that He loves you, that He delights in you, and that He rejoices over you as one of His own children.

Lord, thank You for being a mighty warrior who loves me so affectionately and joyfully.

DAY 279
TWICE BORN

*Jesus replied, "Very truly I tell you, no one can see
the kingdom of God unless they are born again."*

JOHN 3:3 NIV

We're born male or female. We're born into a certain family. We're born with a certain ethnicity and skin color.

And we're all born with a will to break God's law.

Since the very beginning, mankind has struggled to trust that God's laws are worth following. We've wondered if perhaps He is withholding good things from us.

God has things for us to do, and we ignore Him. He has things for us to stay away from, and that's what we find ourselves attracted to. God didn't *create us* to defy His law—we do that on our own.

God forgives, offers mercy, extends grace, and loves humanity because Jesus paid the price. God is holy, which means He's perfect, sinless, and set apart. Grace isn't a free pass, forgiveness isn't a green light to sin again, and mercy is a gift, not an entitlement.

We are born into sin. We are reborn to follow Jesus. The first birth is into the family of mankind. The second birth is into the family of God. Only one of those families has eternal benefits and life-changing impact. Have you been born again? And if you have, how have you been treating the grace, forgiveness, and mercy that God has extended to you?

---

*Lord Jesus, thank You for paying the price for my sins so
that I can be born again into Your eternal kingdom.*

HE STARTED AND FINISHED WELL

Whoever walks in integrity walks securely.
PROVERBS 10:9 NIV

———

The Bible is filled with stories of men who started well (like King Saul) with great hopes of doing something big for God. Many of these men ended poorly. Others (like Peter) struggled at the beginning but ended well. Still others started well—and finished well.

Daniel's story fits the last category.

He was born during an era of conflict. He existed in a time of struggling leaders and citizens who often only did what was right in their own eyes. As a teenager, he was taken from his country and taught a new culture. Somehow, in the middle of the crazy world where he found himself, Daniel wholeheartedly attached himself to the God of his people.

As a teenager, he knew God's law, including dietary requirements. He and his godly friends stood up to those who took them from their families by asking for food they knew they could eat in good conscience.

Daniel refused to compromise when he knew it was out of sync with God's will.

This man's life is an open book on what godly integrity looks like. His integrity was noticed by three kings, and Daniel was a trusted adviser to all three.

Be encouraged. No matter where you find yourself in following God, you have the opportunity to finish well.

Lord God, help me to walk, talk, and live with integrity. Help me to consistently live and think like the man You've called me to be.

DAY 281
WHOSE AUTHORITY?

"Tell us by what authority you are doing these things,"
they said. "Who gave you this authority?"
LUKE 20:2 NIV

———

A s Jesus was speaking, the teachers of the Law, the chief priests, and the elders gathered thick around Him, questioning His authority. He had, after all, just thrown the entire temple complex into an uproar by driving out the corrupt merchants, whose greedy presence they had approved and profited from. How dare He? As if only *He* had the right and authority to be there!

What authority did Jesus have? John the Baptist had declared that the Messiah was coming and would baptize them with the Holy Spirit and fire (Luke 3:16). And this Messiah performed miracles and even predicted His own death. For those who wanted to hear the truth about Jesus and His authority, the evidence was available. His words were just as trustworthy about His nature then as they are now.

You may find yourself in a situation in which you're doubting the authority of Jesus over your sexuality, your finances, or your status. The culture around you is telling you something different than Jesus tells you, and you may wonder if it's correct.

Doubt no more. Jesus is God incarnate and His authority is from on high. But you already know that. The question is, whose authority will you submit to this day?

Lord, help me in my unbelief and weakness to recognize
You as the sovereign authority over my life.

DAY 282
CONFIDENCE TO LIVE GOD'S WAY

[Jehoshaphat's] heart was devoted to the ways of the LORD.
2 CHRONICLES 17:6 NIV

"Fake it until you make it" may be a popular slogan, but it's terrible advice. Granted, it's meant to shore up self-confidence in a world that works overtime to demean you and put you down.

During which times in your life did you feel the most confidence? Perhaps it was as a student, musician, athlete, artist, actor, techie, or collector. Perhaps it was your first promotion or big win in the work world. What stole that confidence? Was it something you did or failed to do? Or something someone said or did to you?

Imagine hearing what God has to say to you and about you: "My son, how much I love you! There is nothing you could do to make Me love you more. There is nothing you could do to make Me love you less. I created you, planned your days, adopted you into My family forever, and indwell you. I want to fill you, lead you, guide you, empower you, and bless you!"

The key is hearing, trusting God, and allowing Him to work in and through you.

Like good King Jehoshaphat, you can enjoy great confidence to live the way God wants you to live. Receive that confidence today.

Lord, I hear You, trust You, and ask You to
give me Your confidence today.

DAY 283
WITHOUT EXCUSE

*And the LORD hath sent unto you all his servants the
prophets, rising early and sending them; but ye have
not hearkened, nor inclined your ear to hear.*

JEREMIAH 25:4 KJV

Ever since Moses had given the Law and the Israelites had been disobeying it, God had sent one prophet after another to warn His people. He "rose early and sent them," meaning that He didn't wait till the last moment to send a warning voice but sent His messengers at the first sign of trouble, before things got way out of hand.

People today are very much like the Israelites in Bible times. Many of them refuse to believe that they're headed for disaster. They wonder what God's making such a big fuss about. But if your heart is tender toward God, you'll trust that He knows what He's talking about and change your ways.

Today God can speak to you through your pastor, a friend, or your wife. Don't be stubborn and resist what they're saying. Don't think, *If God wanted me to know that, He'd have told* me. Trust Him and tune in. He *is* telling you—through *them*. Their delivery may not be perfect and they may get a couple facts wrong. But don't seize on that as an excuse to ignore their message.

---

*Father, help me to listen to those whom You have
sent to speak into my life. Give me the humility to
trust that You have inspired their counsel.*

DAY 284
GODLY PAYBACK

Do not repay evil with evil or insult with insult. On the
contrary, repay evil with blessing, because to this
you were called so that you may inherit a blessing.
1 PETER 3:9 NIV

How do you respond when someone, intentionally or unintentionally, does you wrong or insults you? It's a rare man who doesn't feel anger and a desire for some payback when someone has done or said something that insults him. But while the anger may sometimes be justified, God tells you that your response to those who do you wrong should be to. . .well, *bless* that person.

Your fallen human nature being what it is, you're prone to think that you're entitled to a little vengeance when you've been wronged or to a few sharp, biting comebacks when someone speaks unkind words to you. But God tells you that your responses to evil should be compassionate, kind, and understanding.

On a purely practical level, you need to remember that you can't know what's going on inside the mind of the person who does unkind things and speaks unkind words to you. But God does, and that's one of the reasons He tells you to repay evil and insults with blessings.

No one likes being hurt or insulted. But as a Christian, you must see those unpleasant moments not as negatives but as opportunities to bless those who need God's touch in their lives and to receive God's blessings on yourself.

Heavenly Father, help me not to repay evil with evil or
insult with insult, knowing that You bless me when I bless
those who hurt me with their words or actions.

CHARACTER THAT MATTERS: HONESTY

An honest answer is like a kiss on the lips.
PROVERBS 24:26 NIV

Very few would disagree with the old maxim coined by Benjamin Franklin that "honesty is the best policy." But there are times when honesty seems like the worst possible "policy"!

We aren't always as honest as we could or should be. We shade the truth to avoid embarrassment, save money, or stay out of trouble. Sometimes we exaggerate or downplay the truth so others will think better of us than they would if they knew the whole truth. Some men are pretty clever in the ways they are less than honest. They may not be lying, but they certainly aren't "truthing" either!

The problem with being less than honest is that the truth always and inevitably comes out. Then we are not only guilty for whatever we tried to hide but guilty of not being honest about it. Often the dishonesty ends up hurting us more than whatever we tried to hide.

Honesty can be painful and costly for us and sometimes for others. But in the end, honesty always costs less.

Lord, help me always to be honest, even when it seems like I can benefit by being dishonest.

DAY 286
ENCOURAGEMENT FROM ABOVE

"'Yet now be strong, Zerubbabel,' says the LORD; 'and be
strong, Joshua, son of Jehozadak, the high priest; and
be strong, all you people of the land,' says the LORD,
'and work; for I am with you,' says the LORD of hosts."

HAGGAI 2:4 NKJV

It's safe to say that nearly every father has been faced with a situation in which his son or daughter called to him for help to complete some task—maybe something as simple as learning to ride a bike. A wise dad knows when to step in and complete the task for his child and when to simply speak words of encouragement. Above all, however, he knows the value of just being there.

The Bible is peppered with examples of God encouraging His people with this simple promise: "I am with you." That includes today's verse, which includes amazing words of encouragement straight from the mouth of God: "Be strong. . .for I am with you."

God has arranged His affairs here on earth such that He uses people to accomplish the work He wants done. But when He sends people out, He speaks words of encouragement and promises to be with them.

He'll do the very same for you today.

Father, thank You for being there for me always. Thank You
for having the wisdom to know when I need You to accomplish
a task for me and when I just need Your encouragement.

DAY 287
GIVING AND TRUSTING

"I tell you the truth," Jesus said, "this poor widow has given more than all the rest of them [the rich]."

LUKE 21:3 NLT

━━━━━━━

I magine Jesus standing at the back of *your* church, watching what everybody puts in the collection basket. He knows every penny that every person drops into the basket.

A poor widow, He said, gave more (in proportion to her means) than all the rest of them, even though she only offered two small coins. She had given everything she had (Luke 21:4). This was a genuine act of trust.

Are you struggling with the amount you give to your church every week or month? Are you willing to ask yourself a hard question, such as what's at the *heart* of your struggle? Are you fearful that if you give too much, God won't provide enough to pay the bills? If so, God offers you this challenge from Malachi 3:10 (NLT): "'Bring all the tithes into the storehouse. . . . If you do,' says the LORD of Heaven's Armies, 'I will open the windows of heaven for you. I will pour out a blessing so great you won't have enough room to take it in! Try it! Put me to the test!'"

Lord of Heaven's Armies, thank You for offering such assurances regarding Your faithfulness as I give to You. May I never hesitate to do so, from this day forward.

DAY 288
ENJOYING INNER PEACE

Great peace have those who love your law,
and nothing can make them stumble.
PSALM 119:165 NIV

One of the great promises of the gospel message is peace. Somehow, though, many have interpreted that promise as meaning that a new believer's life will be free of troubles and concerns, that God will somehow rid us of all our problems when we commit ourselves to Him.

But nowhere in the Bible will you receive any promise of peace in terms of what life throws your way. The Bible warns that we all have to endure our share of storms and crises. Jesus Himself warned, "In this world you will have trouble" (John 16:33 NIV).

But this same Jesus said, "Peace I leave with you; my peace I give you. I do not give to you as the world gives. Do not let your hearts be troubled and do not be afraid" (John 14:27 NIV).

Jesus wanted His followers to understand that peace isn't about a lack of problems in this world, but about the inner tranquility His followers can and should enjoy even in the most difficult of times.

We enjoy God's inner peace when we do two things: commit to walking with Him daily as His true disciples, and focus on Him and not our outer circumstances when we are going through difficult times.

Jesus, thank You for giving me peace. Remind me to walk in that peace every day by focusing on You and not on my circumstances.

DAY 289
TRUST THE LORD, NOT YOURSELF

The people of Judah were victorious because they
relied on the LORD, the God of their ancestors.
2 CHRONICLES 13:18 NIV

As a man, you have a built-in drive to win, succeed, and achieve. As a man created in the image of God, you have built-in abilities, strengths, and talents. And as a man indwelt by God, you have more power inside you than you could possibly imagine.

The Lord God, Creator of heaven and earth, resides in you. He merely spoke the word and the universe was created. One moment, nothing. The next moment, an infinity of incomprehensible beauty, complexity, and design.

That Lord God lives within you and earnestly desires to fill every fiber of your being. Are you willing to let Him do that?

- *Are you willing to ask God to search you, know your anxious thoughts, point out your hurtful ways, and lead you in the way everlasting? (Psalm 139:23–24)*
- *Are you willing to ask God to teach you His ways, pledge to walk in His truth, and unite your heart to fear His great and holy name? (Psalm 86:11)*
- *Are you willing to ask God to create in you a clean heart, renew a right spirit within you, restore to you the joy of your salvation, and sustain you with a willing spirit? (Psalm 51:10)*

Lord, thank You for living within me! Please fill every
fiber of my being. Please search me, cleanse me,
teach me, and empower me, I pray.

DAY 290
MAKING TIME FOR GOD

*"If they'd have bothered to sit down and meet with
me, they'd have preached my Message to my people.
They'd have gotten them back on the right track."*
JEREMIAH 23:22 MSG

Many men are so busy with their work, their marriage and family, leisure time, and hobbies that they give little thought to hearing from God. They couldn't be bothered to sit down and meet with Him in the morning. The fact that you're making time for God now by reading this devotional is wonderful.

As you let the Word of God sink down into your heart daily, it increases your knowledge of His ways. Then the thoughts you think and the words you say come more and more into line with God's thoughts and words. And you'll find that the advice you give others will be more helpful to them and get them back on the right track.

Some men see no need to meet with God, to sit quietly before Him, to be still and know that He is God (Psalm 46:10). They assume they'll be able to figure out whatever problems come their way. Don't make that assumption. There are some monstrous waves out there that can absolutely sink your ship if you're not drawing strength from God and staying in tune with Him.

*Lord, I'm meeting with You now. Please give me the wisdom
and the strength to face today's problems, I pray.*

DAY 291
STEPPING OUT IN FAITH

Has [God's] unfailing love vanished forever?
Has his promise failed for all time?
PSALM 77:8 NIV

While the difficulties that the psalmist refers to in today's verse aren't necessarily known, you can probably relate to his lament. Tremendous hardship might cause you to look back at your past and the way God faithfully brought you through it, much like the psalmist contemplated (see Psalm 77:5). But God doesn't always work the same way.

Bible commentator John Gill makes this observation: "Unbelief says [God's unfailing love] is gone, that no more will be shown, and that the treasures of it are exhausted; but Faith says it is not gone, and observes that God is the God of all grace, is rich in mercy, and abundant in goodness."

What a beautiful hope and reassurance!

How can you, in your current turmoil, grasp such a faith? Maybe you need to spend some time with a fellow believer who can remind you that God always comes through. Maybe you need to spend an entire day in fasting and prayer, seeking God's face and His assurance. Or maybe you need to spend some extended time in worship. Take a step in faith. The Lord will respond.

Lord, I confess to giving in to despair at times—to wondering if Your promises have dried up. But I know better. As I step out in faith today, meet me and show me Your faithfulness.

DAY 292
SET FREE FROM SIN

"If the Son sets you free, you will be free indeed."
JOHN 8:36 NIV

It's tough to argue with the truth that you sin (see Romans 3:23). God wants you to admit your sin so He can forgive you (1 John 1:9). You can't undo what you've done. You can't justify your actions in God's courtroom. You come to Him burdened with sin debt and leave as His adopted and forgiven son.

Unlike those who dredge up your old sin to use as a club against you, God takes an entirely unexpected course. He forgives. He forgets (Psalm 103:12). God offers freedom, but Christians often remain incarcerated by choice. You may not feel ready to forgive yourself, but you can't ignore the truth that God can, and does, forgive you. You can accept His forgiveness and discover the freedom your soul has always craved.

Of course, you need to understand the depth of your sin before you can accept and appreciate the freedom found in Christ. But accepting God's forgiveness is important because He has an incredible future awaiting you, and you won't experience it by living in the past while clutching the sin rags that God has already forgiven.

Jesus shared His plan for your life in John 10:10 (NIV): "I have come that they may have life, and have it to the full." Jesus sets you free. Believe and accept His freedom.

Thank You, Lord, for setting me free from the effects of sin. May my mind always focus on the freedom You've given me to live for You.

KNOW WHO YOU TRUST

Pay attention and turn your ear to the sayings of the wise; apply your heart to what I teach, for it is pleasing when you keep them in your heart and have all of them ready on your lips. So that your trust may be in the LORD, I teach you today, even you.

PROVERBS 22:17–19 NIV

A n actor commits to feasting on a script. He starts by reading to make sure he understands the story line. He keeps reading because he wants to learn more about his role and what the director expects from him. He reads to learn how he thinks the character will speak the lines. There will come a point when he no longer needs the script because he has explored the story enough that he knows his role and has memorized every word.

You can have that same connection to God's Word. The way you read the Bible might change from reading to discover comfort to reading to discover your place in God's plan. You should get to the place where it's your guidebook on how to respond to others, when to speak, when to be silent, how to pray, when to pray, and how to step up boldly for truth.

Lord, my trust should always be a gift to You. May I never withhold trust, because You speak wisdom, offer perspective, and give me purpose. Teach me. I want to know You better.

DAY 294

OUTWARD APPEARANCES

*But the LORD said to Samuel, "Do not consider his appearance
or his height, for I have rejected him. The LORD does
not look at the things people look at. People look at the
outward appearance, but the LORD looks at the heart."*

1 SAMUEL 16:7 NIV

Ours is a culture that puts a lot of emphasis on physical appearance. If you don't believe that, just take a look at a good percentage of the advertisements and infomercials that make their way onto television broadcasts on what seems like an hourly basis.

Want to lose weight? Then there's any number of new diets and exercise programs to make it happen, countless companies looking to separate you from your hard-earned cash. Looking to get rid of that wrinkled skin or gray hair? Then there are countless companies pushing creams and hair care products.

Most of us would tell others that we're more concerned with what's "inside" another person than we are with his or her physical appearance. For some, that's just a pleasantry they don't really mean when it comes right down to it. But our God says that very thing. . .and He means it.

There's nothing wrong with taking care of yourself, nothing wrong with trying to look better by staying physically fit. But where your relationship with your heavenly Father is concerned, never forget that He's far more interested in the condition of your inner man than He is with the outer man.

---

*Lord God, help me to focus first and foremost
on the condition of my "inner man."*

YOUR SOURCE OF POWER

"This is the word of the LORD to Zerubbabel: 'Not by might nor by power, but by my Spirit,' says the LORD Almighty."
ZECHARIAH 4:6 NIV

Men tend to admire the self-reliant, independent types, those who seem able to solve any problem and accomplish any task, seemingly without any outside help. Here in the West, that is sometimes referred to as "rugged individualism."

There's no question God can use such a man to accomplish great things for His eternal kingdom. However, that can only happen when he humbles himself and learns to trust not in his human strength or abilities, but in the empowerment of the Holy Spirit.

Zerubbabel led the first wave of Jewish exiles returning to their homeland from the Babylonian exile. God had charged him to lead in the rebuilding of His temple, which had been destroyed decades earlier. He had also provided him with some very able men to accomplish this huge task. Still, God let them know they wouldn't accomplish the task through their own strength, but only by His empowerment.

God is not interested in sharing His glory with anyone, and He wants men to learn to rely completely on Him in all areas of their lives. So if you want to accomplish something for His kingdom, never forget that you can only do it by His Spirit.

*Lord, may I never forget that all I do,
I do through the empowerment of Your Spirit.*

WHO WE CAN CALL "BROTHER"

*"He [Ananias] came and stood beside me and said, 'Brother Saul,
regain your sight.' And that very moment I could see him!"*

ACTS 22:13 NLT

I magine God asking you to place a phone call to speak with a murderer who has just been released after nearly twenty years in a maximum-security prison. When he answers the phone, what will you say?

Brother may not be the first word that comes to mind.

Yet when Jesus used the word *brothers* throughout the Gospels, who did He have in mind? A lot of different kinds of men. First, His earthly half brothers. Second, His twelve apostles. Third, all of His disciples. Fourth, their relationship with each other. And fifth, their relationship with "the least of these" (Matthew 25:40 NKJV).

In the book of Acts, this broadens to include all men, even the most outspoken enemies of Jesus Christ (Acts 7:2; 22:1; 23:1, 5–6). The implication is clear: you can use *brothers* whenever you speak with other men as a means to reinforce the value of your common humanity—and to seek a rapport.

Yes, this may seem counterintuitive, but you have the clear examples of Jesus Christ, the Gospel writers, the martyr Stephen, the apostle Paul, and others. So you're on firm biblical ground.

---

*Lord, I want to be Christlike and grace-filled in all of my interactions.
So, help me learn to say "brother" to every man I meet.*

SPIRITUAL TREASURES

*Seek those things which are above, where Christ is,
sitting at the right hand of God. Set your mind on
things above, not on things on the earth.*
COLOSSIANS 3:1–2 NKJV

To set your mind on things above is to make spiritual things your primary focus. If your main goal, however, is to have a well-paying job, a luxurious home, wonderful vacations, and plenty of retirement money, then those are the things you'll spend years pursuing. Mind you, it's no sin to have those things. But you should have the kind of attitude where, if God removed those things from your life, you'd still be satisfied. Would you be?

Jesus commanded, "Do not lay up for yourselves treasures on earth, where moth and rust destroy and where thieves break in and steal; but lay up for yourselves treasures in heaven. . . . For where your treasure is, there your heart will be also" (Matthew 6:19–21 NKJV).

God knows you need "daily bread" to survive, which is why He told you to pray for it (Matthew 6:11). But later in the same chapter, He explains that you are to "seek the Kingdom of God above all else. . .and he will give you everything you need" (Matthew 6:33 NLT).

*Lord, as the old hymn says, "This world is not my home.
I'm just a-passing through." Help me to seek You
and heaven and my treasures there, above all.*

FAITH AND CONFESSION

Confess your sins to each other and pray for each other so that you can live together whole and healed. The prayer of a person living right with God is something powerful to be reckoned with.

JAMES 5:16 MSG

Dysfunction is a by-product of secrets and hurtful words. There has to be trust for a family or community to thrive. When you make a mistake, break a promise, or sin—own it. Confess to those you trust, and ask them to pray for you. Make this your template for functioning in your family and with friends.

If you insist on hiding skeletons in the closet, refuse to wash your dirty laundry, or hold tightly to secret sins, you're hurting yourself most of all—and potentially preventing others from finding healing, or helping you heal. Of course, wisdom in broaching sensitive information is crucial.

A person living right with God will own their own failure. God said you would miss the mark of His perfection. Don't pretend you don't. Pray, and trust that the God who made you to be righteous will help.

Lord, I want to be honest. If I feel I'm protecting others by being silent about the past, show me if I'm actually trying to protect myself. Help me speak truth in a loving way, at the right time. Help me own my sin and then let You take it away. Help me practice personal honesty with You and others.

DAY 299
GOD DELIVERS

*"Shall I yet again go out to battle against the children of
my brother Benjamin, or shall I cease?" And the LORD said,
"Go up, for tomorrow I will deliver them into your hand."*
JUDGES 20:28 NKJV

After losing forty thousand men in two successive battles against Benjamin, Israel sought the Lord, asking whether they should do battle a third time. You can understand why they were leery of doing so after losing one-tenth of their troops (Judges 20:2). But the Lord promised to deliver Benjamin into their hand—and He did so.

Israel exhibited great trust in God's promise by going back into battle.

Are you experiencing continued defeat in carrying out a work project, in communicating with your family, or in sharing the gospel with a coworker, friend, or neighbor? Are you seeking the Lord, asking Him if you should attempt to do something once more?

If you are, and if you're sensing His leading to go back, will you exhibit the same sort of faith and trust that Israel exhibited? Israel obeyed God, and He delivered Benjamin into their hands. He can do the same for you.

*Lord, I'm not always quick to seek Your guidance, and I've
experienced setbacks as a result. Strengthen my faith to seek
Your face and Your wisdom so I can engage in battle with
boldness and confidence, believing that You will go before me.*

DAY 300

KINGDOM WORK—JUST KEEP AT IT!

Let us not become weary in doing good, for at the proper time we will reap a harvest if we do not give up.

GALATIANS 6:9 NIV

Think of some of the great preachers in Christian history. From the apostles Peter and Paul all the way through the centuries to men like Billy Graham, certain preachers are exceptional in our eyes because the results of their work are both obvious and tremendous.

But it's not like that for every kingdom laborer. Far from it!

God never promised us that working for Him would be easy—or that we'd see a huge harvest of souls or large numbers of lives changed through that work. We don't always see the results of our hard work for the kingdom of God in the short run; in fact, we may not see them at all this side of heaven. But Galatians 6:9 promises us that if we persevere in our good work for the Lord, we *will* share with Him in the joy of seeing the furthering of His eternal kingdom.

So when you begin to wonder whether you're making a difference in the world around you, don't give up. Just keep doing what God has laid on your heart to do, and He'll take care of the rest.

Lord Jesus, sometimes it seems like the things I do for Your kingdom aren't making much of a difference. So help me to be persistent in doing what You've called me to do for You.

DAY 301
DARK DAY REDEMPTION

*[God said,] "I myself will search and find my sheep. I will
be like a shepherd looking for his scattered flock. I will
find my sheep and rescue them from all the places where
they were scattered on that dark and cloudy day."*

EZEKIEL 34:11–12 NLT

I f the book of Ezekiel were a newspaper, its first half was all bad news. The people of Israel were entering a time of national discipline. Many other nations found themselves on God's list of sinning peoples. It seemed there was no end to bad news.

Buried in a story in chapter 34 was a big surprise. This story said there was a 100 percent chance dark and cloudy days wouldn't last.

God promised to search for His people. God promised He would find them. He promised He'd rescue them. Forget the classifieds. Leave the business section unread. If Ezekiel were a newspaper, then you just found the best news of the day.

As a Christian, you're among those God searched for, found, and rescued. This story is a snapshot of what it looks like when God redeems you. It doesn't mean you'll never face dark days, but with access to the rescuer, you no longer have to face those days alone.

*Lord, thank You for Your rescue of me, the hope of a
better day, and the promise of finding other people just
like me. You made a promise, and I trust Your truth.*

DAY 302
WORDS THAT RUIN

By our speech we can ruin the world, turn harmony to chaos,
throw mud on a reputation, send the whole world up in smoke
and go up in smoke with it, smoke right from the pit of hell.
JAMES 3:6 MSG

First Thessalonians 5:20–21 urges you to test the messages you hear from others. Why? The words you speak and those spoken by others can "ruin the world, turn harmony to chaos, throw mud on a reputation, send the whole world up in smoke and go up in smoke with it."

Some messages can't be trusted because even those who share them don't understand them. Some can't be trusted because they're intended to confuse. Some messages can't be trusted because they make enemies of friends.

Words have incredible power. They can hurt or heal, confuse or enlighten, invite trust or instill fear. The only words you can trust completely are the words God placed in the Bible. Be careful about trusting just anything you hear from others. Be careful about the words you speak to others. Ponder what you say before you speak.

Dear God, it's easy to say words full of hatred, anger,
pain, and deceit. It's easy to find those who speak the
same kind of words. Give me wisdom to know what
words can be trusted and what words are to be rejected—
whether they're words I hear or words I'm about to say.

TRUST THE LORD AT ALL TIMES

When all the Israelites saw the fire coming down and the glory of the LORD above the temple, they knelt on the pavement with their faces to the ground, and they worshiped and gave thanks to the LORD, saying, "He is good; his love endures forever."

2 CHRONICLES 7:3 NIV

Was there a time in your life when you made a public commitment or statement of faith? Perhaps you raised your hand, stood up, or went forward to confess your faith in Jesus Christ. Or perhaps you've publicly declared that you're a Christian or talked about some aspect of your faith in a group setting.

If it's hard to do *that*, you already know it's much harder to continue to live for God day in and day out, year in and year out, decade in and decade out.

How few men have dedicated their life fully to the Lord *and* won't let anything prevent them from finishing well spiritually. A hundred trials will assail the man who won't go back on his promises to God. The trials may come in the form of loss, pain, or suffering. Or the trials may come in the form of success, comfort, and pleasure.

Despite King Solomon's astounding achievements and unparalleled lifestyle, he didn't keep the faith. Later in life, he turned his back on the Lord and openly worshipped false gods.

Lord, Solomon's story scares me. No matter what, I'm going to continue worshipping and praising You.

HOW GOD SEES YOU

But now he has reconciled you. . .to present you holy in
his sight, without blemish and free from accusation—
if you continue in your faith, established and firm,
and do not move from the hope held out in the gospel.
COLOSSIANS 1:22–23 NIV

Jesus reconciled you to God His Father, and take note of Paul's choice of words in this verse. When Jesus reconciled you, He presented you to God as His holy son, without the smallest blemish to mar you in God's eyes, someone free from every accusation of sin or wrongdoing.

You may not normally believe such wonderful things about yourself. Perhaps you come from a rough background, or you're repenting of recent sins, and you're very aware of your blemishes and shortcomings. Maybe you think the most God sees in you is a partially redeemed believer, a "sinner saved by grace"—with an emphasis on "sinner."

But that's not how God sees you. Remember "the Great Exchange"? When Jesus took your sin on Himself, God "made him to be sin" while you were "made the righteousness of God in him" (2 Corinthians 5:21 KJV). All you need to do is continue to walk with Jesus, hold fast to Him, and remain firmly rooted in the gospel.

God, thank You for the amazing beauty of this truth from Your
Word. Thank You that You see me as pure and wholly acceptable.

MORE THAN A PEP RALLY

Do not merely listen to the word, and so deceive yourselves.
Do what it says. . . . Whoever looks intently into the perfect law
that gives freedom, and continues in it—not forgetting what they
have heard, but doing it—they will be blessed in what they do.
JAMES 1:22, 25 NIV

You can believe something, but without acting on it, you'll end up in self-deception. You can hear a sermon, read the Bible, or have conversations with Christian friends but through inaction leave people thinking that what you learned isn't worth trusting. Why? If you say you follow Christ but won't actually do what the Bible says, then those who observe you may feel it's not worth following either.

Church isn't a pep rally. Reading God's Word isn't just spiritual comfort food. And following God isn't simply a matter of well-placed bumper stickers, witness wear, or learning the top ten Christian phrases.

God probably won't ask you about your collection of spiritual quotes or T-shirts, but He *will* be interested in whether trust in His plan led you to obedience. God's Word changes lives. Changed lives require obedience. Obedience requires action.

Lord, I don't want to just listen and walk away from You unchanged.
I don't view Your truth as merely an opinion to consider. I don't
want to leave time in Your Word with a lazy "That's nice" on my lips.
Help me continue in Your grace and find freedom in Your Spirit.

DAY 306
TELL THE NEXT GENERATION

We will tell the next generation the praiseworthy deeds
of the LORD, his power, and the wonders he has done.
PSALM 78:4 NIV

A saph, the likely writer of this psalm, had a deep desire to pass on the deep spiritual truths that he had received from his godly parents (Psalm 78:2–3). The psalm, which is a historical account of Yahweh's (God's) faithfulness to Israel in narrative form, is one such way of passing along the faith. Presumably, Asaph had used other methods of sharing his belief as well.

How did your parents tell you about God's power throughout history? How did they tell you about the great deeds He had done in their lives? Did they read Bible story books with you? Did they tell you stories? How are you picking up the torch to do the same thing with the next generation—whether your own children, nieces and nephews, or the younger generation at church?

You'll need to be intentional as you trust God to help you pass on the faith to them. If you aren't, entertainment, hobbies, and the cares of this world will take priority.

Lord, I share Asaph's heart to tell the next generation about Your greatness, but I confess that at times, I've allowed the cares of this world to take priority. That ends today. Give me ideas for reaching the young with the gospel and I'll be faithful to carry them out.

DAY 307
THE STABLE ONE

Jesus Christ is the same yesterday, today, and forever.
So do not be attracted by strange, new ideas.
Your strength comes from God's grace.
HEBREWS 13:8–9 NLT

Mankind looks for the new and improved. They are distracted by the shiny. New packaging inspires renewed interest. But in today's verses we read that Jesus thrives on eternal sameness. This can seem boring or counterproductive to what humanity seeks.

You might make bad choices, but believe that you can make better choices in the future. If you want to earn more money, you do the hard work to move you from where you are to where you want to be. You read books to improve your marriage, parenting, and disposition. You believe it's natural and normal to change actions, ideas, and maybe even beliefs.

Humans change because they're imperfect. Jesus is perfect, so He doesn't change. When you trust the one who is unchanging, you end up with a belief system that stands the test of time. You never have to wonder where you stand. And you discover a walk with someone who never turns His back on you.

Dear God, You never change, but I do. Change me into the man You want me to be. May I rely on You like a cave in a rainstorm or bread in a time of hunger. I thank You that You have always brought stability to my life.

DAY 308
ABSOLUTELY TRUSTWORTHY

Do not be anxious about anything, but in every situation, by prayer and petition, with thanksgiving, present your requests to God.
PHILIPPIANS 4:6 NIV

This is the age of superheroes. They fill comic books, television series, and big-budget movies. They have distinct personalities and impressive abilities. Have you ever wondered why they're so popular?

Confidence is hard to find when life seems uncertain. The result is high anxiety. Superheroes become substitutes for diminished personal confidence. God has always had a better idea. In every circumstance you can pray and ask a loving God for help. He is looking out for you. Be grateful. Above all, refuse every delivery of anxiety. Be confident in the God who rescues and delights in taking care of His family.

You don't need to wear a cape, have a secret cave filled with expensive supertoys, or look for help from super-powered friends. Psalm 20:7 (NIV) says, "Some trust in chariots and some in horses, but we trust in the name of the LORD our God."

Anxiety diminishes your ability to trust, fills your mind with scenarios that aren't acquainted with reality, and has an odd way of diminishing your ability to hear others speak truth. Anxiety tells God that you're not convinced He's strong enough to handle your deepest struggles.

Find your greatest confidence in the one who has always been *super* trustworthy.

Trustworthy God, I bring my worries and stress to You today. Help me to leave those things with You so that I can enjoy the peace only You can give.

DAY 309
WHAT WOULD YOU SAY?

*"I have had one message for Jews and Greeks alike—
the necessity of repenting from sin and turning to God,
and of having faith in our Lord Jesus."*

ACTS 20:21 NLT

If you had one last opportunity to talk with some of your closest friends, what would you say?

Would you say that you're the real deal? That you love the Lord wholeheartedly and serve Him with humility? That you love others deeply and have shed many tears for them? That you've endured many things and stayed true to God's call?

Would you say that you're a one-message man? That you can't stop talking about the need to repent, turn to God, and have faith in Jesus? That you can't stop talking about it publicly and privately? That you stick to that one message regardless of what other men will say and think and do?

Would you say that you're an openhanded man? That you constantly guard your heart's affections? That you don't covet a nicer house, a more expensive car, or a world-class vacation? That you give generously to those in need? That you never compromise your standards for the sake of making more money?

Lord, help me walk the talk. I want to be proud of the life-changing gospel of Jesus Christ. I want to be a generous man who meets the needs of many. Work in and through me, I pray.

DAY 310
MORNING MEETINGS WITH GOD

*My voice shalt thou hear in the morning, O LORD; in the
morning will I direct my prayer unto thee, and will look up.*

PSALM 5:3 KJV

When David penned these words, he was probably surrounded by his enemies (see vv. 6, 8)—perhaps during the reign of King Saul. No matter what the circumstances, David made a point to meet with God every morning. He was intentional in turning his face toward heaven and directing his voice toward God, being confident that the Lord would hear him.

On this day, he reminded God about His character—how He didn't take pleasure in wickedness (v. 4). He also reminded God that the foolish would not stand before Him (v. 5). But David knew he wasn't perfect either. David was resolute in communicating with God every morning, not because he was without blemish or fault, but because he knew God was merciful (v. 7). So he approached Him in the morning with a healthy dose of fear, knowing he deserved judgment, but trusting in God's mercy.

What does your morning routine look like? Does it include approaching God, knowing He will hear you? Do you come before Him with a proper amount of reverent fear, no matter what the circumstances? Or do difficulties, business dealings, or sloth keep you from meeting with Him? Even if you're surrounded by enemies, God will hear you. You're not alone.

*My loving God, help me to understand just how important it is
to You that I spend quality time with You every day. May I start
each day with prayer and the reading of Your written Word.*

DAY 311
LET GOD AVENGE YOU

"Is there not still someone of the house of Saul,
to whom I may show the kindness of God?"
2 SAMUEL 9:3 NKJV

When God's Spirit departed from Israel's first king, Saul hunted his replacement, the young shepherd who had killed a giant and played peaceful harmonies to lull his troubled soul. David lived on the run for years, refusing to fight back against God's anointed, even when presented with two ideal opportunities to end Saul's life.

David not only passed up taking revenge, but after Saul died in battle, he sought out his remaining descendants, not to kill them and consolidate his power but to see if he could do them any good.

In David's day, mercy was seen as weakness. To refuse to retaliate or return a slight to your honor tainted you in most eyes as unreliable. The whole "turning the other cheek" thing would have been as ridiculous to them as wearing a clown nose to meet your future in-laws would be to you.

But, as David demonstrated, the higher virtue is in being able to avenge yourself but refusing to do so. It takes faith to refrain—a belief that when God said vengeance belonged to Him (Proverbs 25:21–22; Romans 12:19), He meant it. Not only will He hold you accountable for all you've said and done; He'll do the same for everyone else. Have the faith to let Him.

God in heaven, so often my human nature moves me toward
vengeful thoughts and actions. Help me to remember
that You will one day set all things right for me.

DAY 312
REMEMBER ME

"Jesus, remember me when you enter your kingdom." He said,
"Don't worry, I will. Today you will join me in paradise."
LUKE 23:42–43 MSG

You know the story. Two criminals. Both guilty. One mocked Jesus, while the other admitted his guilt and called out to Jesus for mercy while hanging on the cross. That very day, both the wretched, dying criminal—who could do nothing but confess his need for salvation—and Jesus, the almighty Son of God, were together in paradise.

Christians trust Christ with eternity but not always with the temporal. They know He has saved their souls but often wonder whether He'll save their marriage, their job, their finances, or their home. Of course, every circumstance is different, and God has varying reasons for dramatically intervening in one situation and not the next, but He always has your best interests at heart.

How could He not? He allowed His Son to die for your redemption. Do you believe God has your best interests at heart? Do you trust that, in spite of what you see?

God's deliverance is not dependent on your performance—only your expression of need. Praise God for that. Turn to Him today, and wait expectantly for Him to act.

Lord, You know my need. I'm burdened by it. It distracts me,
worries me, and pulls me away from You, when in reality,
it should drive me to You. I need You, Lord. Remember me.

TRUSTING IN GOD'S JUDGMENTS

"Yes, Lord God Almighty, true and just are your judgments."
REVELATION 16:7 NIV

Humans, especially those living in the West, tend to be very democratic in their thinking, sometimes overly so. For example, when public opinion polls show a certain position, people tend to take that position as absolute truth.

But a preponderance of people believing something as incontrovertible fact or truth doesn't always make it true. Human opinion, even when it's held by a large majority, can be—and very often is—wrong. But God's opinions? Well, since opinion has been defined as a position or judgment formed about something that isn't necessarily based on absolute fact or knowledge, then God doesn't hold "opinions" but bases His judgments on His absolutely perfect knowledge of what is right and just.

The apostle Paul stated it well when he wrote, "Let God be true, and every human being a liar" (Romans 3:4 NIV).

You can't always trust in the judgments of fallen humanity, even when it involves something most everyone believes. People can be wrong about things, and they can be wrong in overwhelming numbers. That's simply because no man, no matter how well educated, possesses perfect knowledge of all things. But God's judgments are 100 percent true and just, 100 percent of the time.

Lord God, I'm so grateful that I can always trust in
the truth of everything You say in Your Word.

DAY 314
TROUBLES? PRAY!

*Whoever is wise will observe these things, and they
will understand the lovingkindness of the LORD.*
PSALM 107:43 NKJV

Today's passage, Psalm 107:39–43, reinforces the wisdom of choosing "life" abundant and free instead of "death" and all that implies.

A king or prince can choose "death" and suffer accordingly. His wealth, military power, and fierce reputation will prove useless when the Lord executes judgment. That judgment, of course, often comes at the hands of enemy nations.

Conversely, the neediest person can choose "life" and enjoy peace, security, blessing, and prosperity for many years. The Lord is happy to offer such abundance to those who take Him at His Word and choose His way to life.

This doesn't mean that all disasters or crises are forms of the Lord's judgment. This also doesn't mean that all prosperity comes from God's blessings.

Still, the godly take notice of the difference between choosing "death" and "life," choose the latter, and rejoice. The ungodly choose "death," realize their great error, and wallow in remorse.

The wise man gives heed to the Lord's words of wisdom presented in Psalm 107. May you do the same.

Lord, this is a no-brainer. I choose You and Your life. No matter what the world offers, I reject any and all ways that lead to death.

SPEAK, LORD

In the daytime he led them by a cloud,
and all night by a pillar of fire.
PSALM 78:14 NLT

One of the great wonders of the Christian life is that God is always with His people—just as He was always with His people in the Old Testament in the form of a cloud during the day and a pillar of fire at night. He most likely won't appear to you that way today, but He's still always with you and loves you so much that He guides you in multiple ways.

"That cloud which was a shade by day was as a sun by night," wrote Charles Spurgeon in his commentary. "Even thus the grace which cools and calms our joys, soothes and solaces our sorrows. What a mercy to have a light of fire with us amid the lonely horrors of the wilderness of affliction."

How does God typically lead and guide you? Does He speak through other people? Through His Word? Or maybe you hear a still, small voice during times of prayer? It's probably a combination. The key is to be so tuned in to Him that you can't miss His voice.

Father, tune my spiritual ears to Your voice. May I never miss a single message You have for me, and may Your instruction be so clear that I can't mistake it. Make me sensitive to the ways in which You speak to me.

DAY 316
DO JUSTICE

Don't let anyone look down on you because you
are young, but set an example for the believers in
speech, in conduct, in love, in faith and in purity.
1 TIMOTHY 4:12 NIV

On February 18, 1943, German college students and siblings Hans and Sophie Scholl, leaders of the resistance group The White Rose, were arrested by the Gestapo for distributing pamphlets criticizing Hitler and the Nazi regime. They were tried in a kangaroo court reserved for political dissidents and beheaded five days later, their young lives cut short because of their willingness to stand against tyranny.

Inspired by their parents' outspoken criticism of the Nazis, Hans and Sophie chose nonviolent resistance even though they knew it could lead to their deaths. They looked at the world around them, saw injustice, rallied their Lutheran principles and their courage, and acted.

A key mark of a man of God, whether young or old, is a love of justice. Over and over, the Bible calls God's people "to do right; seek justice. Defend the oppressed. Take up the cause of the fatherless; plead the case of the widow" (Isaiah 1:17 NIV).

Along these lines, the apostle John asked a probing question: "Whoever has this world's goods, and sees his brother in need, and shuts up his heart from him, how does the love of God abide in him?" (1 John 3:17 NKJV). No matter your age, what will you do with what God has given you?

Generous God, show me today how I can take action on
behalf of those who need someone to stand up for them.

DAY 317
TRUST THE TRAINING

*God is educating you; that's why you must never drop out.
He's treating you as dear children. This trouble you're in isn't
punishment; it's training, the normal experience of children.*

HEBREWS 12:7 MSG

You might find yourself in difficult situations because of choices you've made. Your struggles could be due to the choices others make. But you might discover that hard days are God's best training ground.

Soldiers learn to trust their training. From boot camp to obeying orders, they don't always understand the reason for the watching and the waiting. However, there comes a time when all the training pays off.

Following Jesus means not dropping out. You're not being punished. You're being trained much like a parent trains a child. You may need to repeat certain steps before you really understand how to do what God is training you to do.

Trouble delivers education and an opportunity to draw close to the God who educates. You serve a God who said there would be trouble. You were saved by Jesus, who overcame trouble in this world (see John 16:33). But you often first have to overcome the resistance you have to His plan for your life.

---

*Lord, help me see Your discipline as training and not
punishment. You're approachable and compassionate,
but I'll need Your training if I'm to move to the place
where I'm following You. Help me trust in the training.*

DAY 318
PROCLAIMING TRUTH

John bore witness of [Jesus] and cried out, saying,
"This was He of whom I said, 'He who comes after
me is preferred before me, for He was before me.' "
JOHN 1:15 NKJV

John the Baptist knew his calling. He was simply a forerunner to Jesus—one born to be a witness for Christ—and he freely admitted it. He knew Jesus was preferred over him. But then John says something astounding: Jesus was *before* him, which can only mean that John understood that Jesus was the preexisting Messiah, the eternal "Son of Man" who had dwelt in heaven in ageless past (Daniel 7:9–10, 13–14).

What truths and revelations in scripture are clear to you? How about the resurrection of the saints? Or the second coming of Jesus? Or His role during the coming great white throne judgment?

Are you proclaiming Jesus to anybody who will listen, the way John the Baptist did? Are you excited to point people to the Messiah, God's Son, knowing that you must decrease so He can increase? Or are you sometimes more preoccupied with building your own kingdom while staying quiet about the kingdom to come?

Lord, I trust You and Your Word. I'm so grateful to live
in a day and age when the Bible is readily available.
As a result, I know what the future holds. Keep me on
point as I seek to direct people toward Jesus.

DAY 319
HELPING GOD

*If you help the poor, you are lending to
the LORD—and he will repay you!*
PROVERBS 19:17 NLT

———

A pply for a loan and you find it usually requires collateral. The word *collateral* is described as "something committed as security for loan repayment." It's subject to being seized if you default on your loan. In other words, if you want a loan, you have to agree to transfer ownership of something you possess, should you fail to repay the loan.

God offers a very unusual loan repayment program. It's infused with both His love for people and an invitation to trust that He will honor His Word.

If you want to be a good manager of the resources God has given you, then you're encouraged to give some of those resources to people who are in need. In return, God will repay your generosity in ways that go above and beyond mere money.

God doesn't need to offer collateral. He always repays a compassionate heart. He wants men like you to see others the way He does. If they need help, God wants to help them. When you help Him, He considers it a loan—and He'll pay you back with interest! Be compassionate. Care like God cares.

Dear God, if there's anyone who can be trusted to repay compassion, it's You. Help me remember I'm never more like You than when I demonstrate Your love by helping others.

DAY 320
YOUR GOD, YOUR PROVIDER

Ask the LORD for rain in the springtime; it is the LORD
who sends the thunderstorms. He gives showers of rain
to all people, and plants of the field to everyone.
ZECHARIAH 10:1 NIV

Have you ever been in a place financially where you felt like you had nowhere to turn? In a place where you wondered how you'd manage to pay all your monthly bills with enough left over to feed your family?

If so, you would be far from the first, and that's why Jesus once told His followers, "Look at the birds of the air; they do not sow or reap or store away in barns, and yet your heavenly Father feeds them. Are you not much more valuable than they?" (Matthew 6:26 NIV).

Jesus' point? God is aware of your needs, and He wants to meet them.

You, however, have an advantage birds don't when you're in need. God has created you to relate to Him as a son relates to his father, and that includes the ability to ask Him for what you need, knowing He *wants* to provide for you.

When you're under stress, wondering how you're going to get by financially, keep your eyes on your heavenly Father, not on your circumstances. God provides for the birds, so you can count on Him to provide for you too.

Lord, help me to look beyond my circumstances
and trust You as my provider.

DAY 321
CONVINCED AND TRUSTING

The fundamental fact of existence is that this trust in God,
this faith, is the firm foundation under everything that
makes life worth living. It's our handle on what we can't see.
HEBREWS 11:1 MSG

Hebrews 11 is often called the Faith Hall of Fame. Readers meet men and women who believed and followed God even when they weren't sure where He was leading. The trust (faith) they had in God gave their lives purpose and provided a foundation for building on. They demonstrated that people don't need to see God or observe His map of their life to know He has a purpose and a plan they need.

Today anyone can be part of the Faith Hall of Fame. Accept God's plan, embrace His purpose, and share His love. Be encouraged, and encourage others. You'll need the strength and friendship of trusting believers to walk with God, determined to reach the finish line.

Read the entire chapter, and get caught up on the stories of faith that made each of these men and women heroes. And take the time to remember people you've known who expressed great faith when they weren't sure where that act of trust would lead.

Lord, I want to be a man of faith. I want You to lead. Help me to
follow. Help me truly believe You know where I need to go. May I be
fully convinced that trusting You is the best decision I can make.

DAY 322
DIVINE FORGETFULNESS

"I, even I, am he who blots out your transgressions,
for my own sake, and remembers your sins no more."
ISAIAH 43:25 NIV

If you think about it, part of the message behind today's verse might seem to contradict the very nature of God. Sure, we can grasp—and celebrate—the fact that God forgives our sins and cleanses us from all unrighteousness. But how can a God who knows everything that has happened in eternity past or will happen in eternity future forget something?

Let's put this in human perspective for just a moment. Suppose your spouse—or someone else close to you—does or says something to cause you pain or loss. It may be a matter of simple carelessness, or it could have been something done intentionally. Either way, you've decided that it is far better to forgive that person and restore the relationship than to cling to wrongs done and let it die. You can't literally forget the offense committed, but you can forget any thought of punishing that person for what he or she has done to you.

God's "forgetfulness" is a lot like that. He remembers sins we've committed against Him, but when we come to Him in humble repentance, He forgives us and casts away any thought of vengeance against us.

God of forgiveness, it's beyond my human understanding,
but You have said that when You forgive me for my sins, it's
as though they never happened. Help me to forget them too.

RETURN TO THE LORD

*So Samuel said to all the Israelites, "If you are returning to the
LORD with all your hearts, then rid yourselves of the foreign gods
and the Ashtoreths and commit yourselves to the LORD and serve
him only, and he will deliver you out of the hand of the Philistines."*

1 SAMUEL 7:3 NIV

Samuel's admonition to Israel included a call to change both their hearts and their actions. A heart change always leads to behavioral change. Israel had accumulated many idols during conquests, and Samuel knew they couldn't serve the Lord while trusting in false gods.

What are you trusting in today to bring you comfort, peace, joy, or deliverance? Is it an enjoyable relationship that leads you away from God? Or a status symbol, like a luxury vehicle? Or maybe a hobby that has taken over your waking hours?

Whatever it is, ask God to help you recognize any false gods that have taken up residence in your life. Then return to Him with your whole heart. Rid yourself of idols, and commit yourself to the Lord and serve Him only. When you do, you'll find true comfort, peace, joy, and deliverance.

*Lord, my heart is often quick to embrace idols. Search
my heart, O God, and root out my most persistent sins.
Loosen their grip on me, and make me wholly dependent
on You. For apart from You, I can do nothing.*

DAY 324
MEANT FOR MORE

*Our people have to learn to be diligent in their work so that
all necessities are met (especially among the needy) and
they don't end up with nothing to show for their lives.*

TITUS 3:14 MSG

The life of a Christ follower is identified by action. When you work, it means you can help those in need. Christians demonstrate love to others by being generous. They demonstrate they're trustworthy when they provide for their families. They do the hard things because they know the work they do is done for God.

Today's verse isn't one you should use to promote self-reliance. You still need to depend on God for everything, but He's given you a job to help you be productive. Your salary helps provide for your family. That same effort can benefit others who can't work.

God has a plan for your life, and you can show your trust in that plan by taking the necessary action to finish well. Whatever plan God has for your life will also impact others. You serve a relational God. Money never advances God's objectives when it takes up permanent residence in your bank account. Use it wisely, yes, but use it to bless others as well.

---

*Dear God, Your plan can be trusted. Help me be
trustworthy by partnering with You. Let my work help
my family. Let my sweat equity help others. May You be
glorified in a life that wants to count for something.*

DAY 325
TRUE WISDOM

*"The wise will be put to shame. . . . Since they have rejected
the word of the LORD, what kind of wisdom do they have?"*
JEREMIAH 8:9 NIV

Sometimes when intelligent people realize how much smarter they are than the average person, they get to trusting their own intelligence so much that they get cocky. They think that their brilliance in, say, mathematics extends to all areas of life. They then haughtily pass judgment on issues of faith, assuming that they know a lot more than the "ignorant" people who wrote the Bible.

"This is what the LORD says: 'Let not the wise boast of their wisdom . . .but let the one who boasts boast about this: that they have the understanding to know me, that I am the LORD' " (Jeremiah 9:23–24 NIV). To be *truly* wise is to admit that, as much as you know, you haven't even begun to scratch the surface of all there is to learn.

In some matters you may be an expert, but in many, many areas you're wise to recognize that you're a small child compared to God, and place your hand in His. You don't know all the answers, but if you truly know God, you can trust that He knows what He's doing.

*Father, I thank You for the wisdom and expertise You
have given me in certain areas. But I acknowledge that
You are God, the only one who knows everything.*

DAY 326

YOUR GOD-GIVEN MANDATE

*Sing to GOD, everyone and everything! Get out his
salvation news every day! Publish his glory among the
godless nations, his wonders to all races and religions.
And why? Because GOD is great—well worth praising!*

1 CHRONICLES 16:23–25 MSG

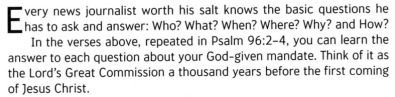

Every news journalist worth his salt knows the basic questions he has to ask and answer: Who? What? When? Where? Why? and How?

In the verses above, repeated in Psalm 96:2–4, you can learn the answer to each question about your God-given mandate. Think of it as the Lord's Great Commission a thousand years before the first coming of Jesus Christ.

Who? Everyone, sing to God!

What? Proclaim good tidings of His salvation.

When? Every day!

Where? Among all nations, peoples, and tongues.

Why? For the Lord is great and greatly to be praised!

The only question left unanswered is *How?*

Thankfully, Jesus supplied that answer to His disciples before ascending to heaven six weeks after His resurrection.

Matthew 28:18–20; Mark 16:15; Luke 24:46–49; and Acts 1:8 provide a detailed and full answer to the question *How?*

- *With Jesus' all-encompassing authority and constant presence.*
- *Preaching the good news that Jesus suffered, died for every person and their sins, rose again from the dead the third day, and now calls you to repent and receive forgiveness.*
- *Making disciples by baptizing people and teaching them all Jesus taught.*
- *With the Holy Spirit's filling, power, and joy.*

Lord, Your mandate is clear. I will obey!

GOD IS WORKING ON YOU

*There has never been the slightest doubt in my mind that the God
who started this great work in you would keep at it and bring it
to a flourishing finish on the very day Christ Jesus appears.*

PHILIPPIANS 1:6 MSG

G od saved you the day you surrendered to Christ, and He stamped
your heart with the royal seal of His Holy Spirit to certify that you
are His child (2 Corinthians 1:22; Ephesians 1:13; 4:30). Though you're
presently imperfect, God won't abandon you in your unfinished state
but is determined to keep working in you until the very day that Christ
returns to take you to heaven.

At times, you may become discouraged by your many weaknesses,
faults, and stumblings and wonder how a perfect God could put up with
you. But let there be no doubt in your mind: He started a great work
within you, and He'll see it through till it's finished. He knows you're a
work in progress. It's no surprise to Him.

You've probably passed by many construction sites and seen signs
there stating the name of the construction company. They started the
building, and they intend to see it through to completion. The Lord is
like that. "It is God who works in you" (Philippians 2:13 NKJV).

*God, I trust that You who began a good work in me will see it
through to completion. Thank You for never giving up on me.*

DAY 328
WHAT'S REALLY POSSIBLE?

Behold, I am the LORD, the God of all flesh:
is there any thing too hard for me?
JEREMIAH 32:27 KJV

You've met the man who considers it a mark of his intelligence to try to outsmart the Bible. He's the one who knows you're a Christian and makes it a priority to let you know that there's no way Jonah could've survived three days in a whale's belly, or that there must have been some mass hallucination when Joshua and his army fought under a sun that stood still in the sky.

He conveniently ignores the real miracles—that a resistant prophet's message caused the biggest, wickedest city of his day to repent, from the king down to the kids. Or that God actually let a man call the shots for a day and obliged him with a meteorological wonder. Really, though, if you can believe the first line of the Bible—that God created the heavens and the earth—the rest is easy.

And a God who can speak everything you can see and know into existence—and a whole bunch of things you can't—is a God who can take care of your needs. Take your cares to Him, even the one about the guy at the office who thinks he knows better than his Creator. Maybe he's closer to faith than either of you could ever imagine; after all, God's done bigger miracles than that.

Mighty God, thank You that there is nothing You cannot do. Help me to rest in the fact that You can do anything for me. . .and that You love me so much that You're willing to meet whatever need I have.

DAY 329
A TRUE PRAYER WARRIOR

Epaphras, who is one of you and a servant of Christ Jesus, sends greetings. He is always wrestling in prayer for you, that you may stand firm in all the will of God, mature and fully assured.

COLOSSIANS 4:12 NIV

If you've ever watched a *real* wrestling match (as opposed to the spectacle that's called professional wrestling), you see two highly trained, well-conditioned athletes trying to impose their wills on each other. You see two opponents applying the techniques they've learned from practice and from prior experience to achieve their goals.

In today's verse, the word *wrestling* implies contending passionately and continuously for something. It means coming to God again and again and requesting that which you're convinced in your heart He wants to do for you. Epaphras engaged in that kind of prayer on behalf of the Colossians. Jacob prayed like that during his encounter with God too (Genesis 32:22–31). And the good news is that God invites you to pray the very same way.

Can you think of someone you know who could benefit from your prayers? Maybe a pastor or other full-time minister who is doing battle with the forces of evil? Or a married man who is working to save his marriage? Or how about a friend who needs Jesus? If so, learn from Epaphras and from Jacob, and don't stop asking until God gives you what you know He wants to give you.

Father in heaven, make me a true prayer warrior, a man willing to spend as much time as necessary on his knees before You.

DAY 330
COURAGE TO SPEAK UP

Speak up for those who cannot speak for themselves,
for the rights of all who are destitute.
PROVERBS 31:8 NIV

━━━━▋━━━━

You may not like thinking about it, but many millions of people worldwide—even right here in the United States—are in places and situations of overwhelming suffering. The hungry, the homeless, the enslaved, and the infirm can be found in every community, and in many cases, they have no one to stand up and speak out on their behalf. That's a terrible kind of loneliness most people have no idea even exists.

One example of this kind of suffering is that of modern-day slaves. Today, there are more slaves working worldwide than at any other time in human history. Millions of people worldwide are held against their will and forced to work as sex slaves, domestic slaves, and commercial slaves.

God may not have laid it on your heart to speak out against the enslavement and mistreatment of human beings—but then again, He may have—but you don't have to look far to find those who need someone to speak out for them.

Ask God to show you who needs someone to speak for them. And when He shows you who it is, trust Him enough to speak and act with courage.

Father, help me to trust You and what You've
taught me in Your Word enough to be a voice for
those who can't speak up for themselves.

DAY 331
SAFE PASSAGE

But he led his own people like a flock of sheep,
guiding them safely through the wilderness.
PSALM 78:52 NLT

The reading from Psalm 78 today covers God's faithfulness to His people. It chronicles the way He sent plagues on His enemies, destroying their crops, killing their livestock, and revealing His anger against them. Meanwhile, He led His own people to safety, brought them to the border of His holy land, and gave it to them as an inheritance.

Your circumstances might not always seem to be clear-cut. Sometimes the wicked seem to prevail for a period of time, and sometimes God's people aren't kept safe from harm. But you can count on God to make all things right in the end and to bring you home to ultimate safety in heaven.

Don't get so caught up in the news or in observing the way that the wicked seem to prevail that it causes you to doubt God's concern for you. He loves you so much that He was willing to send His Son to die for you. His kingdom will prevail, and you can count on the fact that Jesus has gone ahead to prepare a place for you in heaven, no matter what your circumstances are here on earth.

Father, sometimes I get caught up in the things
of this world. Forgive me for losing focus and for
allowing a lack of trust to creep into my heart.

EVERYDAY DOUBLE AGENTS

A double minded man is unstable in all his ways.
JAMES 1:8 KJV

Aldrich Ames, a CIA operative, was arrested in 1994 and charged with selling secrets to the Soviet Union. The information he sold had led to the exposure, arrest, and deaths of dozens of CIA operatives in the East Bloc. His careless spending on pricey homes and cars led to *his* arrest, and he eventually received a life sentence.

Ames is one of history's most infamous double agents, but a far greater number of men have, in similar ways, sabotaged themselves spiritually. While they haven't sold state secrets to enemy nations, they have secretly tried to have it both their way and God's way. These nominal Christians put on all the airs of discipleship, shaking hands and offering prayers on Sunday morning but carrying on with affairs, shady business deals, and self-serving behavior the rest of the week.

James called this behavior being "double minded." A man like that will fool a lot of people a lot of the time, but never God. As Paul wrote, "Don't be misled—you cannot mock the justice of God. You will always harvest what you plant" (Galatians 6:7 NLT). When you know about God and His ways but try to play both sides rather than giving *all* you are over to Him, you'll destabilize your whole life. Better to trust Him all the way or not at all.

Lord, help me to trust You and focus on
You completely, without reservation.

DAY 333
GOD'S GIFT OF A TRUSTING HEART

*One woman, Lydia, was from Thyatira and a dealer in
expensive textiles, known to be a God-fearing woman.
As she listened with intensity to what was being said,
the Master gave her a trusting heart—and she believed!*

ACTS 16:14 MSG

The world's greatest miracle? Hands down, it's God's gift of a trusting, believing, faith-filled heart. Just as remarkable? God can give that gift to *anyone*. After all, He doesn't want anyone to perish, but for all to come to repentance (2 Peter 3:9).

Who is the one person you know who, humanly speaking, is least likely to receive God's gift of a trusting heart? Are you willing to let God use you in his life? If so. . .

1. Go to that person.
2. Ask questions.
3. Listen to him.
4. Ask him to tell you his story.
5. Ask again until he says yes.
6. Don't interrupt—just listen.
7. Be nonjudgmental.
8. Be unshockable.
9. Keep on listening.
10. Bless him.
11. Ask if you can pray for him.
12. Repeat.

Experience shows that listening is the new loving. Better yet? Even tough guys respond to such unobtrusive love. The greatest miracle you'll experience this year could be right around the corner.

*Lord, it truly would take a miracle for _____ to receive
Your gift of a trusting heart. Then again, I believe You still do
miracles today. Guide my steps as I reach out to him, I pray.*

DAY 334
GOD WILL REWARD YOU

*Work with enthusiasm, as though you were working for
the Lord rather than for people. Remember that the Lord
will reward each one of us for the good we do.*
EPHESIANS 6:7–8 NLT

Paul originally gave this advice to Roman slaves who had become Christians. Though he told them to seek their freedom if possible (1 Corinthians 7:21), he also advised them, if they had to remain a slave, to be good examples of a follower of Christ—trusting that He would reward their work. If they could follow this counsel in such difficult circumstances, you can apply it in your job.

You're not a slave, but you may be experiencing some nearly unbearable things in your life. You wonder how you'll make it, or how God could expect you to put up with aggravating circumstances patiently—let alone accept them and have a triumphant, enthusiastic attitude. The only way you can do this is to trust that God will reward you for following His commands during such difficult times.

Jesus turned many common understandings upside down, declaring that the first would be last and that if you want to be great, you should become the slave of all. You have to trust deeply in Him to follow His commands.

*Lord, may I trust that You have the wisdom to see
me through my problems and the power to turn
all unpleasant situations into good ones.*

HONESTY AND DISHONESTY

Better to be poor and honest than to be dishonest and a fool.
PROVERBS 19:1 NLT

Today's verse links dishonesty and foolishness. It's hard to trust someone who has an open foolishness account. Those who are poor but trustworthy are in a much better position.

An honest and trustworthy man can sleep well at night, has a greater potential for meaningful friendships, and will be remembered for something more than personal struggles. A dishonest man has to try to come up with fresh answers for ongoing deceit, never knows when he'll be caught in a lie, and is remembered for his attempts to avoid the truth.

The emphasis in today's verse is on honesty. You can be honest and poor *or* honest and rich. You can also be dishonest and poor *or* dishonest and rich. Perhaps the reason "poor" is mentioned in the first example is that it's something most people want to avoid, but it *doesn't* have to be a condition that leads to dishonesty.

Lord, may I go on an honesty diet and keep my distance from foolishness. Even when honesty is hard, help me place a strong grip on the truth and invite greater trust in my words, my walk, and my will. Help me accept Your truth so I'll live honestly.

DAY 336
LEAVE YOUR WATER POT

*The woman then left her waterpot, went her way into
the city, and said to the men, "Come, see a Man who told
me all things that I ever did. Could this be the Christ?"*
JOHN 4:28–29 NKJV

The Samaritan woman who had come to Jacob's well for water had just heard Jesus say that He was the Messiah. Imagine! In her day! The woman was so excited that she abandoned her water pot, left Jesus sitting at the well, and dashed into the city to blaze abroad the news. She clearly trusted what Jesus was telling her, and she couldn't keep it to herself. She was beside herself with excitement.

Has the gospel so penetrated your heart that you too have a burning desire to return to your city, workplace, school, or community to talk about Jesus? Have you ever become so excited about God's promises that you left your "water pot"—your pressing business at hand—behind?

When Jesus called His first disciples, they left their nets, their families, their friends, and everything they knew to follow Him. You can't always drop your duties to share the gospel, but it should still stir you up and excite you. Share while you work!

*Lord, You're in my life, but sometimes my zeal to tell others
about You is lacking. Forgive me. Reignite my heart. Fill me with
boldness—so much so that I'll be moved to be Your ambassador.*

CHOOSING FRIENDS WISELY

Do not make friends with a hot-tempered person,
do not associate with one easily angered, or you
may learn their ways and get yourself ensnared.
PROVERBS 22:24–25 NIV

People with bad tempers can be very unpleasant to be around. Sure, they can be good company—as long as other people and life itself are treating them the way they deserve to be treated. But when some offense comes, the ill-tempered can react with unkind words and unkind (or even violent or dangerous) actions.

The Bible includes some simple but very sound wisdom when it comes to dealing with hot-tempered people: stay clear! Sure, we're going to encounter people with bad tempers (and other sinful attitudes and behaviors), but today's passage advises us to avoid socializing too much with these kinds of people.

Our God is all-knowing and all-wise, and He understands far better than we do that we tend to adopt the behaviors of those closest to us. He also knows that a person with a bad temper is headed for disaster, and He will do everything He can to make sure His people don't end up in the same place.

That includes giving us this simple bit of wisdom: don't spend your time with a hothead!

Lord God, give me wisdom in choosing my friends.
Help me to avoid close relationships with ill-tempered men.

DAY 338
DON'T FORGET

Let us hold tightly without wavering to the hope we affirm,
for God can be trusted to keep his promise. Let us think
of ways to motivate one another to acts of love and
good works. And let us not neglect our meeting together,
as some people do, but encourage one another.
HEBREWS 10:23–25 NLT

Those who originally read this letter were drawn back to a time when they first heard stories of Jesus' life, death, burial, and resurrection. Some may have met Him personally. But time had passed and the truth needed a good dusting. The life of Jesus was nearly becoming a ritual in the remembering. The people might have been getting a little ho-hum about meeting together.

Humans have always been easily distracted. These three verses invite you to join in a movement that puts hope in perspective, trust in the hands of God, and sets encouragement as a prime human motivation.

God has made promises He *will* keep. You can trust them. You can celebrate them. You can meet with other Christians and proclaim them.

Dear God, life has a way of making me forget. I can leave a church
service on the weekend and slowly forget the hope I affirmed
there. Thank You for having the idea of a place to meet with
others who have the same struggle. Help me remember that You
have promised never to leave me and that You're here now.

DAY 339
WHAT CAN I TRULY TRUST?

The rich think their wealth protects them;
they imagine themselves safe behind it.
PROVERBS 18:11 MSG

Those who have wealth may think that wealth is powerful and that placing trust in money is a good idea. They may believe a fat bank account places a secure barrier between themselves and bad days. Today's verse, however, states that not everything you think is *true* and not everything you imagine is *real*. Believing a lie doesn't make it true.

Every word in the Bible means something, and while this verse leads to the clear lesson not to trust in wealth to save you, it also leads to another logical conclusion: God *can* be trusted when even money fails to provide security.

You can *think* power and prestige bring security. You can *imagine* fame and ability set you up for only the good things in life. But when your trust is misplaced, you'll return to the question whose answer you got wrong: "What can I truly trust?"

Lord, I want to trust You more than anything else in life. Help me rethink my decisions when I consider the possibility that there's anything I can trust that is somehow greater than You. May I return to the wisdom that says my trust is best placed in the hands that made the universe, made me, and were nailed to a cross for me. I no longer have a reason to doubt Your love for me.

DAY 340
A BLESSED INVITATION

*Then the angel said to me, "Write this: Blessed are those
who are invited to the wedding supper of the Lamb!"
And he added, "These are the true words of God."*
REVELATION 19:9 NIV

Remember the last time you were invited to a wedding? Usually, the text featured on the invitation begins something like this: "Tim and Joanne request the honor of your presence. . ."

Did you know that you as a follower of Jesus Christ have been invited to a wedding celebration? Not only that, you've been chosen as one of the guests of honor.

The Bible refers to Jesus as our "Bridegroom" and His Church (meaning all believers) as the "Bride." As a believer, you've been betrothed to Christ, and the "marriage" will be completed when He brings you and the rest of His Church together for an event He calls "the wedding supper of the Lamb."

If you know Jesus Christ as your Lord and Savior, you're one of the "blessed" because you've been assured of an eternity in God's heavenly kingdom. Not only that, you've been invited to the party to end all parties.

You can count on that because, as the angel of God stated, "these are the true words of God."

---

*Heavenly Father, thank You for inviting me to the
wedding feast of the Lamb. Help me to live daily in
the assurance that I'm Yours, now and forever.*

RELATIONAL BLUEPRINT

*A friend is always loyal, and a brother
is born to help in time of need.*
PROVERBS 17:17 NLT

Today's verse describes God's "Friends and Family Bonus Plan." The primary thing God seeks to restore is relationship, and He ensures that friendships and family relationships are included.

God chose to use a word meaning "loyal" to describe friends. He chose to describe "brothers" as individuals assigned to help in times of need. That means you have a lot to live up to. You aren't perfect, and there will be issues standing between your actions and God's requirements.

You're probably thinking of family and friends who fit this description, and those who don't. This verse describes God's ideal. It doesn't always describe people's actions. Well, that gives you something to work on.

This one verse provides a relational blueprint that sounds easy, but living it is often hard. It's easy to expect loyalty from others, but it can be hard to *be* loyal. It's easy to want someone to help you but hard to *offer* help.

Loyalty and being helpful are two expressions of trust. They can prove your trustworthiness and inspire others to trust you.

*Lord, help me learn how to reflect Your plan to be loyal to
friends and responsive to the needs of family. May I see it as a
sure path to trust and be trusted. May Your example of being
trustworthy guide me as I'm inspired to be worthy of trust.*

DAY 342
ONE HOPE

Now there have been many of those priests, since death prevented them from continuing in office; but because Jesus lives forever, he has a permanent priesthood. Therefore he is able to save completely those who come to God through him, because he always lives to intercede for them.

HEBREWS 7:23–25 NIV

Jesus isn't a short-term Savior. He's not up for reelection. He doesn't need to adapt His platform to match poll numbers. He always has been. He always will be. And He saves completely. His rescue plan has no limitations. His authority is without question. His kindness is assured.

Because you *will* fail, Jesus reminds His Father that He paid the price for your sin. No more death sentence, separation, or condemnation. He brought life, offers real forgiveness, and wants to be your friend. Every person gets a *trust invitation*. No exclusions. He came for all.

Jesus is the one way to God. He's the one hope for mankind. He provides the only answer for your future. The sacrifice of one Man brought an end to your old life. It established the beginning of something new, something permanent. His faithfulness is bigger than the combined faithlessness of every believer.

Lord, I'm overwhelmed by Your gift, impressed by Your friendship, and humbled by Your mercy. One of the greatest benefits of living for You is that I'm no longer condemned. I'm amazed at how much You offer when I have nothing to bring but myself.

DAY 343
UNSELFISH CONVERSATION

Fools have no interest in understanding;
they only want to air their own opinions.
PROVERBS 18:2 NLT

———

Spend time on social media and you'll encounter posts stating that the opinion they express is not open to discussion. People have been *defriended* for suggesting there's another perspective to consider.

This isn't a judgment against those who have a narrow conversational acceptance on social media. But it's a potent illustration of what it's like to carry on a conversation with someone without ever hearing and understanding what they're saying.

It's hard for someone to trust you with their opinions or share their life's toughest moments when you only seem to be waiting for a moment to share what's on your mind—even when it has nothing to do with what they've been talking to you about. That's selfish conversation. You can be sure that if you refuse to really *listen*, the other person will either stop talking or cease attempting to share anything meaningful with you in the future.

Not everyone can be trusted with knowing what you're going through. Can you be trusted with the words others share with you?

Dear God, help me discover the compassion needed to really
listen when people share things that are important to them.
Lead me to those who can be trusted with my thoughts
and concerns. Even when I don't agree, may my ability to
listen prove a good reflection of Your love for mankind.

REVEALING GOD'S HEART
FOR PRODIGALS

*"Say to them, 'As surely as I live, declares the Sovereign LORD,
I take no pleasure in the death of the wicked, but rather that
they turn from their ways and live. Turn! Turn from your
evil ways! Why will you die, people of Israel?' "*
EZEKIEL 33:11 NIV

While there's no mistaking the consequences that await those who turn away from God, perhaps our shame and guilt hide the true desires of God from us. If you imagine an angry God eager to judge or to catch you in your sins, let this passage change your mind. Ezekiel shows us a God who pleads with His people and begs them to change their ways. Rather than threatening His people, the Lord shows His people that there are two paths set before them and passionately calls on them to choose the life of God found in obedience.

Each day we face choices and opportunities to move toward God or to shut ourselves off from God. If you've failed or closed yourself off from the Lord today or for as long as you can remember, the same desperate message applies to you: turn from your evil ways! Seeing His beloved people undone by sin devastates the heart of God. The unraveling of our lives under the sway of sin is the absolute last thing He wants. God stands ready to forgive, to welcome us, and to lead us back to life. His plea for us today is simple and heartfelt: turn back.

*Loving heavenly Father, please remind me daily that
You want me to bring my sin to You so that I can be
forgiven. . .and so I can enjoy the life You have for me.*

DAY 345
IT'S WORTH TRUSTING GOD

"What fault did your ancestors find in me,
that they strayed so far from me?"
JEREMIAH 2:5 NIV

G od described how He had done great miracles to bring the Jews'
ancestors out of slavery in Egypt, had provided for them in a barren,
unforgiving desert, and had done miracles to bring them into the Promised
Land. Despite all this, His people turned from Him to worship useless
idols. Hence His rhetorical question above.

The truth was the Israelites had found *no* legitimate fault with
God. "He is the Rock, his works are perfect, and all his ways are just. A
faithful God who does no wrong" (Deuteronomy 32:4 NIV).

But many modern people think they *have* found fault with God. They
say, "He allows innocent children to suffer. Christianity is outdated, out
of touch with modern liberated worldviews." So they disrespect Him
and stray in their hearts. Do *you* sometimes find yourself doing this?

Trust God. His works are still perfect, even though you can't yet see
the end from the beginning. "You *are* good, and *do* good (Psalm 119:68
NKJV, emphasis added). Even what may now seem only to be senseless
tragedies will be recycled into a meaningful design. Believing this takes
great trust in God, but He is worthy of your trust.

Father, help me to trust that You are good and that You do good—
both in my life and in the world around me. In Jesus' name, I pray.

DAY 346
AN INVITATION TO TRUST

*"When the time is ripe, I'll free your tongue and you'll say,
'This is what GOD, the Master, says:. . .' From then on it's up
to them. They can listen or not listen, whichever they like."*

EZEKIEL 3:27 MSG

God had a message for a people determined to rebel. Ezekiel was one of several prophets God used to ensure that the people had every opportunity to turn away from the things they had done. He wanted them to have a mindset that matched His own. Ezekiel was bold in sharing the message because it came from God, was honest, and contained an invitation to trust.

God knows it's hard to fully trust someone who offers no choice. Maybe you've heard people make decisions for others then say, "Trust me. This is for your own good." The decision might *be* good, but imposing it on someone doesn't generally cause them to trust—only comply.

Ezekiel spoke God's truth, but the people had to decide for themselves if they'd trust. As today's verse says, "It's up to them. They can listen or not listen, whichever they like."

God has a message for you. He asks you to accept it. But receiving His truth will require trust.

---

*Dear God, You have given me a mind to think with. Help me
to do so. You've given me an invitation to trust. Help me
believe. You've given me a choice. Help me choose wisely.*

DAY 347
GRATEFUL FOR FRIENDS

Be careful then, dear brothers and sisters. Make sure that your own hearts are not evil and unbelieving, turning you away from the living God. You must warn each other every day, while it is still "today," so that none of you will be deceived by sin and hardened against God. For if we are faithful to the end, trusting God just as firmly as when we first believed, we will share in all that belongs to Christ.

HEBREWS 3:12–14 NLT

The writer of Hebrews laid out a clear battle plan when it came to retaining a strong belief and trust in God. What was that plan? Keep your mind from all kinds of deception, and do everything to keep your heart from being hardened. Keep in contact with other Christians who feel comfortable pointing out any red flags in your behavior.

It's easy to get defensive when someone points out your flaws. No man likes to think he's failing. But you're asked to accept such candid observations from other Christians.

Trust is something God requires of you. He wants you to finish your journey well. Christ-following companions can help you stay focused on the finish line.

Lord, it's a gift to find a Christian friend who can see failings in my life that I've missed and love me enough to point them out. Remind me why trusting Your rebukes through godly friends is wiser than trusting the praise of fools.

DAY 348
FRIENDS WITH GOD

*"I no longer call you servants, because a servant does not know his
master's business. Instead, I have called you friends, for everything
that I learned from my Father I have made known to you."*
JOHN 15:15 NIV

When we approach the work we do for a living in the right way, we
can take great joy in that work. But there is something extra special
about the work we do in helping our friends. There's something about
getting your hands dirty in simple tasks like helping a friend move or
spending a Saturday helping him paint his home, or in more "emotional"
ways like offering a listening ear during times of trouble, that brings you
closer to your friend.

The same is true of the greatest friend you'll ever know—Jesus, who
demonstrated His love for His friends by laying down His own life for
us (see John 15:13). When we walk closely with Him, listen to Him, and
follow His leading, He calls us His own friends (John 15:14).

Jesus is such a loving friend that He walked the earth for more than
thirty years for us, taught us, died for us, was raised from the grave for
us, and now resides in heaven, where He constantly pleads our case
before His heavenly Father (see Hebrews 7:25).

As the old hymn says, "What a Friend we have in Jesus!"

---

*Jesus my friend, thank You for drawing me so close to
You that You consider me Your friend. Help me always to
remember that You are the best friend I'll ever have.*

DAY 349
MOVED TO COMFORT YOU

"As one whom his mother comforts, so I will comfort you;
and you shall be comforted in Jerusalem."
ISAIAH 66:13 NKJV

God sees your troubles. He hears your groaning. And He's right there with you, beside you, sharing your burden and your sorrow. Trust that He cares for you and will act. He won't remove all burdens and hardships from your life—at least not immediately—but He will reach out with His Spirit to comfort you and to help you bear up under the weight you carry.

God depicts Himself as having the tender heart of a mother responding to the sorrow of a crying child. Tests have been done in recent years that highlight the different reactions of men and women: when hearing a baby crying, most men become aggravated and disturbed; most women, however, feel pangs of empathy and a strong desire to comfort the child.

God says that just like a mother, He's irresistibly moved to comfort you. This is brought out beautifully in the book of Revelation, where John says that when you get to heaven, God will personally wipe the tears from your eyes (Revelation 7:17; 21:4). But know this: He's wiping your tears away even now.

Dear Father, thank You for presenting a picture of Your
love that I can understand. Thank You for responding
to my sorrow and pain. Help me to trust that You
care deeply for me and are comforting me.

DAY 350
TRUST AND RESTORATION

I appeal to you to show kindness to my child, Onesimus. I became his father in the faith while here in prison. Onesimus hasn't been of much use to you in the past, but now he is very useful to both of us. I am sending him back to you, and with him comes my own heart.

PHILEMON 10–12 NLT

———

Philemon was a slave owner, and Onesimus was his slave. Onesimus thought he was being mistreated. Philemon thought the slave was unteachable. Trust had been broken.

Onesimus fled and sought sanctuary with the apostle Paul. The two spoke often and, in time, the heart of the slave softened toward Philemon, so Paul told Onesimus to return to his master. He sent a letter to Philemon asking him to accept Onesimus. Paul said Onesimus had become family to him.

This story requests faith in the faithless and is a reminder that a merciful God wants His people to show mercy.

While the only one worthy of trust is God, He asks that you seek to be trusted and find reason to trust others. The downside to refusing to trust is cynicism, paranoia, and isolation. When trust is broken, you need to extend forgiveness and encourage restoration.

Lord, help me believe You can restore trust in people who have been untrustworthy. There are times I have broken trust, so may I be willing to encourage the restoration of trust in others.

ESTABLISHING—AND PROTECTING— YOUR REPUTATION

A good name is more desirable than great riches;
to be esteemed is better than silver or gold.
PROVERBS 22:1 NIV

The great basketball coach John Wooden once said, "Be more concerned with your character than your reputation, because your character is what you really are, while your reputation is merely what others think you are."

Wooden's words point out the simple truth that character and reputation, while they are closely related in many ways, are not the same thing. However, a life defined by godly character—the kind of life committed to treating people well, conducting business with integrity, building a family with true love, and worshipping God in both word and deed—will almost always lead to a good reputation.

There are few things in life that are worth guarding with great passion, and one of those is a good reputation. You can establish and protect a good reputation by making sure that the thoughts you think, the words you speak, and the actions you take are those that please God in every way.

Lord, my reputation is important to me. . .and to You.
Help me to have a good reputation, but more importantly,
help me to be a man of good character.

A GREATER OBEDIENCE

*My aim is to raise hopes by pointing the way
to life without end. This is the life God promised
long ago—and he doesn't break promises!*
TITUS 1:1–2 MSG

Paul had initiated his work by founding churches in Crete. He then passed the work on to a younger man named Titus whom he called his "legitimate son in the faith" (Titus 1:4 MSG).

For Titus, this letter from Paul was an instruction manual, personal encouragement, and a reminder that every day that Titus shared God's message, he could trust God to lead. Titus was considered trustworthy when he agreed to point the way to endless life by introducing people to God, the author of trust.

God knows He uses people who make wrong choices, which is why He had Paul include a list of qualifications for those aspiring to church leadership (see vv. 5–9). Paul knew that people needed to see those who lead as trustworthy because if they weren't trustworthy when they shared the truth, then how could people trust the gospel? How could they trust the God behind the message?

Greater obedience leads to greater trust. Greater trust leads to greater faith.

Lord, help me keep my word to others. Help me keep my word to You. I fail and will continue to fail, but when others find they can trust me, it's only because I have discovered I can trust You.

GIVING WITH THE RIGHT MOTIVES

*"So when you give to the needy, do not announce it
with trumpets, as the hypocrites do in the synagogues
and on the streets, to be honored by others. Truly I
tell you, they have received their reward in full."*

MATTHEW 6:2 NIV

We may not want to admit it, but it can be easy to wonder, *What's in it for me?* when we think of giving to others. Jesus understood this part of fallen human nature, and that's why He told His followers not to seek human recognition when we give.

When we think of the word *giving*, our minds usually go to the financial. But God also calls us to give of our time, of our efforts, of any other of the gifts He's given us. But no matter what we find ourselves in a position to give, the principle stands the same. When we give, we're to do it in such a way that only God—and sometimes the recipient—knows about it.

So give—give generously. But when you give, make sure your heart and mind are free of any desire for human recognition or any other earthly reward. When you give with a pure heart that is motivated by the desire to glorify God and bless others, God will honor your giving and bless you in return.

*Give me a generous heart, Lord, but also give me a
humble heart—the kind of heart that is unconcerned
with the recognition of men when I give.*

REMEMBER WHAT GOD HAS DONE

Who can list the glorious miracles of the LORD?
Who can ever praise him enough?

PSALM 106:2 NLT

Pop question: Over the years, how many miracles has the Lord done for you and your family?

None? One? Two to five? Six to nine? Ten or more?

If you had a hard time answering today's pop question, you might consider doing what the psalmist recommends.

First, make a list of the miracles God has done for your family. Remember, miracles don't have to be flashy or spectacular. They just have to be God at work to make something happen that wouldn't have happened any other way.

Examples include God's sovereignty, providence, holiness, love, and mystery to—

- *bring two people together who later marry,*
- *give a couple a long-prayed-for child,*
- *heal a family member after a troubling medical verdict,*
- *provide a needed financial gift even though no one knew about the need,*
- *bring a wayward child back home to God and family.*

Then make a list of the miracles God has done for you personally. Examples include—

- *bringing you to saving faith in Jesus Christ,*
- *making you wholeheartedly dedicated to the Lord,*
- *providing your first career job in a remarkable way,*
- *healing you after a tough bout with cancer.*

Now add up both lists. How many miracles has the Lord done? Amazing!

Lord, I truly can't praise You enough. Thank You for all You have done!

CLAY IN THE MASTER'S HANDS

But now, O LORD, thou art our father; we are the clay,
and thou our potter; and we all are the work of thy hand.

ISAIAH 64:8 KJV

You are like clay in God's hands. You must be yielding, moist clay, however, not dry and brittle. God is forming you into a vessel of His own design, but for Him to do that, you can't harden your heart. You must keep your heart soft and yielded to Him, able to be worked. And God often keeps you moist through suffering and tears.

Paul wrote, "If you keep yourself pure, you will be a special utensil for honorable use. Your life will be clean, and you will be ready for the Master to use you for every good work" (2 Timothy 2:21 NLT). You must allow God to remove any unyielded bits from your life, just as a potter picks a hard, dry lump of clay from the spinning vessel.

Is God working and massaging and shaping your life now? Is He removing hard, unyielded areas from your heart to prepare you for service? The process is sometimes painful, but yield to God's loving hands and trust Him. Things may be difficult now, but the end result will most definitely be worth it.

Father God, help me to yield my life to the pressure of Your
skilled fingers, allowing You to shape me as You will.

DAY 356
KINGDOMS AND CURRENT AFFAIRS

"He made the earth by his power; he founded the world by his wisdom and stretched out the heavens by his understanding. When he thunders, the waters in the heavens roar; he makes clouds rise from the ends of the earth. He sends lightning with the rain and brings out the wind from his storehouses."

JEREMIAH 51:15–16 NIV

God founded the world, stretched out the heavens, and created the water cycle. The God who can do all that has the ability to do anything. Seeing such power and creativity should inspire trust.

With today's scripture, this acknowledgment is just the opening statement of what became God's promised judgments against Babylon. That empire had taken Judah captive. God planned it that way. Judah was rebellious, so God used Babylon to help turn their hearts back to Him.

However, Babylon became merciless and deluded with pride. They ruled Israel with an iron fist. They made life unbearable. The prophet Jeremiah recounted Babylon's atrocities then the promises God made to defend His people from an empire that had gone too far.

God's design in creation and weather can be trusted. God can also be trusted with nations and current affairs. No detail escapes His attention. Nothing catches Him by surprise. His plan, for the world and for your life, can be trusted.

Dear God, when I'm discouraged and think things are out of control, help me remember You have a plan, and that plan shows Your faithfulness.

DAY 357
ONE-ON-ONE INTERVENTIONS

Better is open rebuke than hidden love. Wounds from a
friend can be trusted, but an enemy multiplies kisses.
PROVERBS 27:5–6 NIV

Confrontation is uncomfortable for most people. We don't like being told that we're harboring sinful or unhealthy attitudes or taking part in actions that displease God or cause others pain. And it can be even harder to be "that guy"—the one who must somehow summon the courage it takes to confront a friend who so desperately needs it.

But the Bible tells us that a true friend is one who is willing to risk the friendship and say what needs to be said to a brother or sister in the Lord who either is living with obvious sin or has some kind of "blind spot" that keeps him or her from living or thinking in a way that pleases God.

It's easy to decide to just mind your own business when your friend strays from God's standards of living and thinking. But today's verse teaches us that part of being a real friend is being willing, no matter how uncomfortable it may be, to speak difficult truth to those you love—and to do it gently and firmly.

Do you have that kind of friend? And can you *be* that kind of friend?

Lord, help me to be the kind of friend who can
lovingly challenge, even confront, those brothers
in the faith whom You've placed in my life.

DAY 358
TRUSTING ENOUGH TO GIVE

"Bring the whole tithe into the storehouse, that there may be food in my house. Test me in this," says the LORD Almighty, "and see if I will not throw open the floodgates of heaven and pour out so much blessing that there will not be room enough to store it."

MALACHI 3:10 NIV

Recent polls have revealed startling facts about the giving/tithing habits of American churchgoers. One poll found that Christians give at only 2.5 percent per capita, a rate worse than during the Great Depression.

Something is clearly amiss!

In the Bible, God commands His followers to give generously and has also promised blessings on those who obey this command.

If you think about it, you just might find that your reluctance to give toward God's work here on this earth has less to do with simple selfishness and much more to do with your lack of trust in Him to provide what you need to care for yourself and your family.

If I give 10 percent or more of my income, you might think, *then how am I going to pay the mortgage, the car payment, the power bill. . . ?* The Bible teaches that's backward thinking. God promises that when you give, you put yourself in a position to receive blessings from above.

Father, forgive me for my lack of generosity. Even more, forgive me for not trusting You enough to give out of what You've given me.

DAY 359
LET THE SPIRIT WORK

But the one who plants in response to God,
letting God's Spirit do the growth work in him,
harvests a crop of real life, eternal life.
GALATIANS 6:8 MSG

God is the only one who can accomplish anything. This is why Jesus said in John 15:5–6 (MSG), "I am the Vine, you are the branches. When you're joined with me and I with you. . .the harvest is sure to be abundant. Separated, you can't produce a thing. Anyone who separates from me is deadwood."

A dry, withered branch bears no fruit. How could it? It's dead. You wouldn't expect a lopped-off branch to bear fruit. No more can you, unless you remain firmly attached to God, receiving the life-giving sap of His Spirit. "He who is joined to the Lord is one spirit with Him" (1 Corinthians 6:17 NKJV). You have to trust and depend on God to cause you to bear fruit by His Spirit dwelling in you.

God has a job for you—to share the life-giving gospel with people. But apart from Christ, you're dead and withered. You can't cause life to spring forth in anyone else if you aren't connected to God yourself. So stay firmly attached to God, and allow Him to work in and through you.

Jesus, please keep me connected to You so that I can
pass on Your Holy Spirit and eternal life to others.

DAY 360
GUARD YOUR EYES

*"I made a covenant with my eyes not to
look lustfully at a young woman."*
JOB 31:1 NIV

Job was well aware of his weaknesses. He knew that if he allowed himself to look at a young woman for too long, he'd probably lust after her, so he made a pact—an agreement with himself—that he wouldn't purposely look at a woman with the intent to lust. He wouldn't objectify her, nor presume to have the right to do so.

This battle against the flesh is an ancient one. Many a man has fallen into temptation after gazing longingly at a woman he found attractive. What are you doing to guard your eyes? Are you willing to make a similar covenant with your eyes? Are you willing to stay off your computer late at night, if you find that to be a temptation? Are you willing to stay accountable to other men?

As you work out your own salvation in this area, trust the power of the Holy Spirit to keep you strong. You'll be unable to stand otherwise. But as you yield to the Spirit's leading and guidance, you'll find joy and freedom. If this is a new practice for you, consider talking to godly men who show women the respect they deserve.

---

*Father, I'm often tempted to give in and allow myself to lust after
a woman I'm attracted to. Help me to live purely instead.*

DAY 361

WORSHIP IS PREPARATION FOR WORK

One day as these men were worshiping the Lord and fasting, the Holy Spirit said, "Appoint Barnabas and Saul for the special work to which I have called them."

ACTS 13:2 NLT

In Acts 12:18–13:13, Doctor Luke records the death of wicked King Herod Agrippa I after the apostle Peter's miraculous jail break. Then Luke strategically moves the focus of his book to the city of Antioch, the new center for missionary outreach. Antioch becomes such by God's choosing, not man's.

At the beginning of Acts 13, all of the gifted men of Ephesians 4:11—Antioch's apostles, prophets, evangelists, and teachers—have gathered together for a time of dedicated, focused worship. They were so dedicated that they decided to forgo eating. It's easy to imagine them asking the Lord to build up His church in Antioch and in the unreached regions of the empire surrounding the rest of the Mediterranean Sea.

In the midst of their prayers and praise and silence and singing, God speaks. This wasn't just an impression. It was anything but vague or imaginary. On the contrary, it was specific and succinct. These gifted men knew exactly what God had said and had every reason to continue their fasting and prayers. Then they sent Barnabas and Saul (Paul) out on their first missionary journey.

Lord, I understand that worship is preparatory for everything in my life. Therefore, I gladly worship You today.

DAY 362
THE RIGHT THING TO BRAG ON

This is what the LORD says: "Let not the wise boast of their
wisdom or the strong boast of their strength or the rich
boast of their riches, but let the one who boasts boast
about this: that they have the understanding to know me."
JEREMIAH 9:23–24 NIV

If you've ever been around someone who spends a lot of time—not to mention his own breath—bragging about his own accomplishments, possessions, or talents, then you probably have a small clue as to why God isn't pleased with human pride and arrogance.

When we boast about our own accomplishments, about our talents and gifts, in essence we communicate a mindset and heart attitude that what we have and what we can do are a result of our own efforts and not a result of God's blessings.

Indeed, God doesn't want His people carrying around an attitude of braggadocio. He doesn't want us expending our energy letting others know about the great things we've accomplished or about our gifts and skills.

Instead, our God wants us to make sure our words—especially those we speak in relation to our gifts, blessings, and accomplishments—point to Him as our loving benefactor. And, as today's verse instructs us, that should begin with the fact that we know Him as our loving heavenly Father.

Lord, if I must boast about anything, let it be that
I know and love You above everything else.

HOW TO SABOTAGE THE GOSPEL

*Do everything without complaining and arguing,
so that no one can criticize you.*
PHILIPPIANS 2:14–15 NLT

There is one certain way to undermine your ability to communicate the gospel to others: engage in arguments. As we fight to be recognized, to win arguments, to justify our actions, and to make excuses for ourselves, we engage in a practice that is wholly centered upon ourselves and, even worse, has a tendency to cast blame on others. As we fight to justify ourselves, we turn others into our opponents, either blaming them for our problems or eliminating common ground with them as we argue over disagreements.

While communicating the gospel has the potential to create peace and common ground with others, complaining and arguing will give our listeners cause to criticize us. Even if we're completely convinced that we deserve to complain or have every right to win an argument, we are reminded by Paul that there are unintended consequences that will further separate us from either our fellow Christians or those we are hoping to reach with the gospel. As we stop fighting for our rights or to be "right," we remove a major obstacle with others and keep as many doors open as possible for the gospel to take root and flourish in our relationships.

*Father in heaven, help me to avoid conflicts over
things that aren't important to You. Help me to
remember that I don't always have to be "right."*

DAY 364
FAITHFUL IS SUCCESSFUL

Make it your ambition to lead a quiet life: You should
mind your own business and work with your hands.
1 THESSALONIANS 4:11 NIV

In the parable of the talents (Matthew 25:14–30), Jesus told of three men, each of whom was given a different amount of money, "each according to his ability" (Matthew 25:15 NIV). The first two doubled their investment, but the third held on to his money and was condemned for doing nothing with it. That tells you a few things about God's definition of success.

First, success comes when you've done the work in front of you—the work God has "prepared in advance" for you to do (Ephesians 2:10 NIV). It also means that God hasn't assigned everyone the same type of work, or given everyone the same resources, but whatever He has given you is enough for you to do your job. So no matter what you do for a living, do it to honor God.

No amount of money can increase God's kingdom, but one man, whether he's digging ditches or investing in stocks, can make the difference for the people he's working with, one at a time, to build the eternal nation. When you're focused on living the life God has for you, "attending to your own business" takes on a fresh attitude—you're minding God's business. In His view, to be faithful is to be successful.

Lord, may I be faithful to You and to Your
calling on me above all things.

DAY 365
REALITY-CHECK THE PECKING ORDER

But if you show favoritism, you sin.
JAMES 2:9 NIV

It's natural for men to establish a pecking order. Whether it's at work, playing softball, or raking leaves—if other guys are involved, you want to know where you stand. Which guys are stronger, smarter, faster, and which aren't? But while it's fine to get the lay of the land, it can also provide a false standard of a person's worth. What better shows a man's worth—a sports car and a fat stock portfolio, or the way he treats those from whom he has nothing to gain?

The message of the gospel is not about getting in good with the Guy who can get you in the pearly gates—you can't. It's not about impressing heaven with earthly success—you won't. The cross reveals an unsettling truth: we're all on the same footing before God and the earth is shaking. But Jesus offers a hand up to rich and poor alike; the guy in the penthouse and the one in the gutter matter equally to Him.

That's why James spoke against saving seats up front at church for the wealthy contingent; if anything, Jesus wants you to save a seat for the guy who's lost it all, whose sin has messed up his life and hurt others to boot. Save a special place in your heart for the man with the greatest need. It's what Jesus did for you.

Lord Jesus, help me to avoid the sin of favoritism. Help me instead to view all people as valuable in Your sight.

CONTRIBUTORS

Rev. Robin Burkhart, PhD, has served for more than thirty years as a pastor, author, educator, and denominational leader. His varied background includes ministry in Latin and South America, the Caribbean, Europe, Africa, and the People's Republic of China. He is the father of three adult children and five grandchildren.

Ed Cyzewski is the author of *A Christian Survival Guide: A Lifeline to Faith and Growth* and *Coffeehouse Theology: Reflecting on God in Everyday Life* and is the coauthor of *The Good News of Revelation* and *Unfollowers: Unlikely Lessons on Faith from Those Who Doubted Jesus*. He writes about prayer and imperfectly following Jesus at www.edcyzewski.com.

Quentin Guy writes from the high desert of New Mexico, to encourage and equip people to know and serve God. He currently works in publishing for Calvary Albuquerque and has cowritten such books as *Weird and Gross Bible Stuff* and *The 2:52 Boys Bible*, both of which are stuck in future classic status. A former middle school teacher, he serves with his wife as marriage prep mentors and trusts God that his children will survive their teenage years.

Glenn A. Hascall is an accomplished writer with credits in more than a hundred books. He is a broadcast veteran and voice actor and is actively involved in writing and producing audio drama.

Chuck Miller lives in Sylvania Township, Ohio. He worked for fourteen years as a high school English, journalism, and Bible teacher in the public schools of Lexington, Kentucky, and then at Toledo Christian Schools. He worked as a hospital chaplain—nights and weekends, the "disaster shift"—for seven years, and currently works in the surgical instrument department of that hospital and as a freelance writer of devotions and poetry. Some of his devotional work and poetry can be found on his website, BardofChrist.net. He's been married for forty-two years; his four-year-old grandson Preston (a.k.a. "Pres-Tron"!) is the joy of his life.

Jess MacCallum is president of Professional Printers, Inc. in Columbia, South Carolina. He has authored three books—two on marriage and one on raising daughters—and has twice been featured on *FamilyLife Today* with Dr. Dennis Rainey. He also works with two leadership organizations as an executive coach and is a regular contributor to HealthyLeaders.com. Jess is married and has three grown children.

David Sanford's speaking engagements have ranged everywhere from the Billy Graham Center at the Cove to UC Berkeley. His book and Bible projects have been published by Zondervan, Tyndale House, Thomas Nelson, Doubleday, and Amazon. His professional biography is summarized at www.linkedin.com/in/drsanford. His personal biography features his wife of thirty-six years, Renée, their five children, and their twelve grandchildren (including one in heaven).

Ed Strauss was a freelance writer living in British Columbia, Canada, who passed into heaven in 2018. He authored or coauthored more than fifty books for children, tweens, and adults. Ed had a passion for biblical apologetics and, besides writing for Barbour, was published by Zondervan, Tyndale, Moody, and Focus on the Family. Ed has three children: Sharon, Daniel, and Michelle Strauss.

Tracy Sumner is a freelance author, writer, and editor in Beaverton, Oregon. An avid outdoorsman, he enjoys fly-fishing on world-class Oregon waters.

Lee Warren is published in such varied venues as *Discipleship Journal*, *Sports Spectrum*, Yahoo! Sports, Crosswalk.com, and

ChristianityToday.com. He is also the author of the book *Finishing Well: Living with the End in Mind* (a devotional), as well as several Christmas novellas in the Mercy Inn Series. Lee makes his home in Omaha, Nebraska.

SCRIPTURE INDEX

OLD TESTAMENT

NEW TESTAMENT

DEVOTIONS FOR MEN

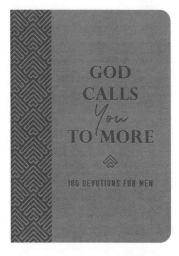

Don't be content to coast—do more! Based on 2 Timothy 2:15 ("Do your best to present yourself to God as one approved"), these 180 devotions encourage you as a Christian man to stretch yourself spiritually—not to earn your salvation but to honor the God who saved you.

Flexible DiCarta / 978-1-63609-596-7